IMAGES
of America

ELKHORN

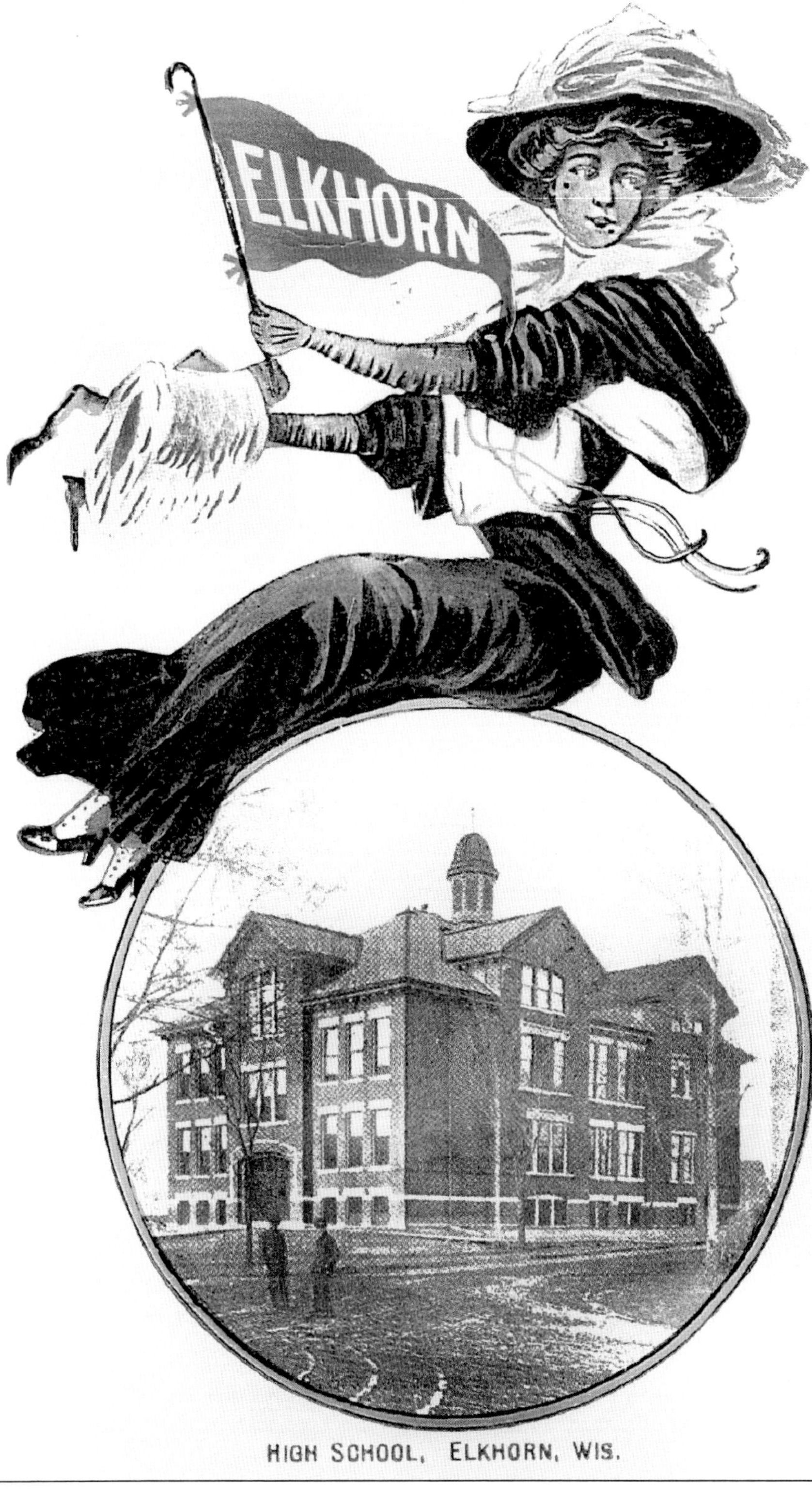

HIGH SCHOOL, ELKHORN, WIS.

IMAGES
of America

ELKHORN

Doris Reinke

ARCADIA
PUBLISHING

ISBN 978-0-7385-3320-9

Published by Arcadia Publishing
Charleston, South Carolina

Printed in the United States of America

Library of Congress Catalog Card Number: 2004107549

For all general information contact Arcadia Publishing at:
Telephone 843-853-2070
Fax 843-853-0044
E-mail sales@arcadiapublishing.com
For customer service and orders:
Toll-Free 1-888-313-2665

Visit us on the Internet at www.arcadiapublishing.com

Contents

ACKNOWLEDGMENTS

First of all, a very special thank you to Phil Strong, vice president of the Walworth County Historical Society. Without his expertise with computer and scanning equipment, the preparation of the book would have been very difficult.

F.H. Eames Publishing Company, owned by Frank Eames, gave access to the old photographs in its collection.

The Elkhorn Chamber of Commerce gave permission to include pictures of the greeting cards that made Elkhorn the "Christmas Card City."

Ken Amon allowed the use of his ever-growing compilation of area history.

The Walworth County Historical Society provided most of the pictures and postcard views from its voluminous files.

Elizabeth Jobe and Arcadia Publishing guided and encouraged the writing of *Elkhorn*.

INTRODUCTION

In 1995, residents of Elkhorn were excited to learn that their city had been listed in the book *The Best Small Towns in America,* by Norm Crampton. Everyone here had always believed it was a good place in which to live, but did not really expect that nonresidents would feel the same way.

It was great to make that list, but it was even better to see that the city ranked way up near the top. It was Number 14!

As people went over the criteria used to select the winners, they nodded their heads in agreement. Yes, the city they lived in met the qualification with flying colors.

Winners needed to have a spirit of community, a feeling of safety, a commitment to the well-being of its children, and a growing population. Elkhorn residents are proud that over the years these attributes have consistently been part of the city.

Elkhorn is one of several small cities in Walworth County. Today, in the year 2004, it has reached a population of 7,500. It is the fastest growing area in the county. An effort is being made to control this rapid growth by careful zoning and regulation so that the quality of life, treasured by its residents, will not be lost.

A population of 7,500 may seem small to "big city" dwellers, but the only place in the county that has more than 10,000 residents is Whitewater, where one of the University of Wisconsin schools is located. The college students who attend help to swell that city's population.

Situated between a university town and two popular vacation areas, Elkhorn has a style of its own. Life is quieter, the pace is slower, and the standards established years ago are maintained. There is a strong emphasis on home, church, and school. The beautiful churches built years ago have faithful congregations. Also prospering are the many new denominations that have appeared in recent decades.

At first, the major sources of employment were based on agriculture. There was a milk plant and a canning factory. The production of musical instruments was another kind of work. A majority of the labor force had jobs in legal offices, health services, law enforcement, education, banking, and the court house business, because this was the county seat.

In later years, tourism has become very important in Walworth County—but Elkhorn has resisted the idea of becoming a resort town. It welcomes visitors to its upgraded downtown district, but has no desire for noise, litter, or traffic jams.

Much of Elkhorn's growth has come in the last 20 years. In 1980, its population was 4,605. In 1990, the number had increased to 5,337, which was a 15 percent growth rate. Figures for the year 2000 revealed that in those 10 years the population had grown to 7,305. This was a 36.9 percent increase.

It is hoped that the newcomers will blend in well with Elkhorn's way of life. However, as much as heritage and the old ways of doing things are appreciated, we also recognize that progress is inevitable. Places that do not grow often shrivel and die.

Elkhorn prefers to grow.

One

A Reason for Being

At first there seemed to be little reason for the pioneers of the 1830s to choose this particular location for a city. The Territory of Wisconsin had been organized by Congress in 1836 and that same year a number of counties, including Walworth, were created. Those seeking land came into these new counties quickly, paying the United States government $1.25 per acre.

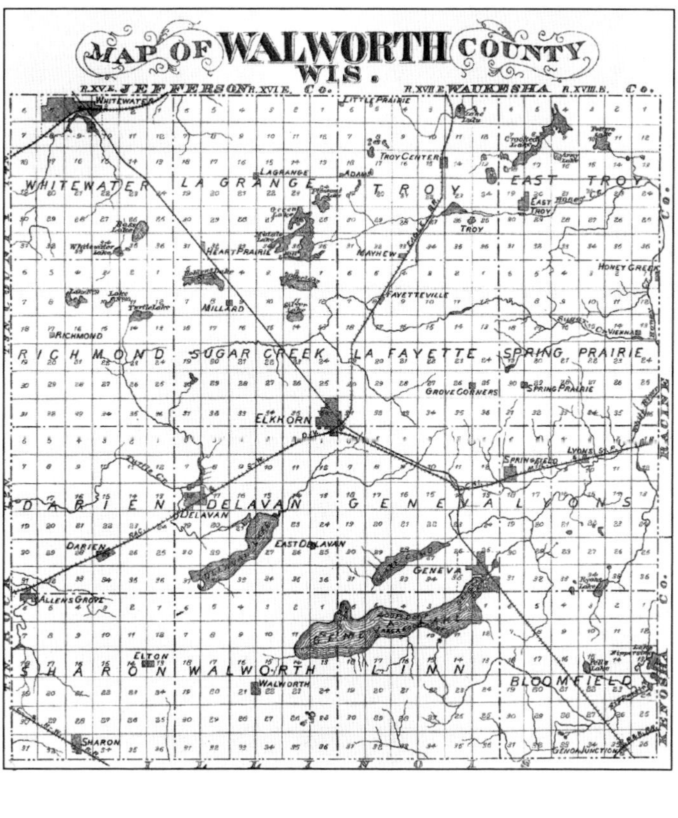

Most settlers looked for favorable natural resources such as a river, stream, or lake, for needed water power. Despite this handicap, land was purchased here because it had one special thing in its favor—when the county was established, it was laid out as absolutely square.

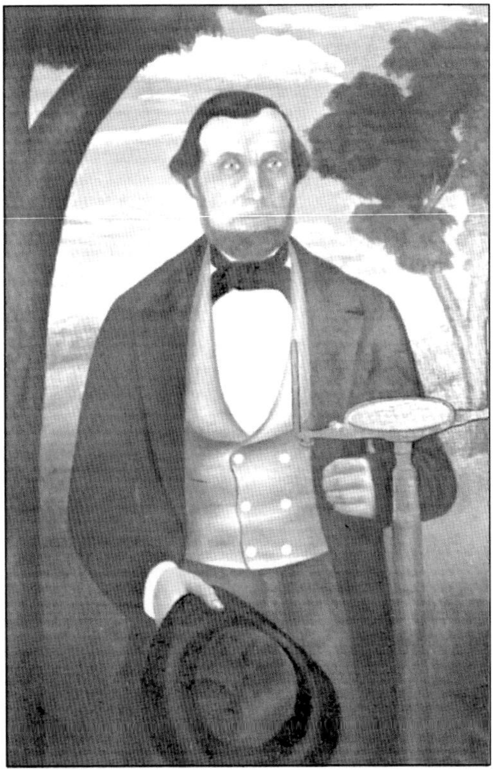

John Brink was one of the first surveyors. He is pictured here with the tools used to measure the new county.

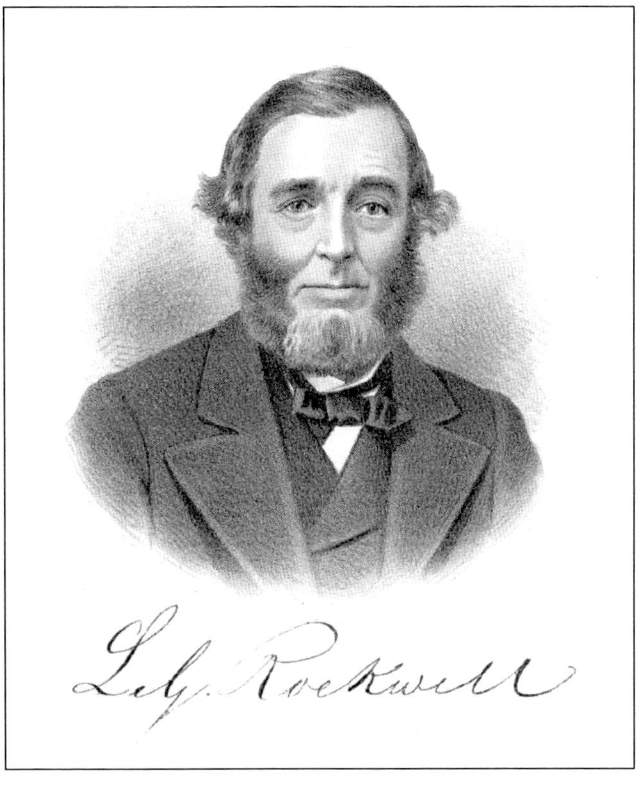

It was the square shape of the site that interested entrepreneurs. A group of Milwaukee men banded together and gambled that acquiring the land exactly in the center of the new square county would be a very profitable move. These men were LeGrand Rockwell (pictured at right), Daniel and Milo Bradley, Hollis Latham, and John Coleman. When the land was put up for sale, they bought large sections, all in the middle of Walworth County.

Although Elkhorn was slow to develop due to the lack of water power, Rockwell soon had an office and store in the dreamed-of village. His partners joined him, establishing a small inn.

One of the people who had looked the area over in order to find a suitable place for settlement was Samuel Phoenix. He is credited with giving Elkhorn its name.

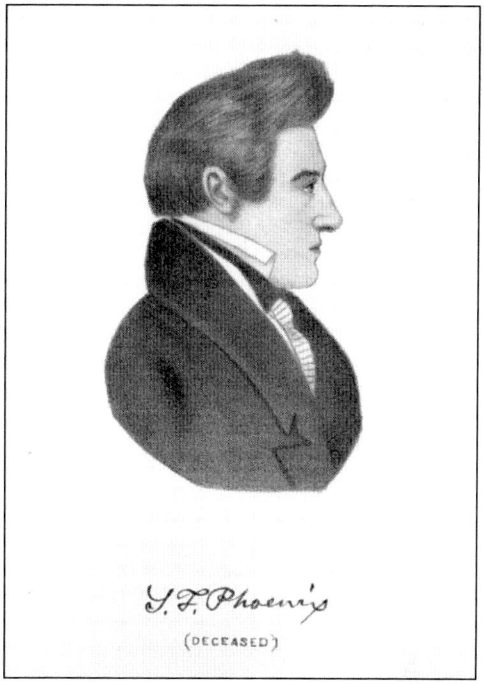

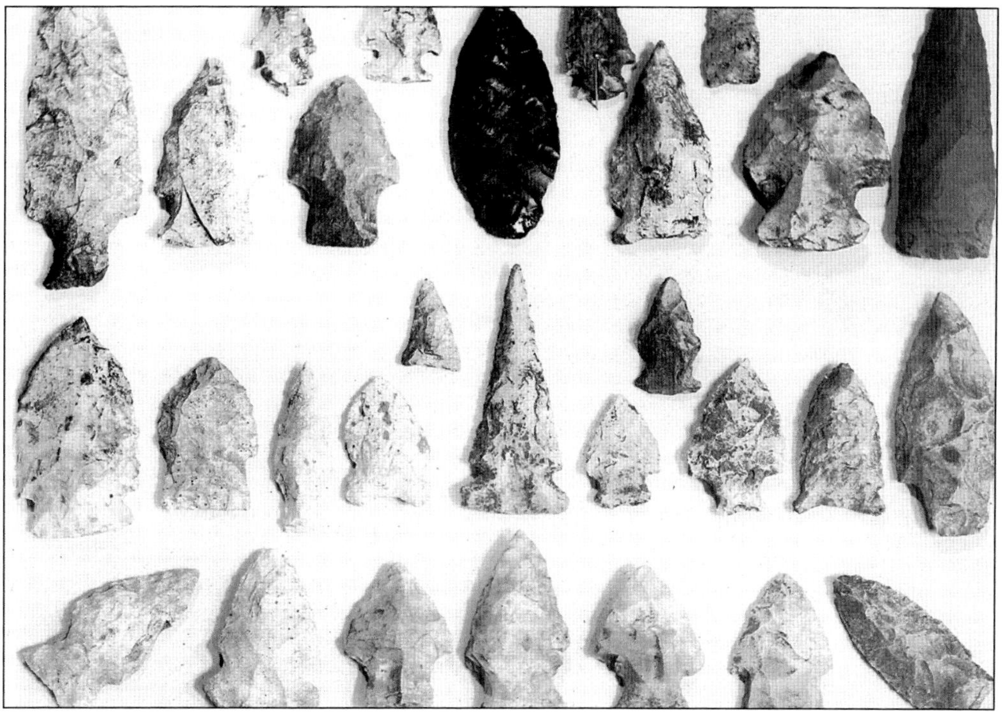

Phoenix had stopped to rest on the prairie and happened to look up into the branches of a tall tree. There he saw a huge rack of elk horns. He surmised that they had been set up in the tree by the Potawatomies who had lived here formerly. They had used the region as their hunting grounds, as evidenced by the large quantity of spear heads and arrow points found, especially during spring plowing time.

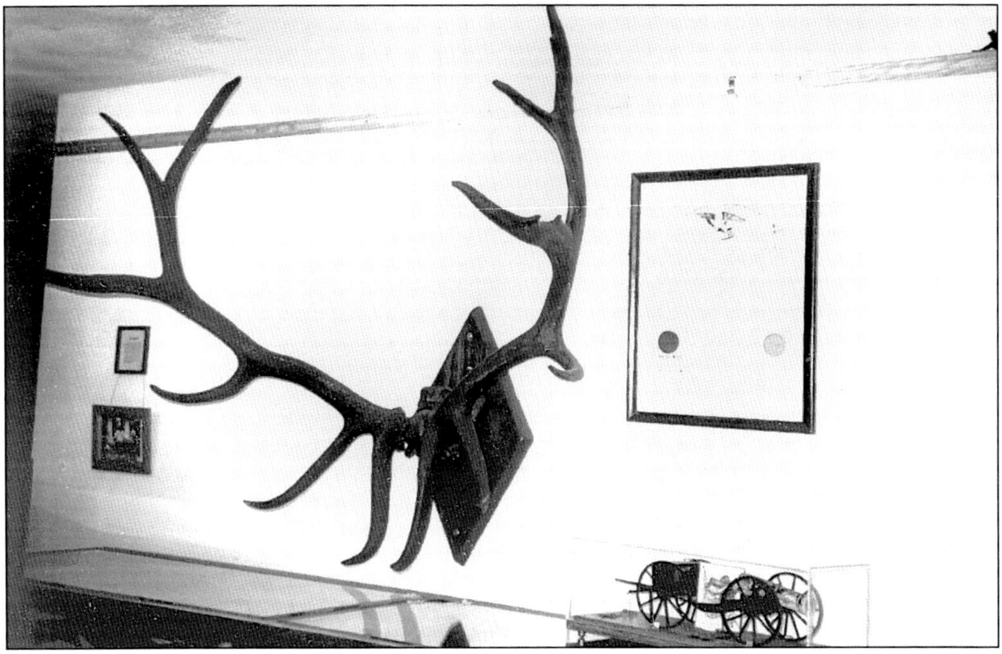

The Indians traded with other tribes and also with army posts, and therefore had a regular network of trails. Phoenix thought that the horns in the tree marked a turn in the trail. He wrote in his journal that this place should be called Elk Horn Prairie.

When the horns were taken down, they were hung in LeGrand Rockwell's office. Eventually, they journeyed to the court house and then to the city's municipal building. A few years ago, the city council decided that the horns belonged in a museum. They were given to the Walworth County Historical Society and are now displayed in the Webster House Museum.

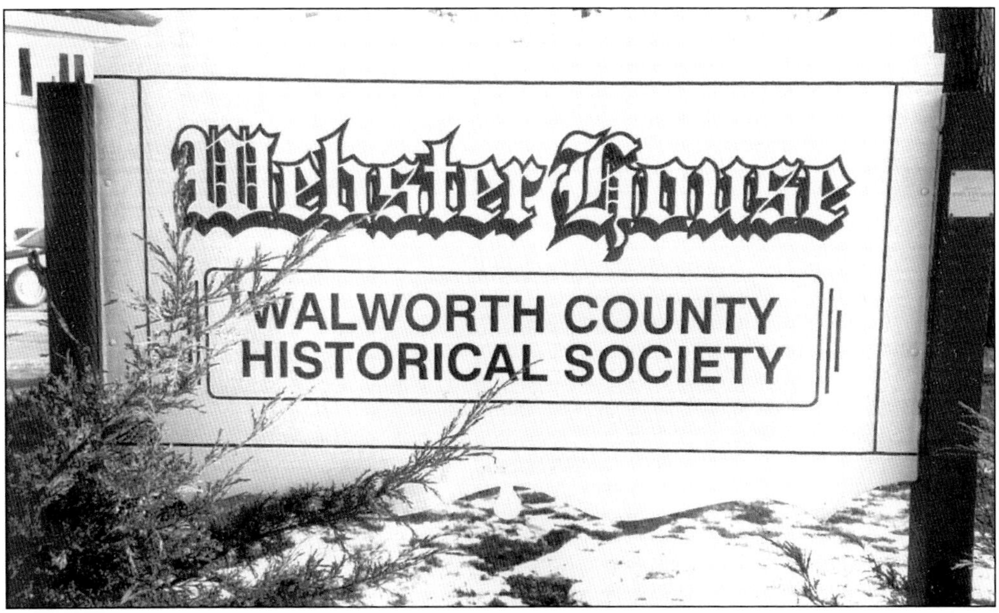

Coincidentally, the museum back in 1837 was Rockwell's office building. The horns have returned to their first home.

Two

CHOSEN FOR THE COUNTY SEAT

In 1838, LeGrand Rockwell's gamble paid off. Elkhorn, despite its tiny population, was selected to be the county seat of Walworth County. Just as Rockwell had hoped, placing the government offices in the exact center of a perfect square was a natural choice, considered fair to everyone in each of the 16 townships.

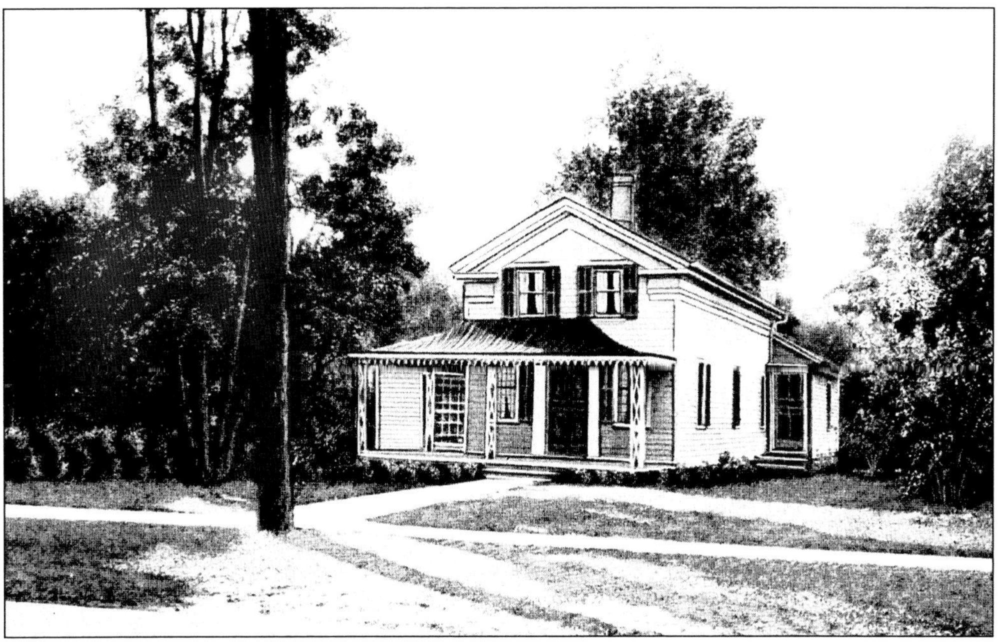

Until a real court house was constructed, Rockwell's multi-purpose building served as court house, land grant office, post office, law office, and general store.

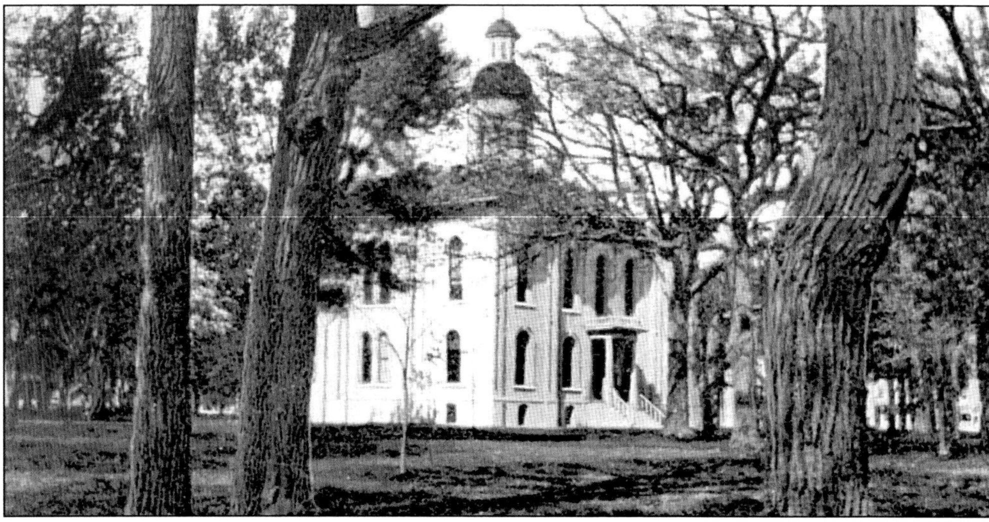

In 1841, the first actual court house was erected in the large square downtown. It lasted 30 years and then a substantial brick building replaced the older wood one.

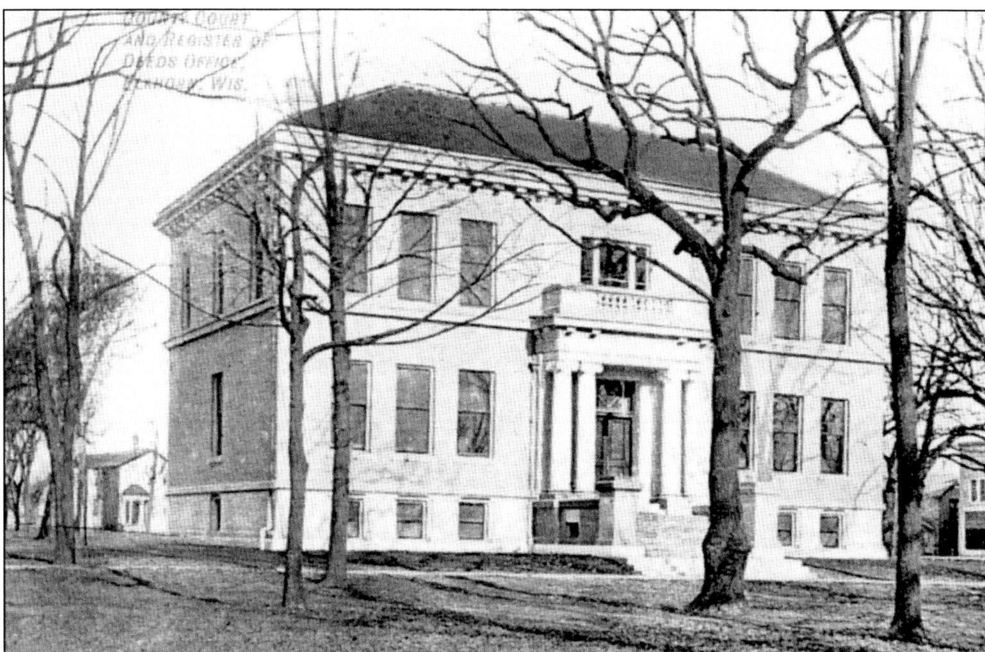

An additional building for the register of deeds' office stood next to it.

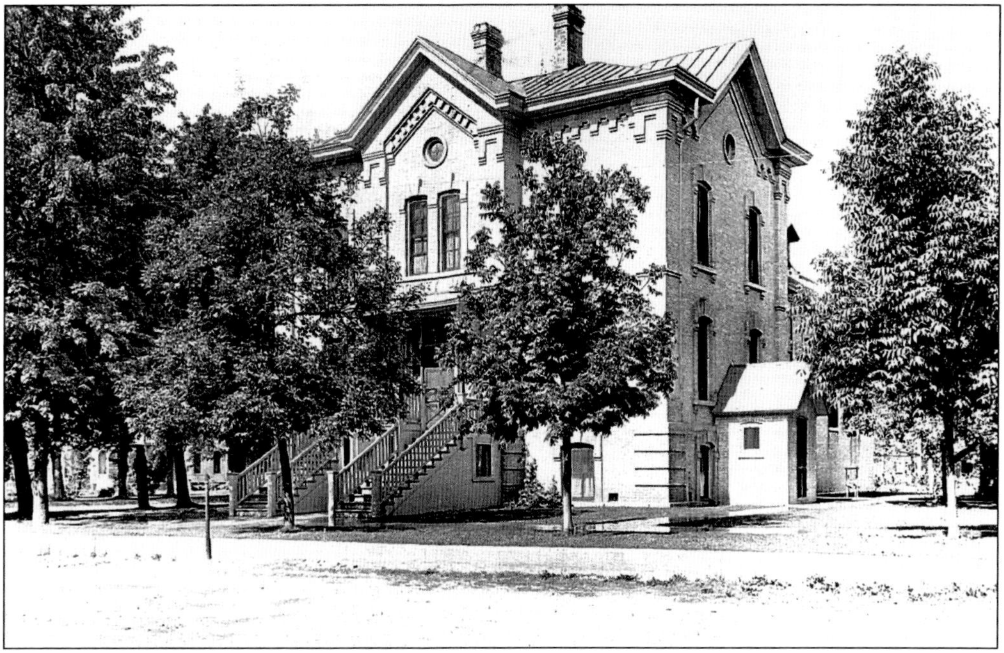

The increasing government business brought more and more regular business, and Elkhorn grew. Hotels were built, law offices opened, livery stables prospered, and general stores flourished—a thriving city had been launched.

County matters continued to dominate. The little log jail that had been little used was replaced by a substantial brick building that had space inside for the sheriff's office. This was in 1877.

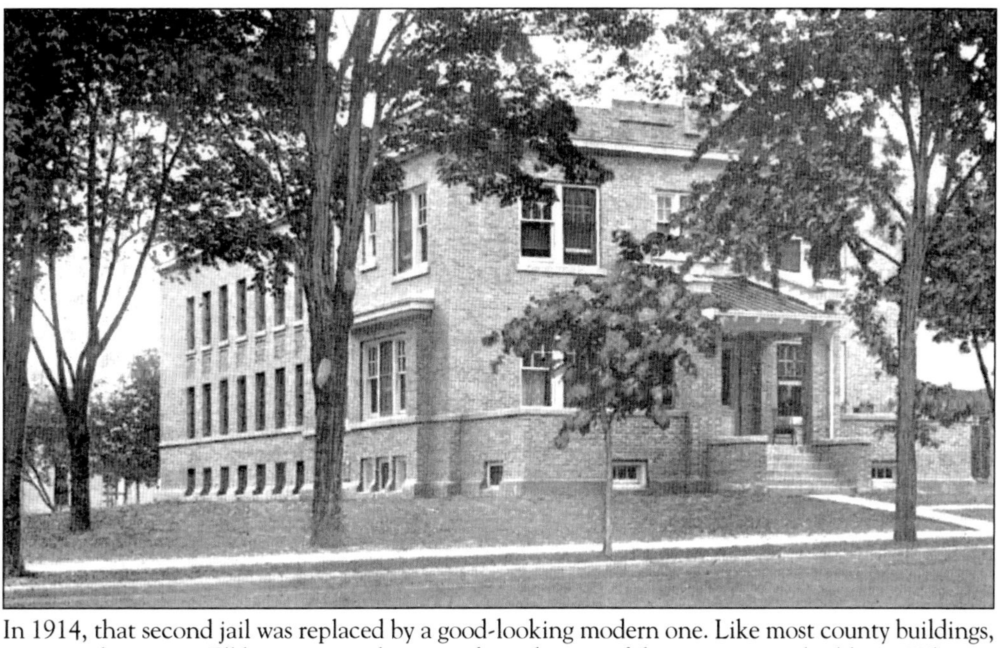

In 1914, that second jail was replaced by a good-looking modern one. Like most county buildings, it was in downtown Elkhorn, across the street from the rest of the government buildings. When it was decided that the time had come for a new court house, the separate jail was eliminated and one wing of the structure was designed to hold prisoners and the sheriff's office.

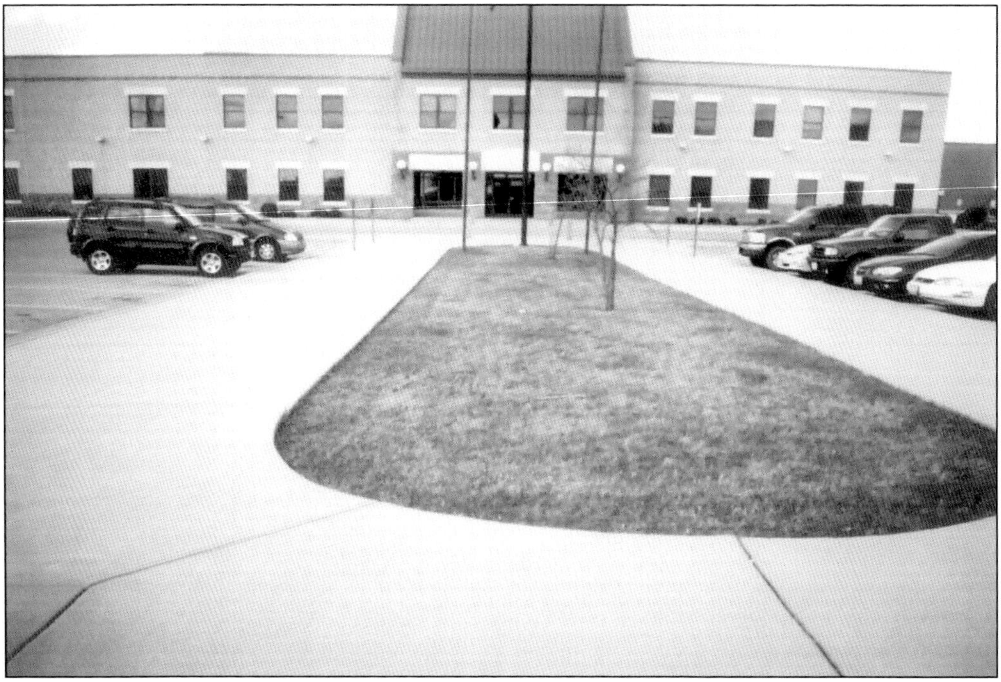

Now, for the purpose of increased security, the newest jail is once again a separate building. The new court house will be next door to it.

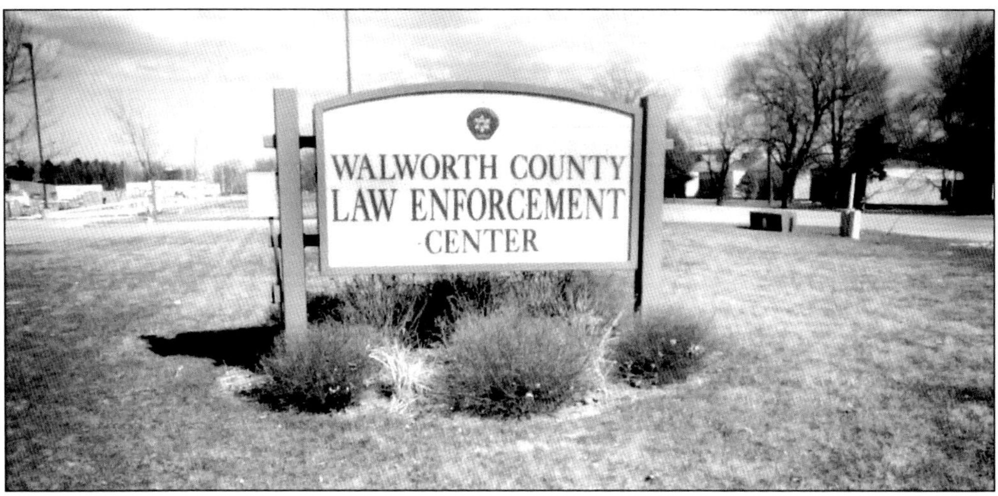

The sign at the entrance to this latest jail informs everyone that it has now become a Law Enforcement Center.

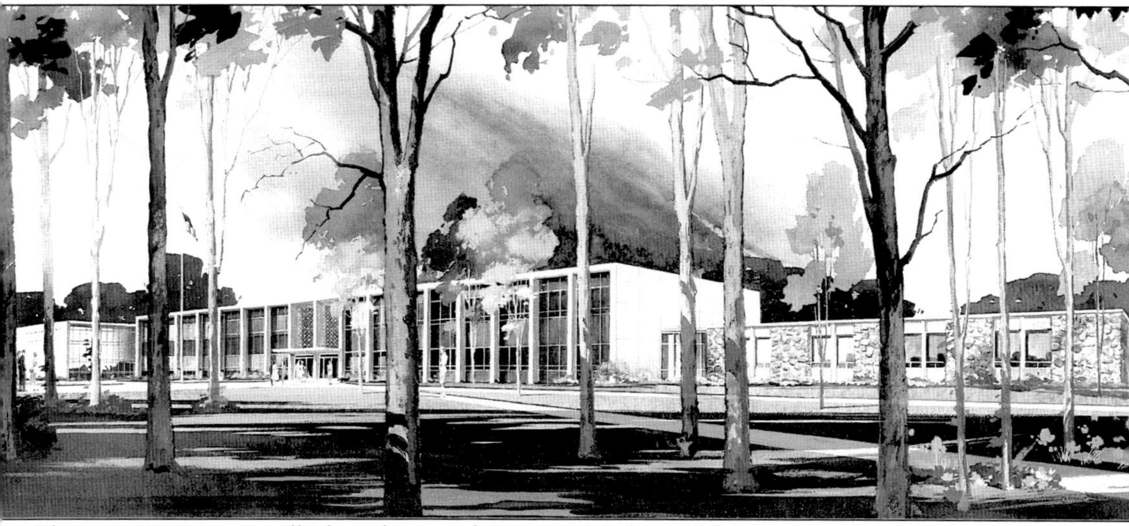

The year 1962 saw really big changes downtown. A beautiful new court house had been commissioned. This modern building's exterior was faced with multi-colored fieldstone to echo the stone foundations of the 19th century houses that lined one side of the square.

The century-old trees in the square were fenced, to prevent heavy construction machines from hitting them. To further save the trees, the existing county buildings were torn down and the new structure was placed right where the old buildings had been. Empty stores and church basements became government offices for a while. (Photo courtesy of Ebling-Plunkett-Keymar-Reginato and Associates—Architects; 6830 West Villard Avenue, Milwaukee, WI.)

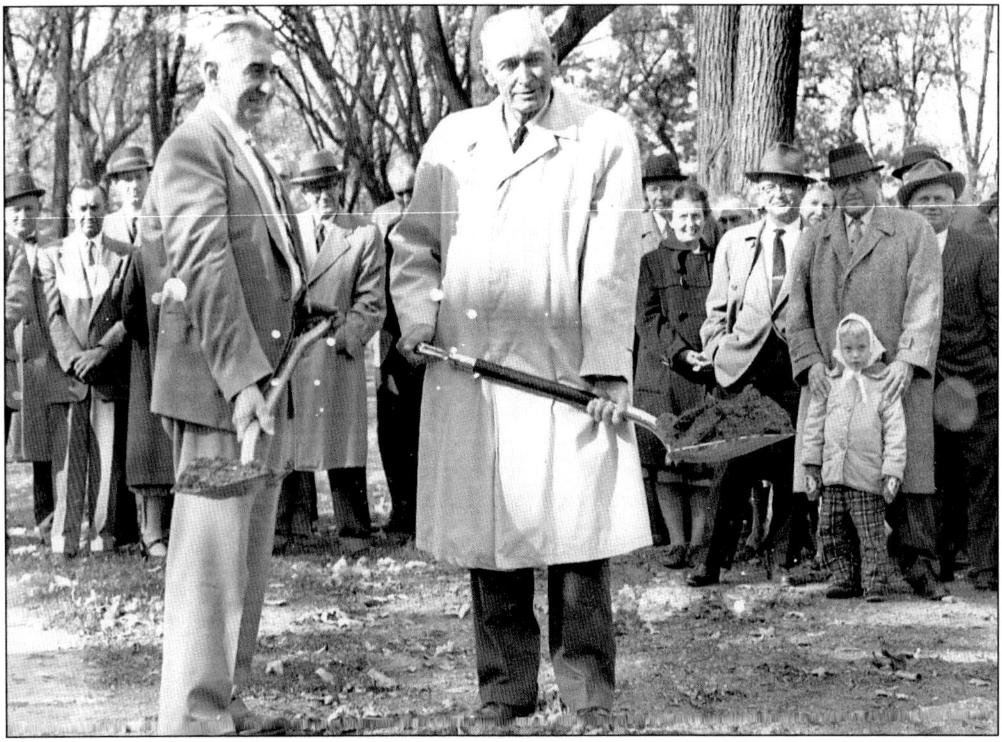

In the fall of 1961, interested citizens gathered to watch ground being broken for the new court house. Wielding the shovels were Clarence Buckholz and Henry Gutzmer.

Objects were collected for placement in a copper box, which was placed in the cornerstone of the soon to be erected building. The box had copies of county newspapers, pictures of old buildings, and also the items that had been sealed in the cornerstone of the two razed buildings.

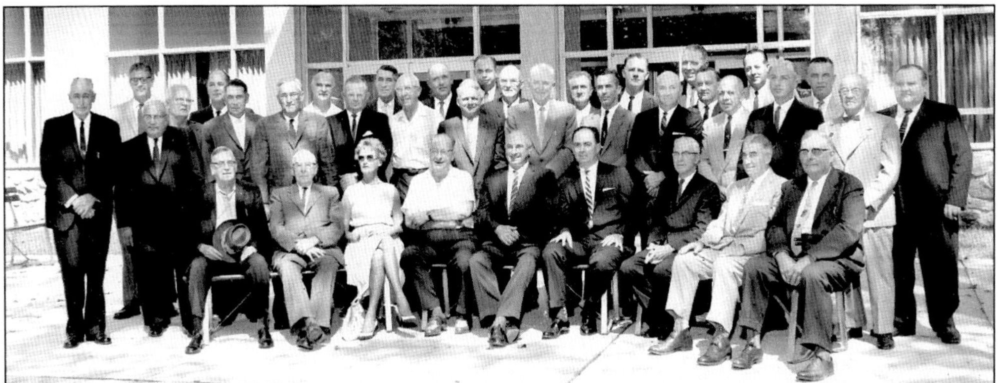

A proud Board of Supervisors posed for a photograph on the grand opening day in 1962. Pictured from left to right are: (front row) Eugene Joslin, H.C. Quass, Rosepha Ambrose, Ralph Gosso, Franklin Walsh (Ch.), C.H. Buckholz, and Ray Fish; (second row) Henry Gutzmer, William Blank, William Steffen, Arnette Peters, Jim Baker, Claud Voyles, Glenn Walbrandt, V.H. Gunyon, Merle Robinson, Richard Behrens, John Deschner, Herman Quade, Jack Fagan, Charles Shager, and Ray Morrissy; (third row) P.B. Morrissey (corporation counsel), Vic Houlberg, Roger Dingman, Gene Nashold, Herb Schaefer, Wilfred Brotz, John Dwyer, Phil Steffanus, B.J. Francover, P.L. Lusignan, Eugene Hollister, Harold Kelley, and Frank Spoerle.

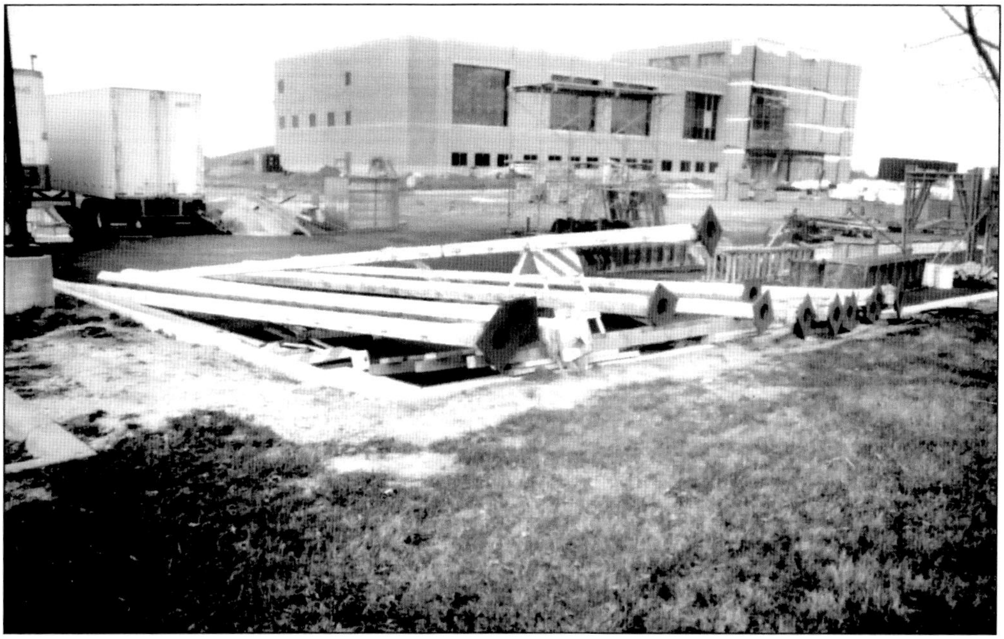

Forty years after the grand opening of the sprawling court house in downtown Elkhorn, government affairs had expanded so much that the facility in the square became too small and not secure enough. A new court house is in the process of being constructed a few miles east of the city. Occupancy is planned for the autumn of 2004.

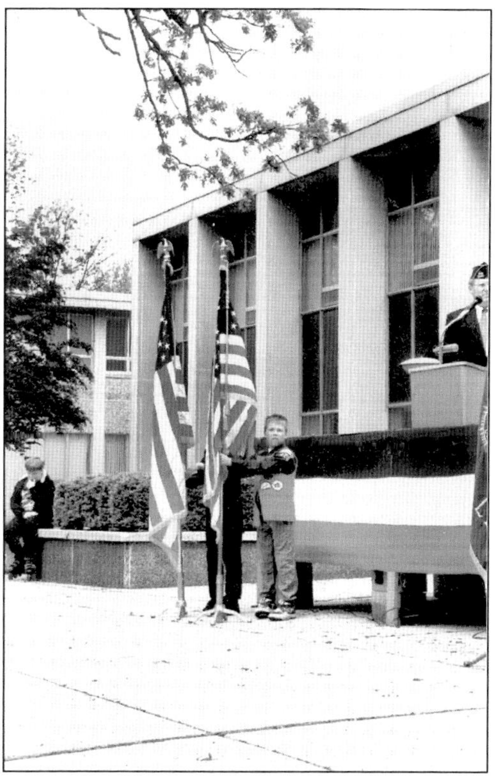

Since the square also serves as a park, it is used for the annual Memorial Day ceremony, which always culminates with music, speeches, and a flag salute. The grassy tree-shaded park will continue to be the scene for such ceremonies and events.

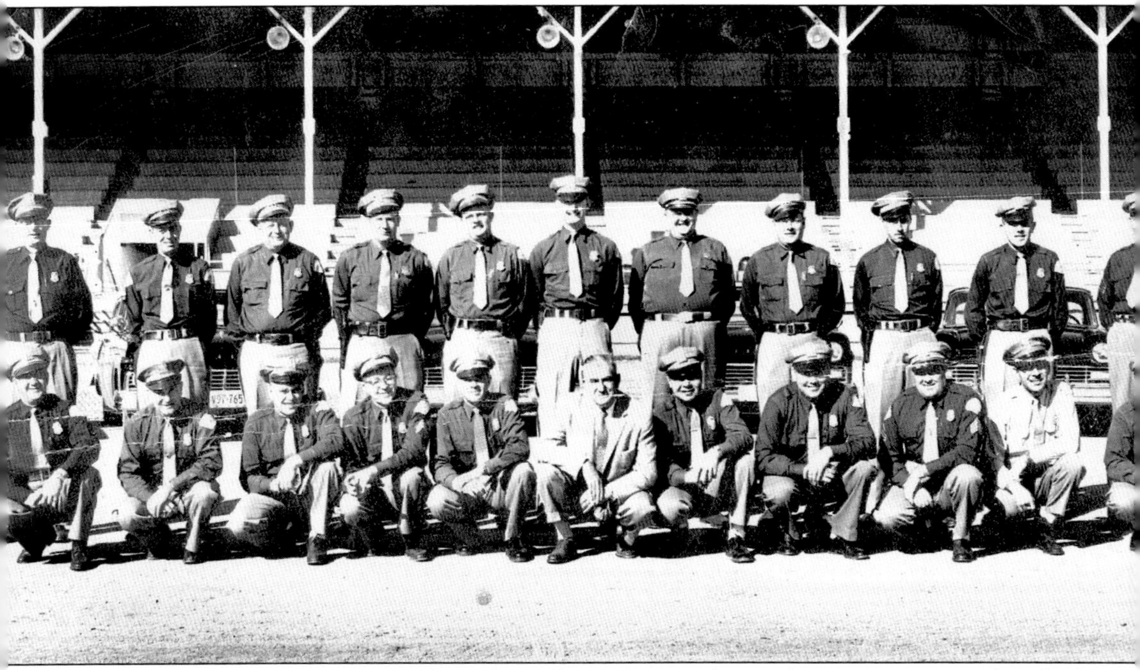

Like everything else, the number of people working in law enforcement increased with the growth of the county. The first sheriff, Walling, was elected in 1839 and took care of all problems by himself. He was the only one on the payroll that year.

In 1927, the men who comprised the department posed for a group picture. Joe Dorr, in civilian clothes, was sheriff at that time.

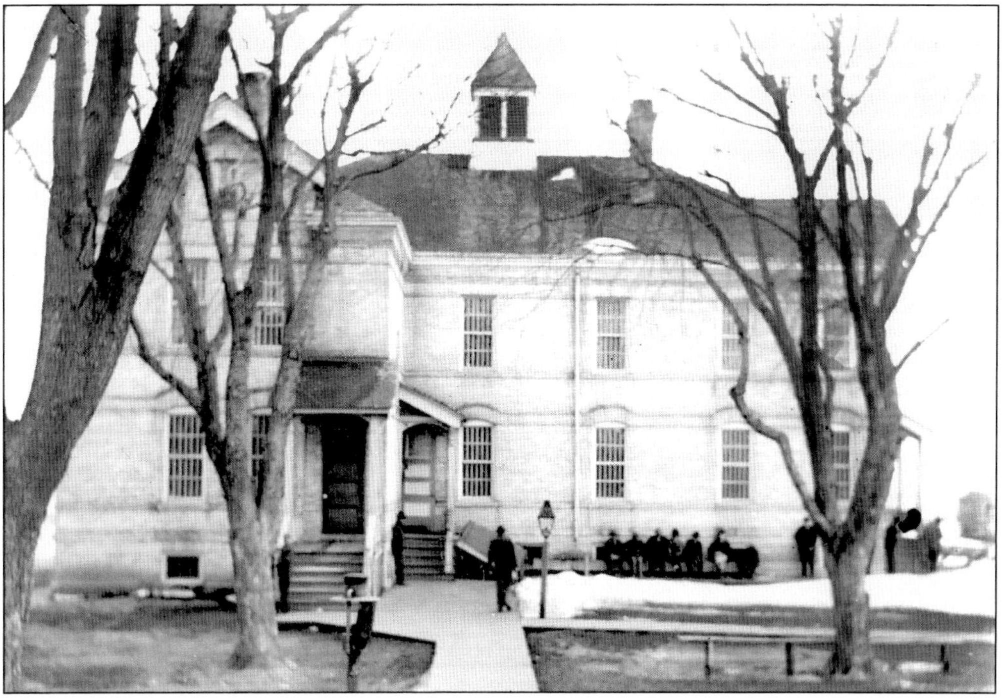

Being the county seat also meant that the "Poor House," established in 1853, would be located near this central city.

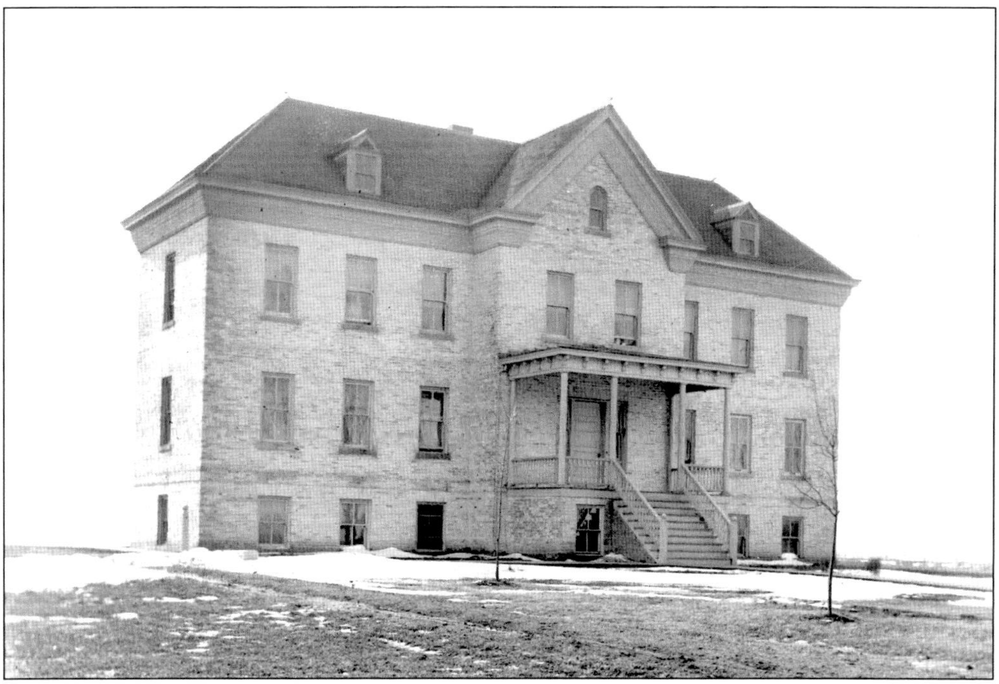

Beside it was another large brick structure known as the Insane Asylum. A County Farm completed this complex of buildings. Many of the inmates worked at the farm. It was considered therapy for them and it helped pay for their support as well.

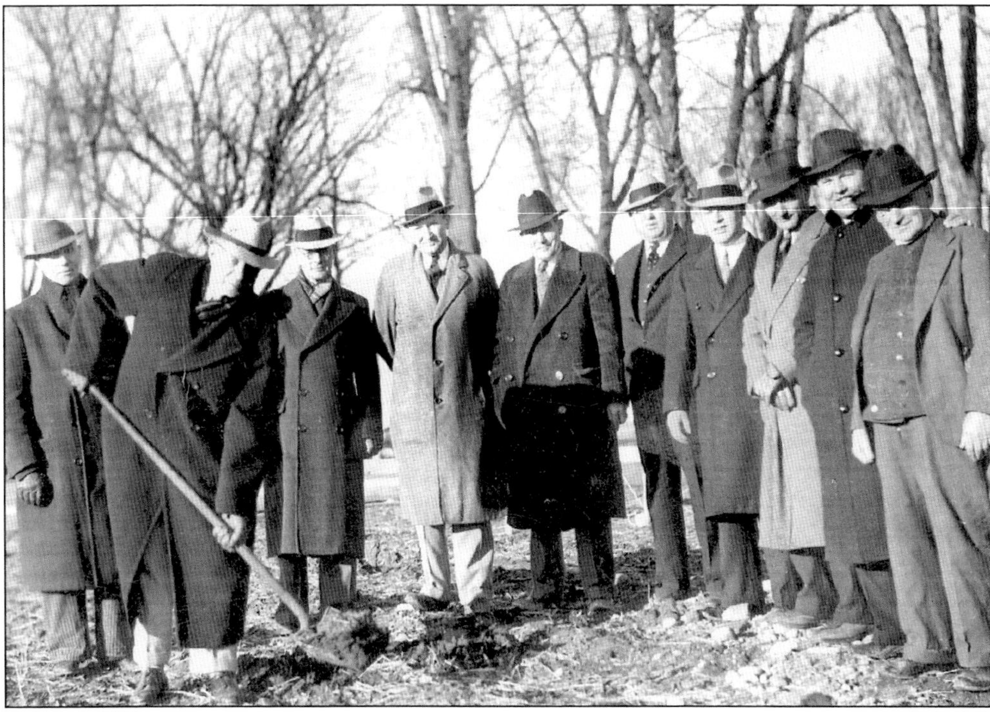

There was a growing need for a hospital, and in 1935, ground was broken for such a facility by members of the Board of Supervisors.

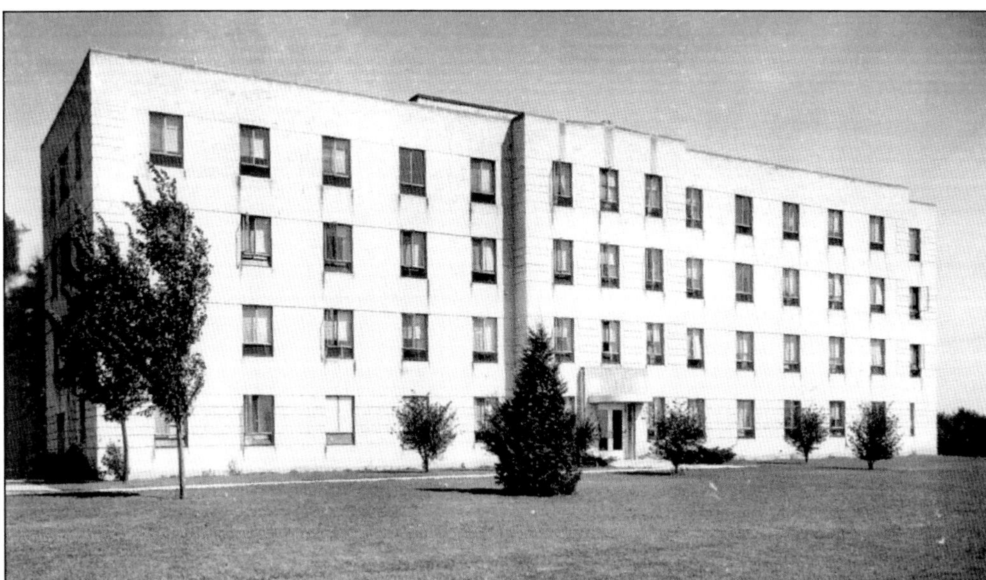

The hospital was east of Elkhorn, near the old Poor Farm and Insane Asylum buildings. As the years went by, even this large facility had to be remodeled and enlarged several times. Originally, there was a residence hall for the nurses next to the hospital.

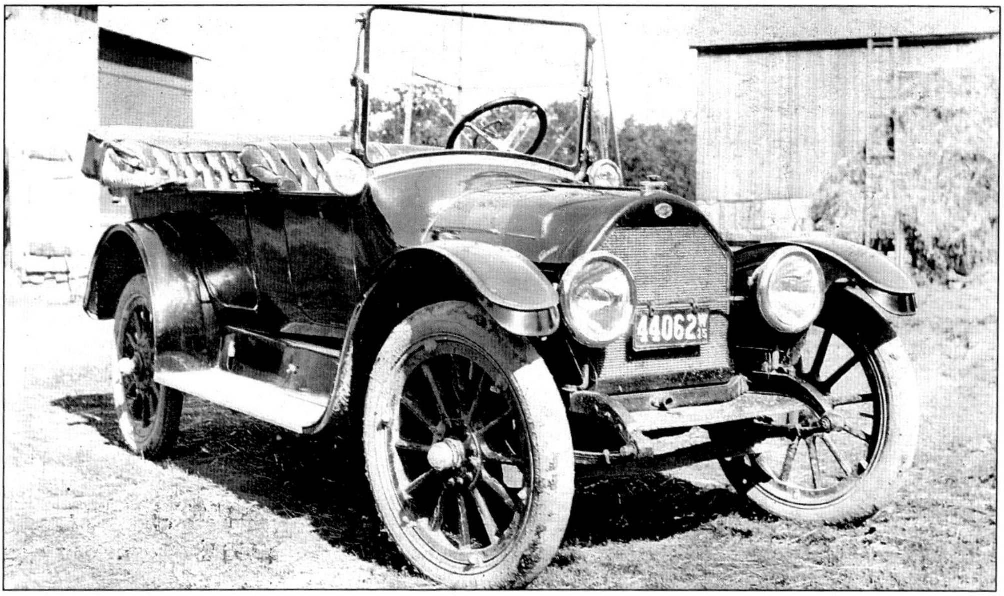

The highway department was situated in Elkhorn too. In the beginning, there was no need for a highway department. Most of the rural roads were maintained by the farmers whose land bordered on them. Work on the road was credited toward local taxes. That changed when motor cars were introduced.

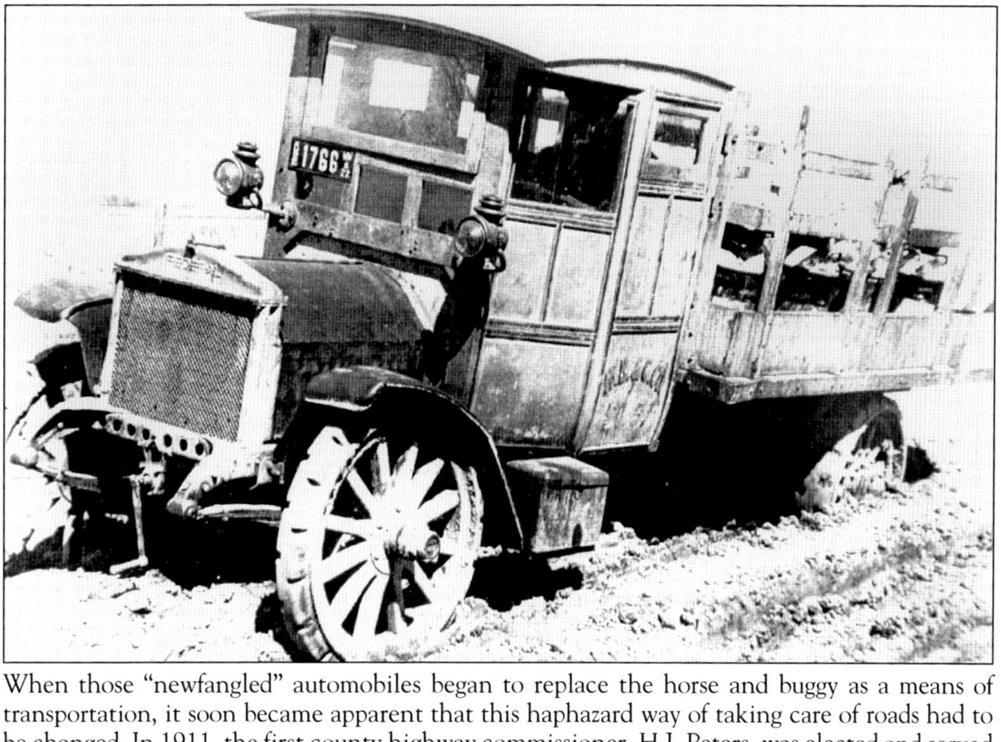

When those "newfangled" automobiles began to replace the horse and buggy as a means of transportation, it soon became apparent that this haphazard way of taking care of roads had to be changed. In 1911, the first county highway commissioner, H.J. Peters, was elected and served for 45 years. He supervised the transition from dirt roads to the modern concrete and blacktop highways. Here, a milk truck is mired in the mud.

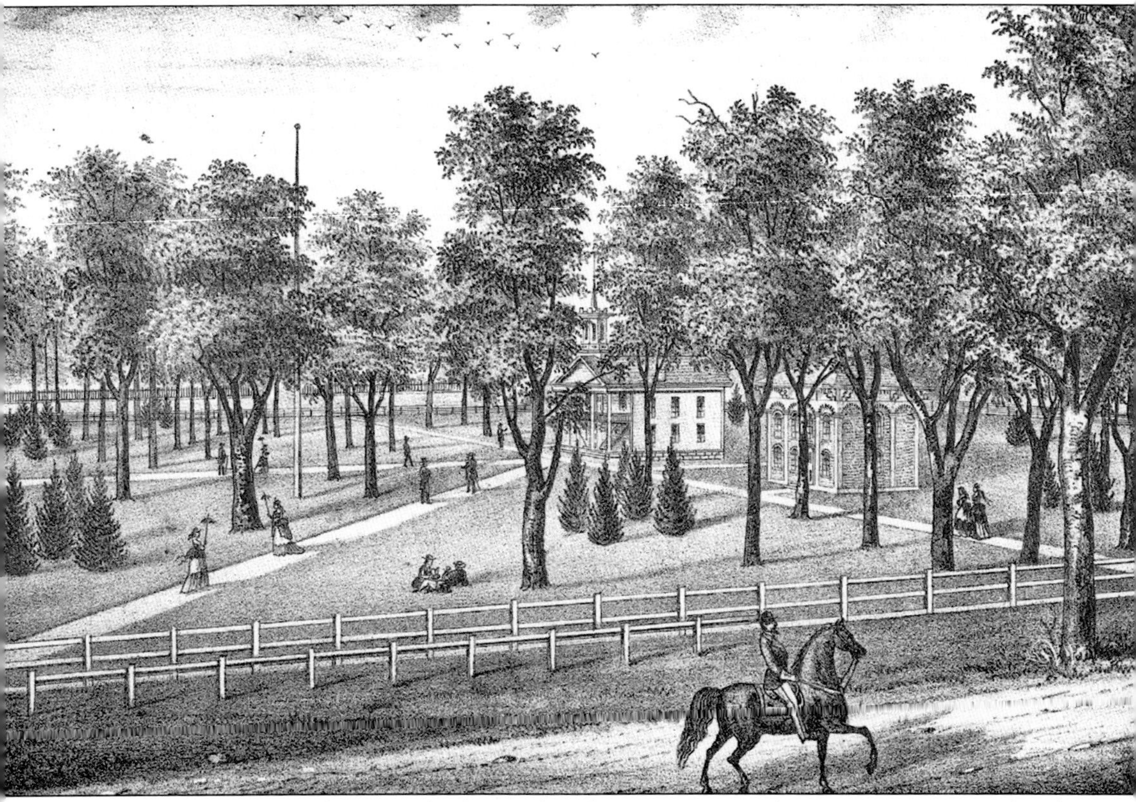

The preceding pages have amply shown that the exact center of a square county was the place to be. This sketch of the downtown park, useful for pleasure as well as business, appeared in an early *Atlas of Walworth County*, dated 1873.

Three

A Roof Over Their Heads

The flat expanses of prairie soil looked good to the incoming settlers, coming from the eastern states and later from Europe. Their first priority after getting land was to put up some sort of shelter for the family. Most of the pioneers built one-room cabins at first, using logs cut from the oak forests which ringed the prairie. The axe was the indispensable tool on the frontier.

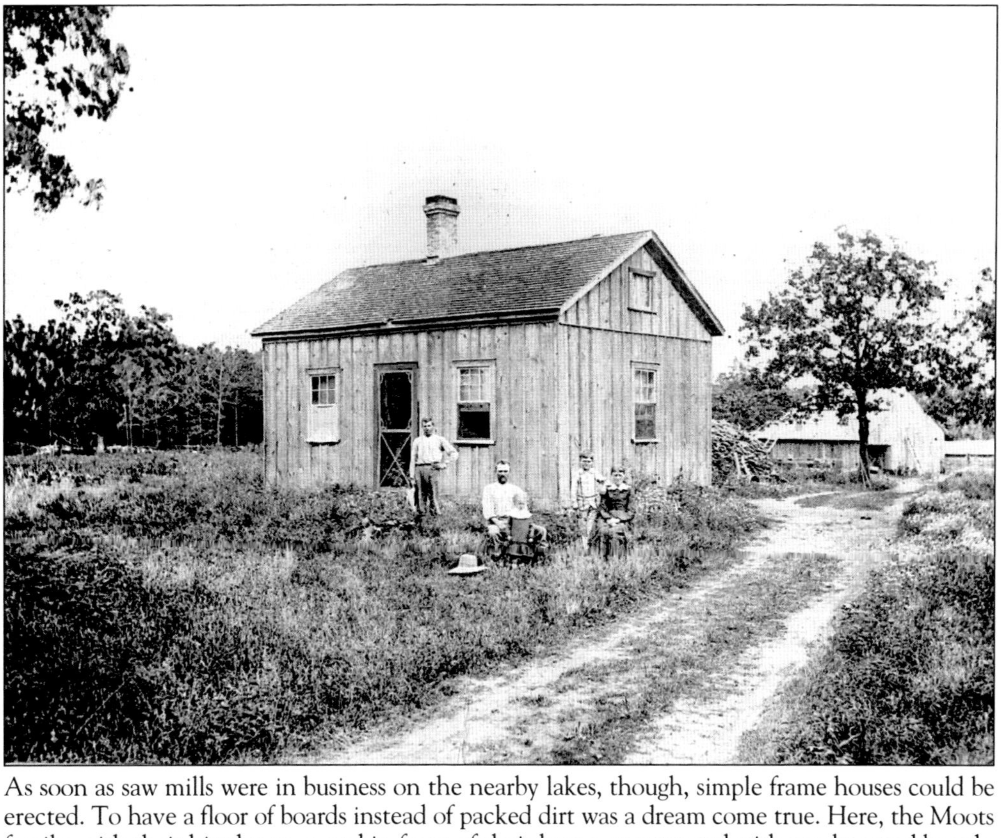

As soon as saw mills were in business on the nearby lakes, though, simple frame houses could be erected. To have a floor of boards instead of packed dirt was a dream come true. Here, the Moots family, with their hired man, posed in front of their home, constructed with newly sawed boards. It even had glass windows, carefully hauled by wagon from the bustling port city of Milwaukee.

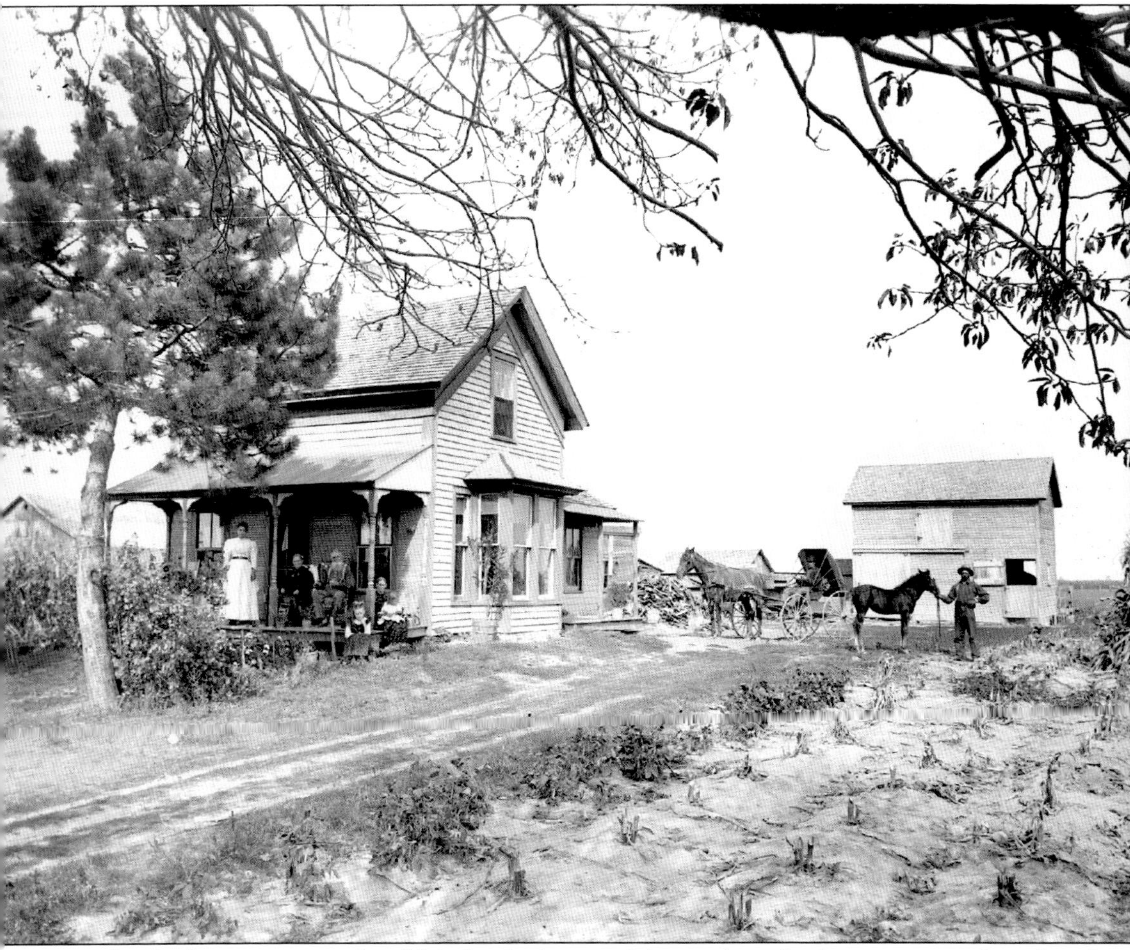

As the farmer prospered and his family increased in number, the houses were enlarged and became more elaborate. Rural property owners were happy to pose with their animals for an itinerant photographer.

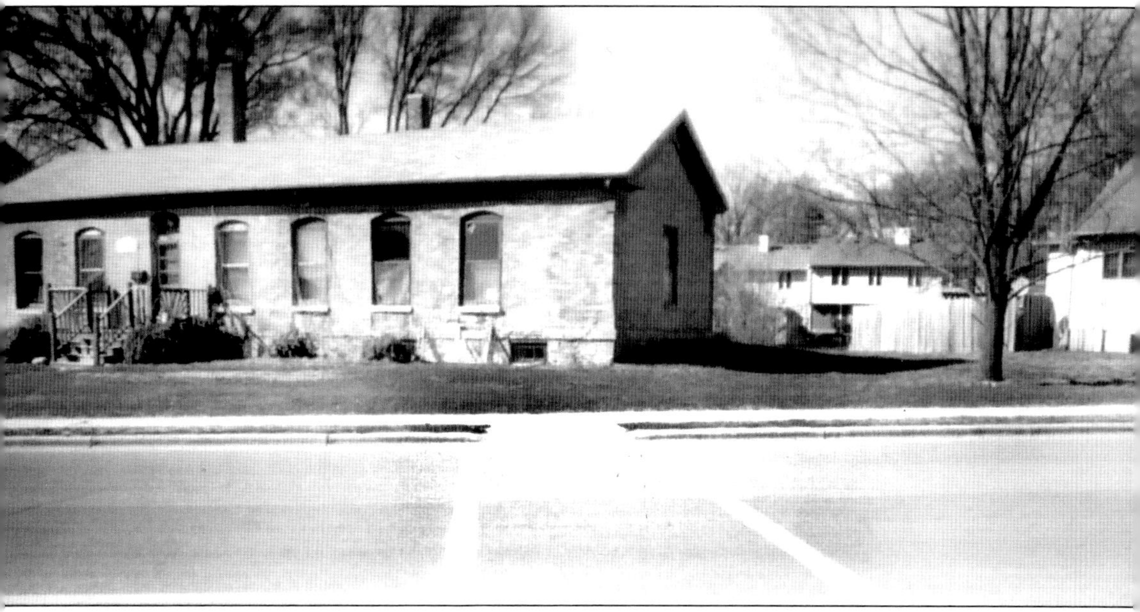

The city inhabitants erected houses on large lots so there was plenty of space for garden, grape arbor, and fruit trees. One of the first houses in Elkhorn was that of Hollis Latham, one of LeGrand Rockwell's partners. Built with yellow brick manufactured from the city's heavy clay soil, it still stands today, just a few blocks from downtown. To make shopping easier, people liked living close to the business district.

"There he goes again," said Mrs. Partington, in the Legislature, as a member stood up for the fifth time to speak on a question. "There he goes like a soda fountain and just as fluidly as water. Now Isaac, mind him, and see if you can't become a speeker of the house and reprehensibles sometime."

The SHANTY, nee Centralia, heard from!

The SHANTY is now fully inaugurated as one of the Institutions of the village of Elkhorn, and the latest and most reliable news may be looked for by the people of Walworth County.

THE PROGRAMME STATED!

The **SHANTY** will give employment to a larger class of persons than any establishment in town.

The **SHANTY** will expect, and require, of its employees, strict and faithful support in its efforts to make for the Institution a creditable reputation.

The SHANTY will be fully stocked up with the latest and most approved styles of STAPLE DRY GOODS of strictly prime quality; and will be the exponent of the advantages of the New Tariff system.

The SHANTY will present the largest and most varied stock of HATS and CAPS to be found in the County, and prices will be straight and equitable.

The SHANTY will present the largest and most complete line of WOOLENS and GENTS FURNISHING GOODS to be found in this section of the State, and will not be undersold. The cutting of Garments a gratuity.

The SHANTY will manufacture all of the extensive range of CLOTHING, and will offer inducements to the Public unsurpassed by any house in the West.

In short, the SHANTY will be a live and equable Institution, and while it will not "*Lie down, Speak, or Roll over*," for any persons cracker, it will seek to command patronage by a faithful adherence to rules of equity in all its transactions.

P. S. The SHANTY will make a strong effort to please all classes, but wishes it understood that those who will not buy unless they can *beat down on prices*, had better not be to the trouble of calling, as it will not practice the *Scalping Art*, "If she knows herself and she thinks she does."

R. C. PRESTON.

Elkhorn, April, 1867.

The county seat brought business to Elkhorn. Merchants established small shops. The newspaper regularly advertised the merits of tailors, milliners, blacksmiths, livery stables, and furniture stores. In 1867, merchant R.C. Preston went all out to bring in customers.

One of the earliest shops was that of Edward Norris. His specialty was the selling of stoves of all kinds, from kitchen ranges to heating stoves for parlors.

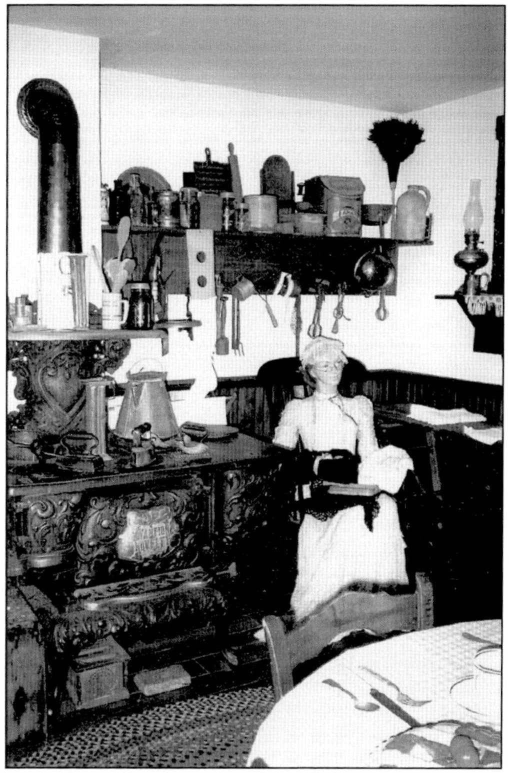

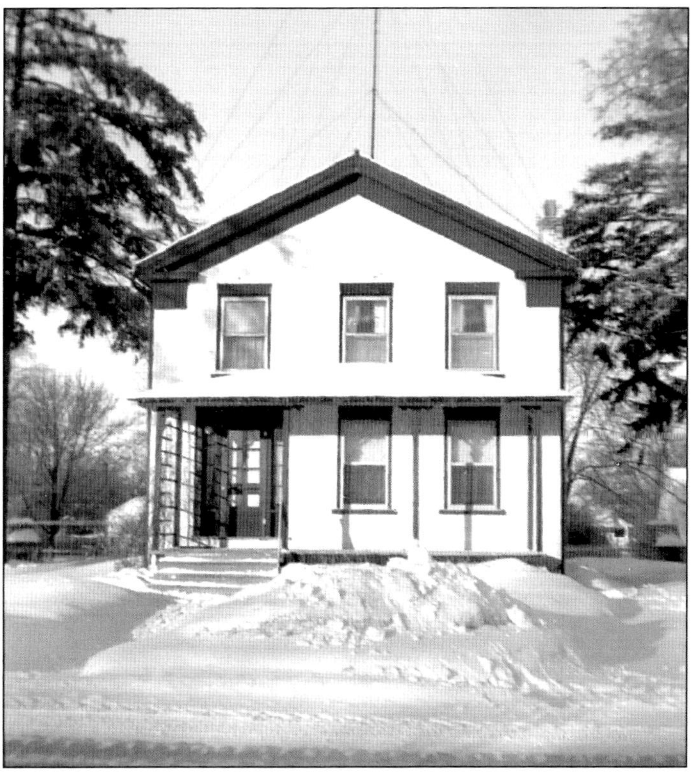

In the 1870s, Norris built a Greek Revival style house on the north side of town. One hundred years later, new owners wondered why a house of that age did not have a single fireplace. The reason was obvious. Norris was the leading stove dealer in Elkhorn. He preferred stove pipe holes in every wall to fireplaces.

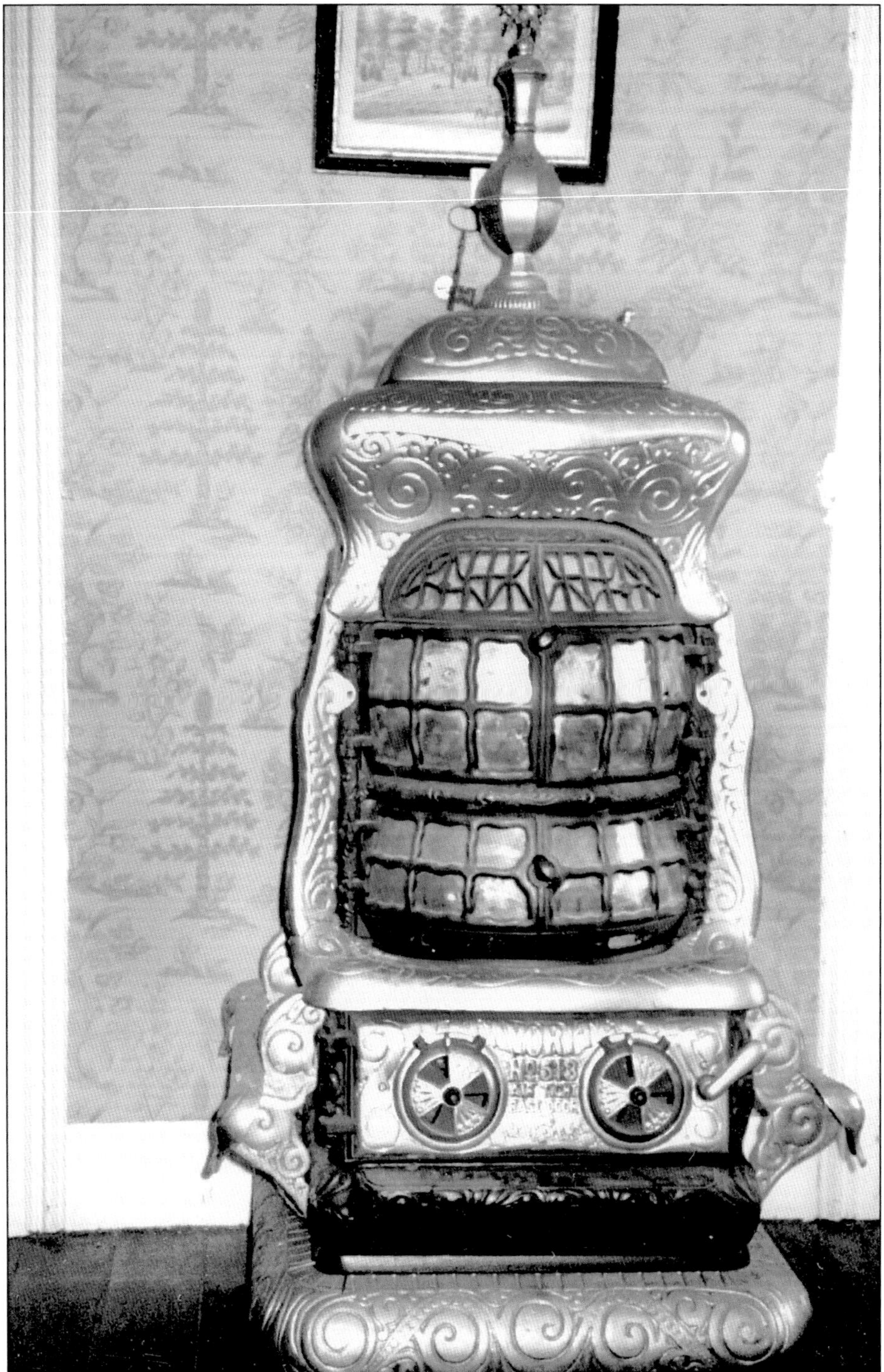

This was typical of the kind of ornate stove Norris sold to heat the rooms in the fancier houses, which were being constructed in prosperous Elkhorn. Norris' son became the first mayor in the 1890s when the city was large enough to have a mayor and aldermen.

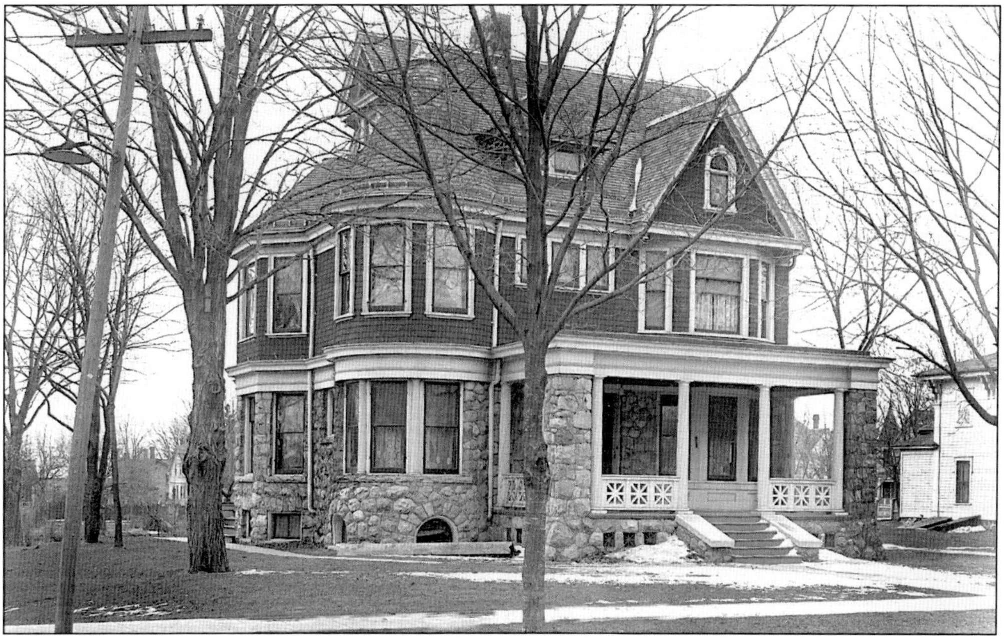

Dr. George H. Young came to Elkhorn in 1843 from New York and was the city's first doctor. His son, George Young Jr., joined him in his practice later. The Young's house, a Queen Anne Victorian, remained in the family until this present day. Dr. Young's wife was the daughter of E.J. Hooper, a banker.

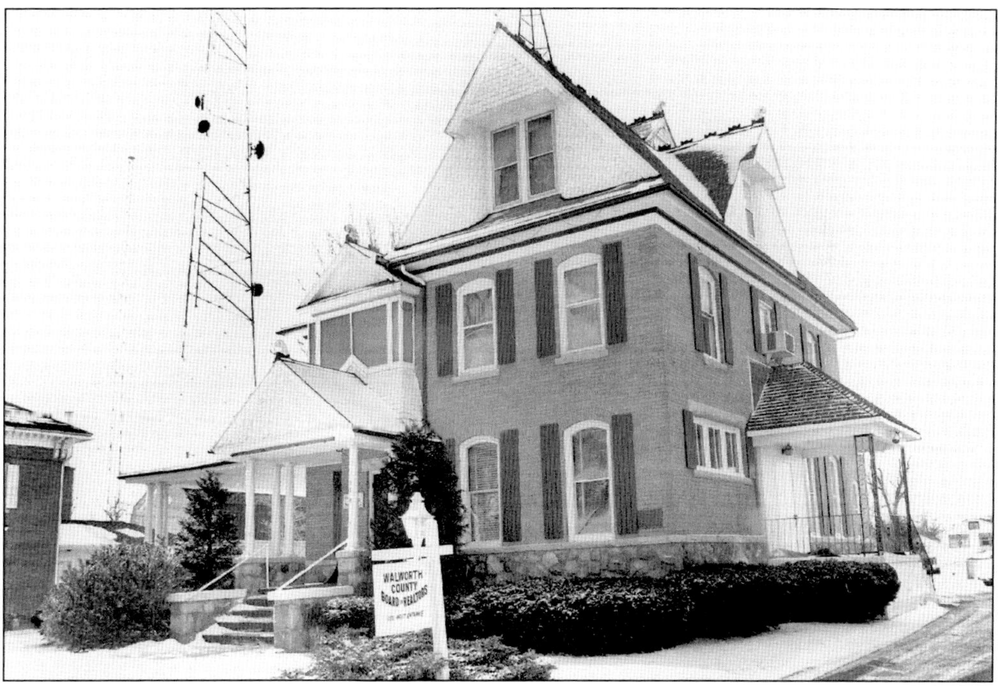

Another banker, Fred Isham, lived in a large three-story house near the square. Today, old houses of that size have usually been remodeled into offices. This one served as a funeral parlor for many years.

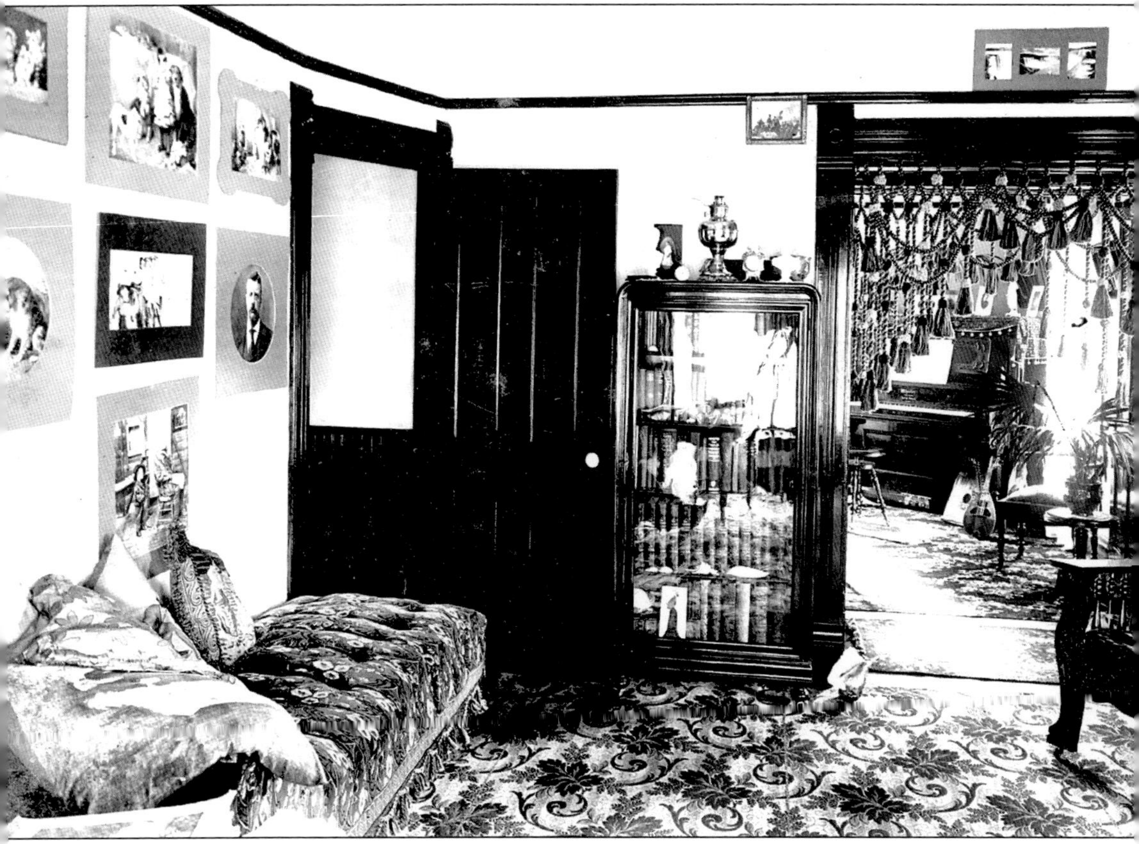

As the merchants and professional people prospered, the interiors of their homes reflected their status. Bright flowered carpets covered the floors. Heavy velvet drapes framed the lace-curtained windows. It was stylish to have beads or fringed satin ropes hang in the openings between rooms. Tall glass cabinets displayed treasured dishes. Colorful pillows made the hard couch comfortable. Pictures, some of sentimental scenes and others of family members, hung on every wall.

The parlor was the room where guests were entertained. The family Bible was displayed prominently on a center table. An intricate kerosene lamp gave illumination. Seldom used by the family, the parlor was preserved mainly for visitors.

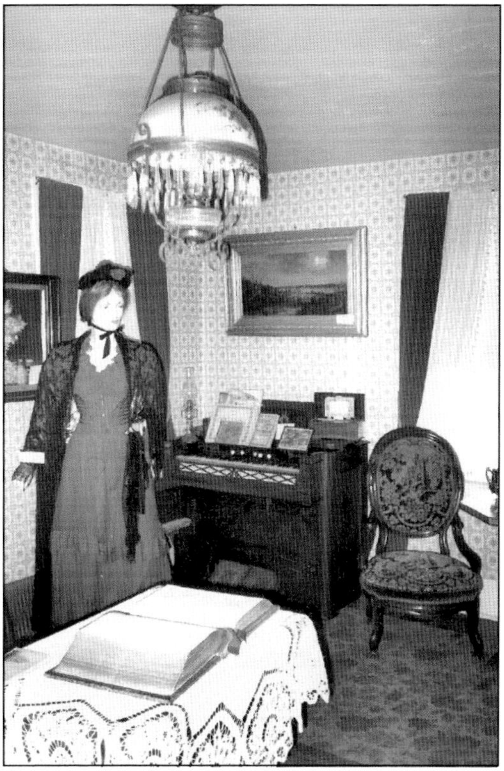

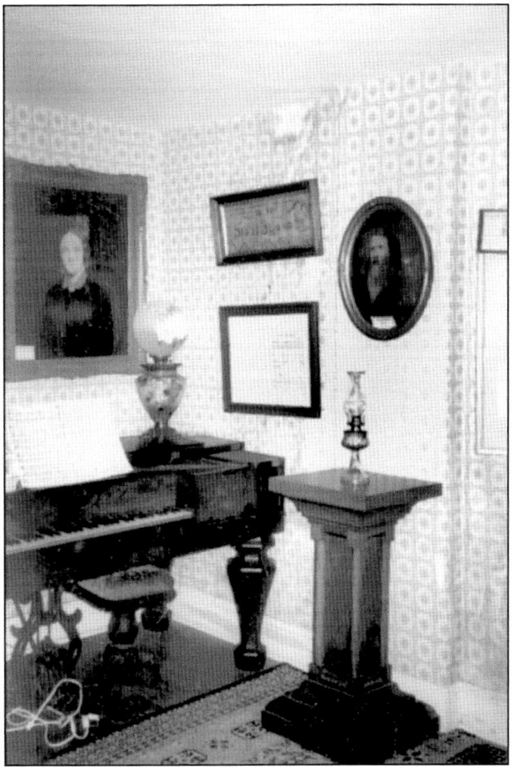

There was usually an organ or piano in the house. Piano lessons were important for the children so that the family could gather together on a cold winter evening and sing the favorite songs everyone knew.

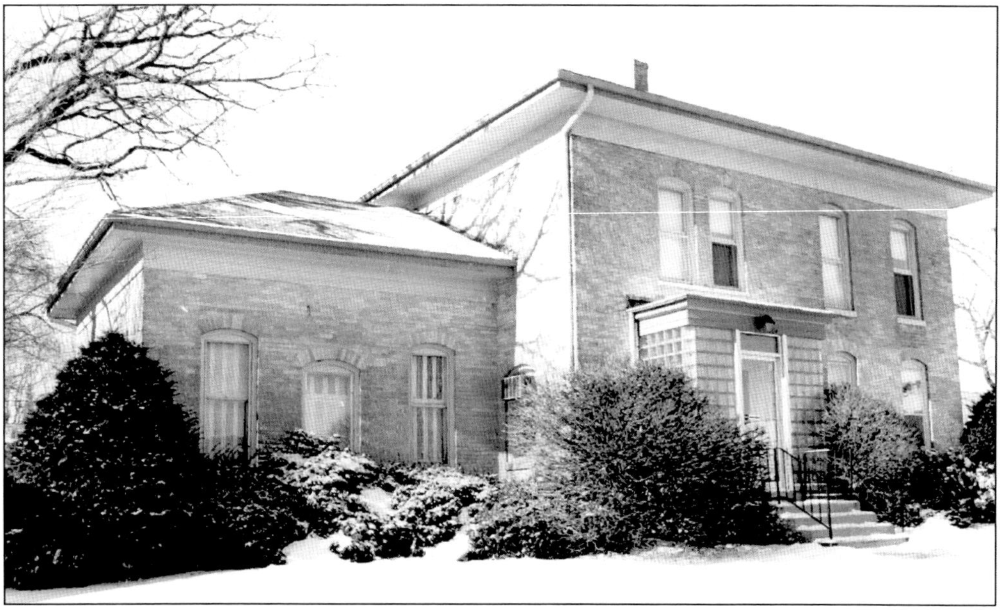

Retired farmers who decided to move into town and let their children run the farm tended to erect big, comfortable houses. This yellow brick house, an office building now, was owned by the Wales family for many years. Descendants of that retired farmer, Charles Wales, have the popular Elk Restaurant. It stands next to the Sprague Theater.

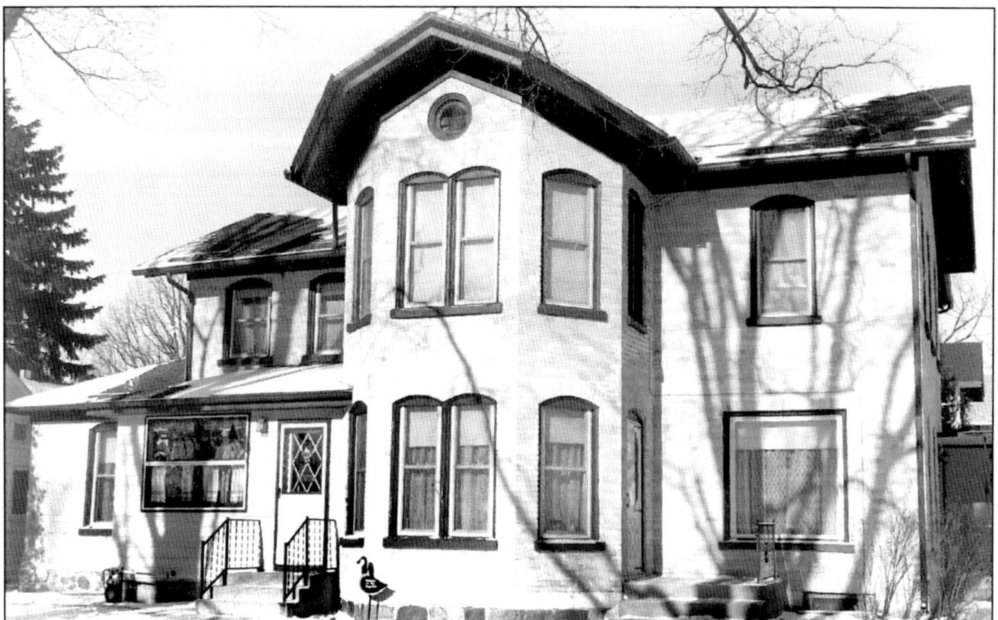

Brick was used for much of the construction jobs in the early years. Heavy clay deposits under the topsoil made for poor drainage, but also made excellent brick. As a result, there were several brick yards in Elkhorn at one time. E.H. Sprague was the owner of one of them. He used his own yellow brick for his big house. His name was an important one here, since he was a very public-spirited citizen.

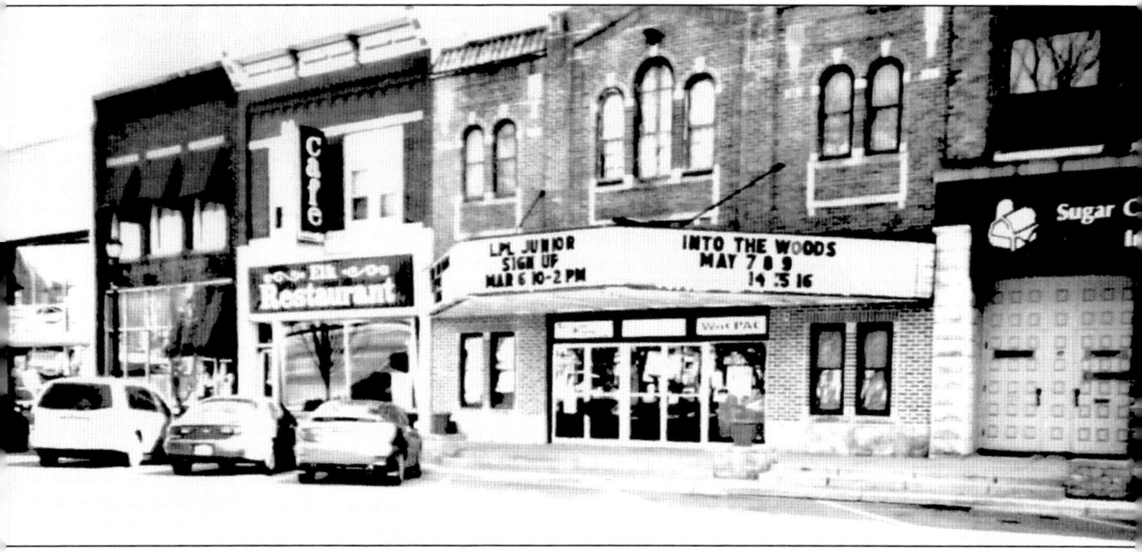

Facing the square was a row of business places, among them Wales' Elk Restaurant and the Sprague Theater. The theater was named in honor of E.H. Sprague, whose own magnificent Opera House had been destroyed by fire. Unfortunately, the theater today is no longer a motion picture palace. Several times a year, though, the Lakeland Players present plays and musicals.

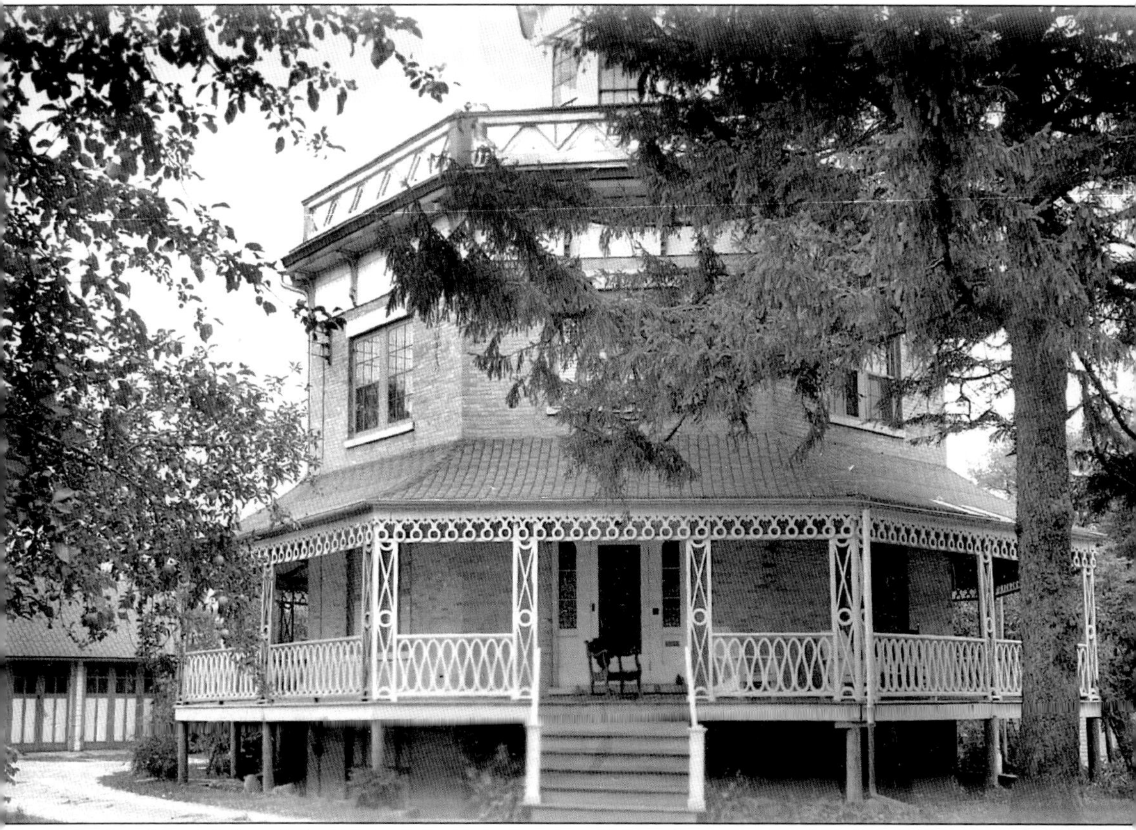

In the middle of the 19th century, a spectacular and unusual type of architecture achieved renown. This was the eight-sided house known as an Octagon house. First designed by Orson Fowler, it intrigued many prospective home owners.

One of these novel houses was constructed here for Colonel Elderkin. He was a teacher, lawyer, and farmer. It was said that he would stand at the top of his house and oversee the progress of his farm workers from the cupola. It is now on the National Register.

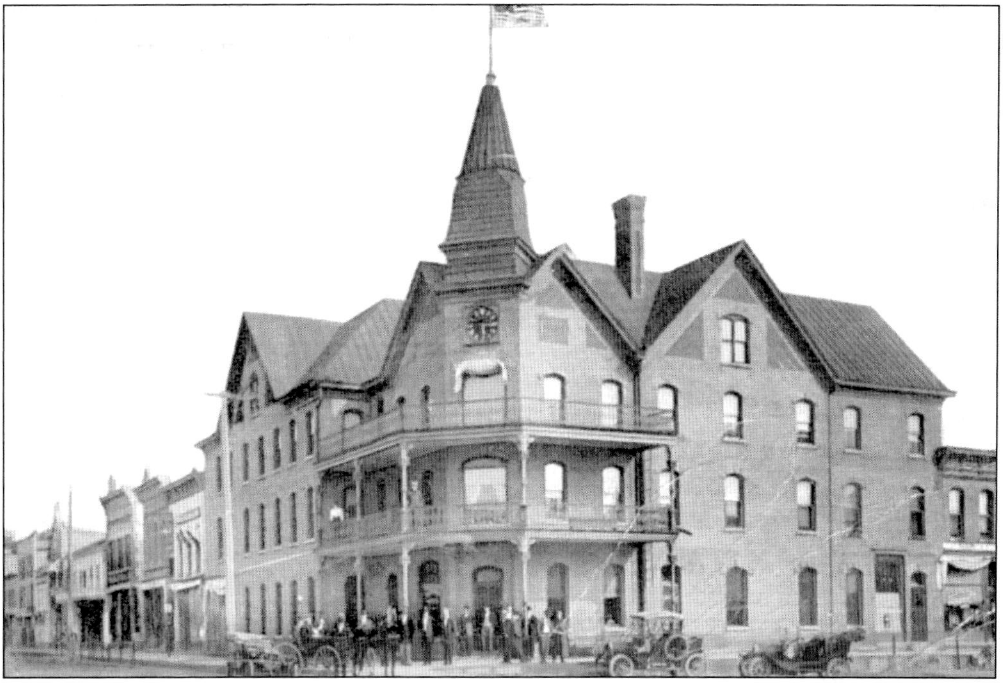

People who were traveling and stayed overnight in Elkhorn needed a roof over their heads too. The Elkhorn House, on a downtown corner, offered a comfortable night's lodging. No longer a hotel, it is now a well-patronized Chinese restaurant, Moy's. At one time, the Snyder family ran it. John Snyder was an artist and some of his oil paintings hang in Matheson Library here.

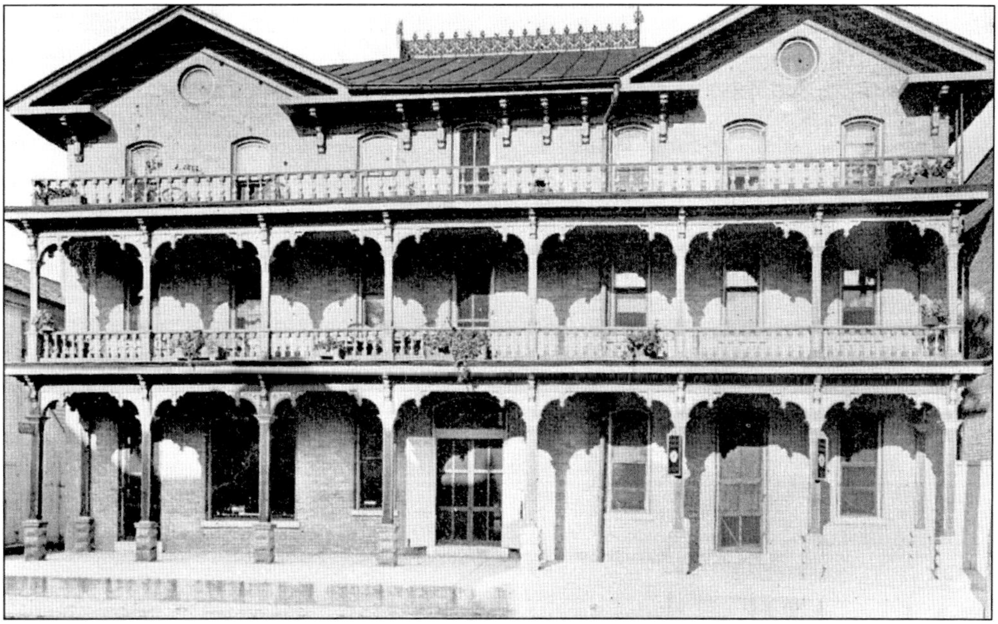

Farther down the street was the Nickel Plate Hotel. Both hotels had long double porches where visitors could sit and watch the downtown doings. Since travel was often done by train when these hotels were started, both of them had a livery stable nearby.

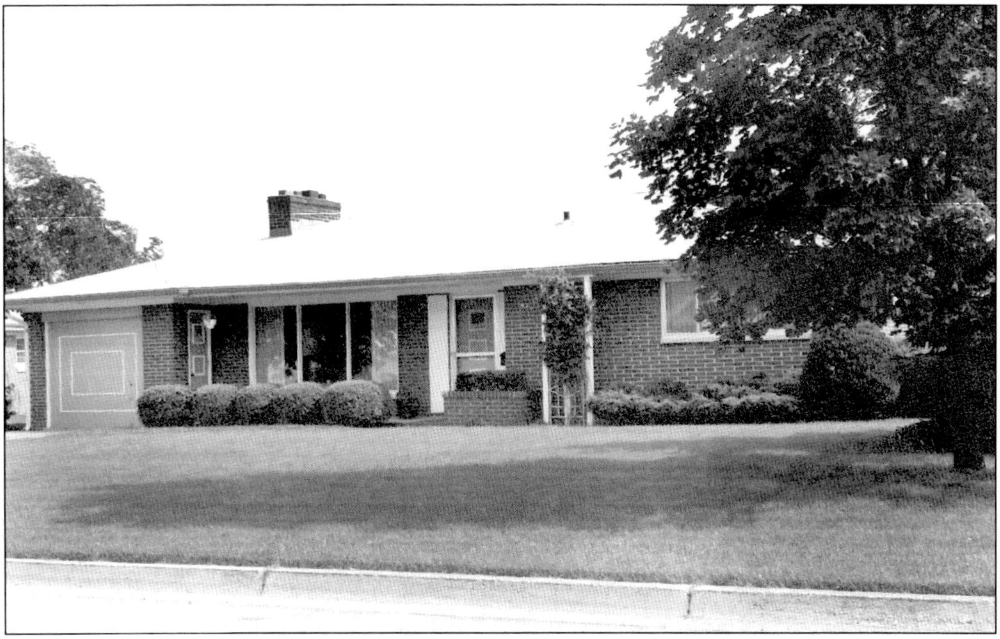

After World War II, the architectural style of houses changed. The new ones were much less elaborate. Ranch style homes, all on one level, became popular. They can be found throughout the city, mixed in with the older traditional styles of the earlier days.

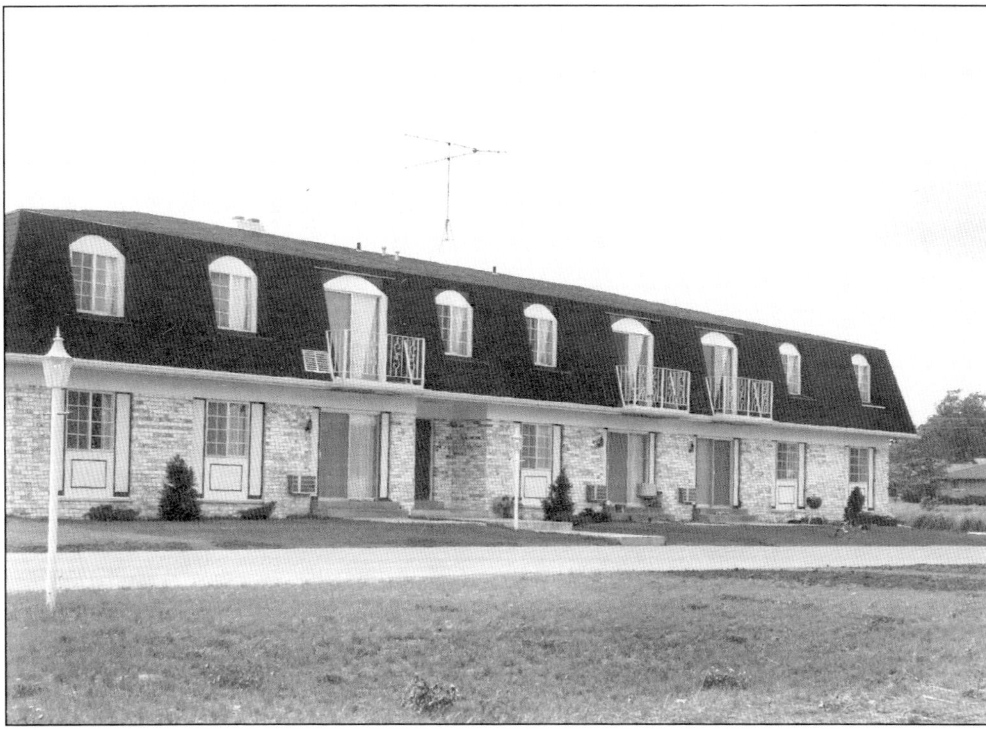

Apartments made their appearance on the scene about then, too. Previously, most multiple-family dwellings consisted of an upstairs "flat" which was rented out by the owner who lived downstairs.

Four

PLACES TO WORSHIP

Along with establishing a shelter, church was also a priority with the Elkhorn pioneers. The churches drew worshippers from the farms. People traveled many miles either on foot or by horse and buggy to attend services. Often the circuit riding preacher could come only once a month, so a Sunday sermon was a real event.

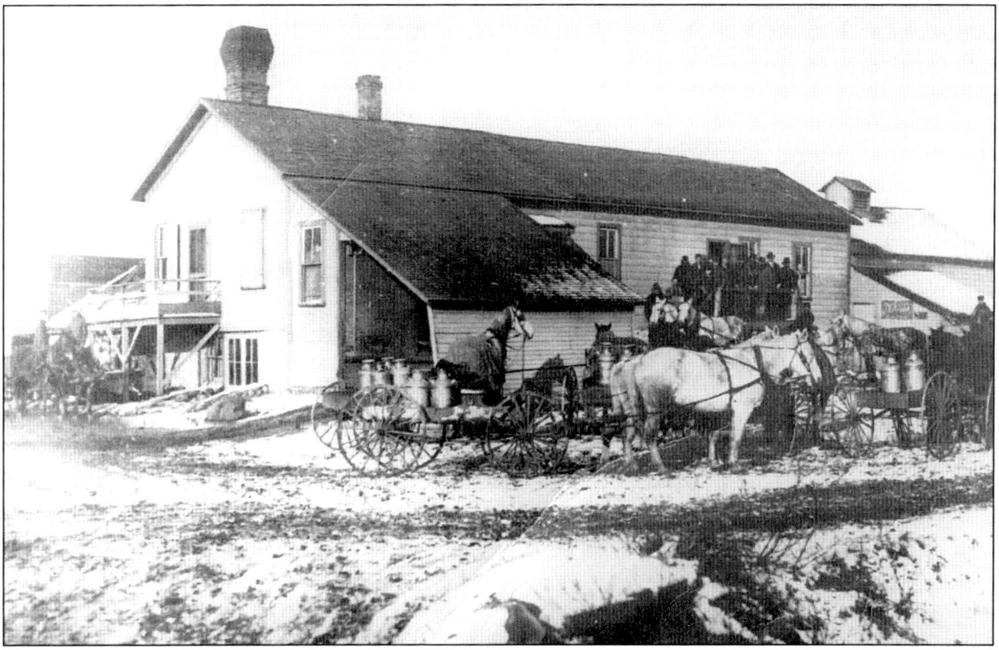

Many of the immigrants who came from Norway in the 1840s chose farmland just to the west of Elkhorn. There were so many Norwegians there that it was designated Jacobsville. They had their own church with services in the Norwegian language. The settlement at Jacobsville grew to have a milk plant, store, and post office.

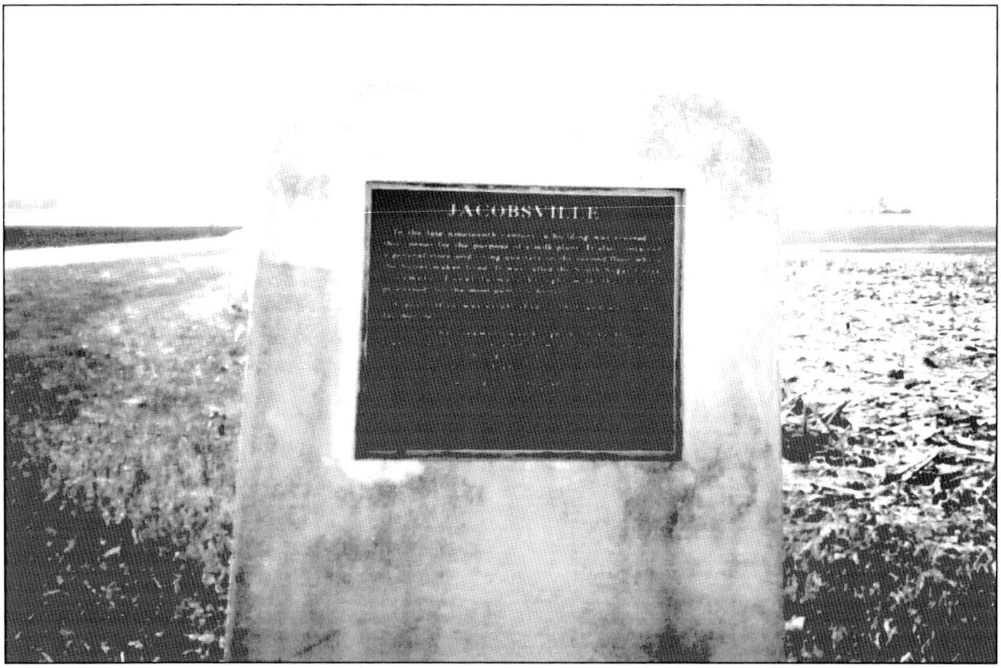

The settlement is gone now. The end came when the milk plant was purchased by Elkhorn's larger butter and cheese company and then was closed. Only a cement marker erected by Ormal Nelson, who farmed the land on the corner, gives any indication that it once was a busy corner hamlet.

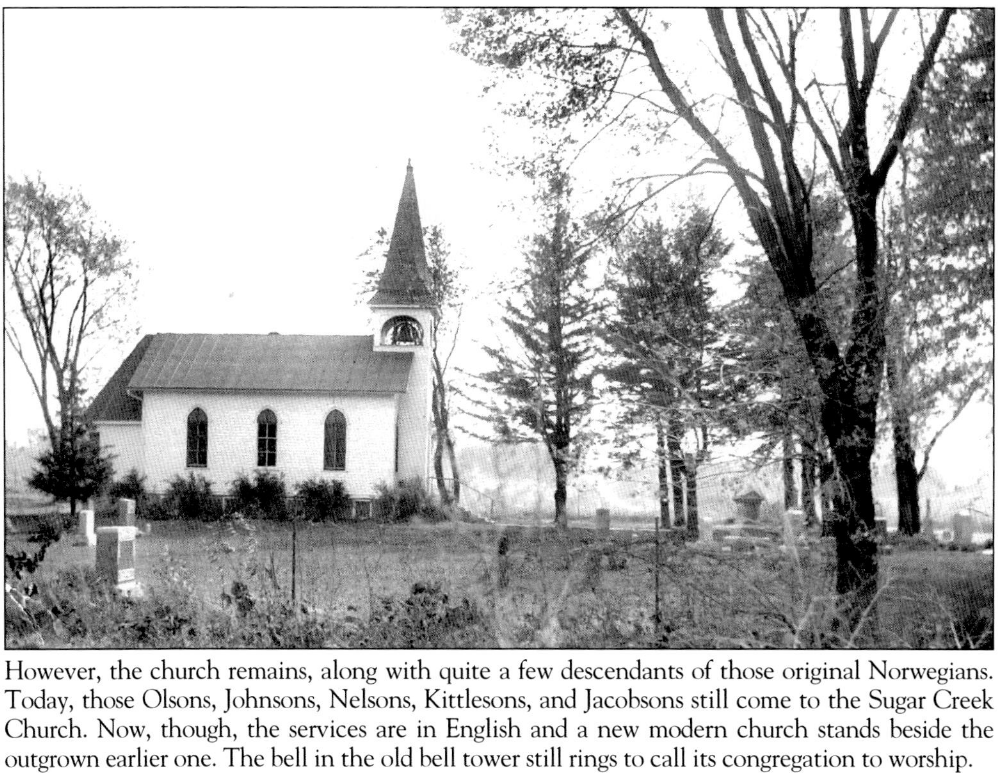

However, the church remains, along with quite a few descendants of those original Norwegians. Today, those Olsons, Johnsons, Nelsons, Kittlesons, and Jacobsons still come to the Sugar Creek Church. Now, though, the services are in English and a new modern church stands beside the outgrown earlier one. The bell in the old bell tower still rings to call its congregation to worship.

Two other rural churches that continue to flourish are Bethel Church and Millard Church. Bethel Church is at the corner of Highway 67 and County Road A. It had its beginning in 1872.

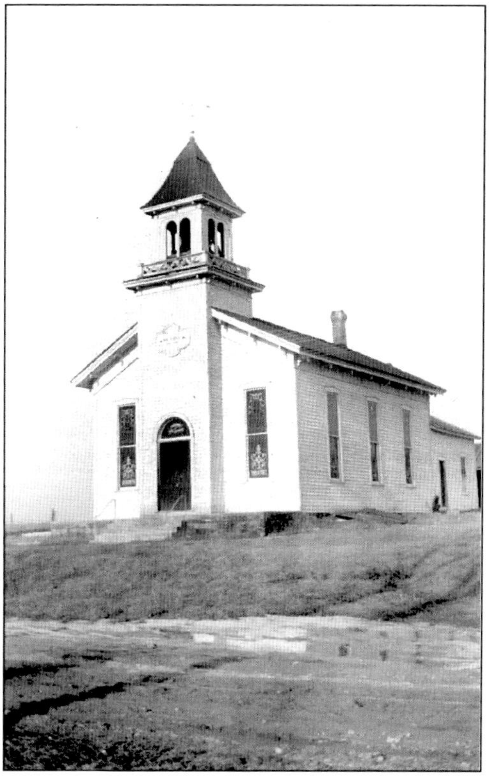

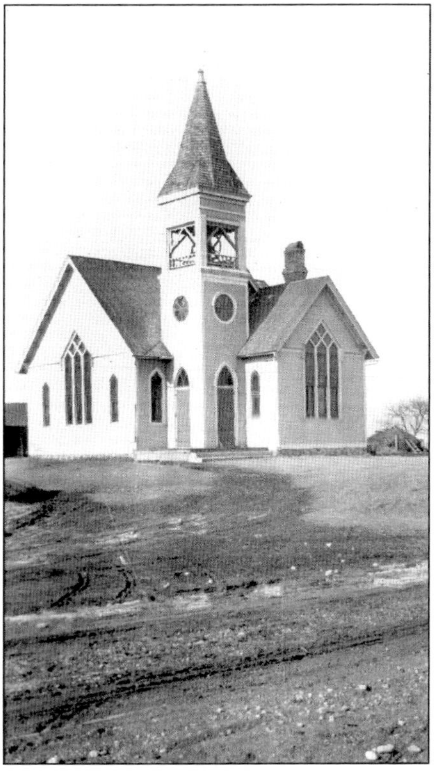

Millard Church was built in 1892, but was hit by lightning in 1950 and burned down. It was quickly replaced by the brick church which stands there now.

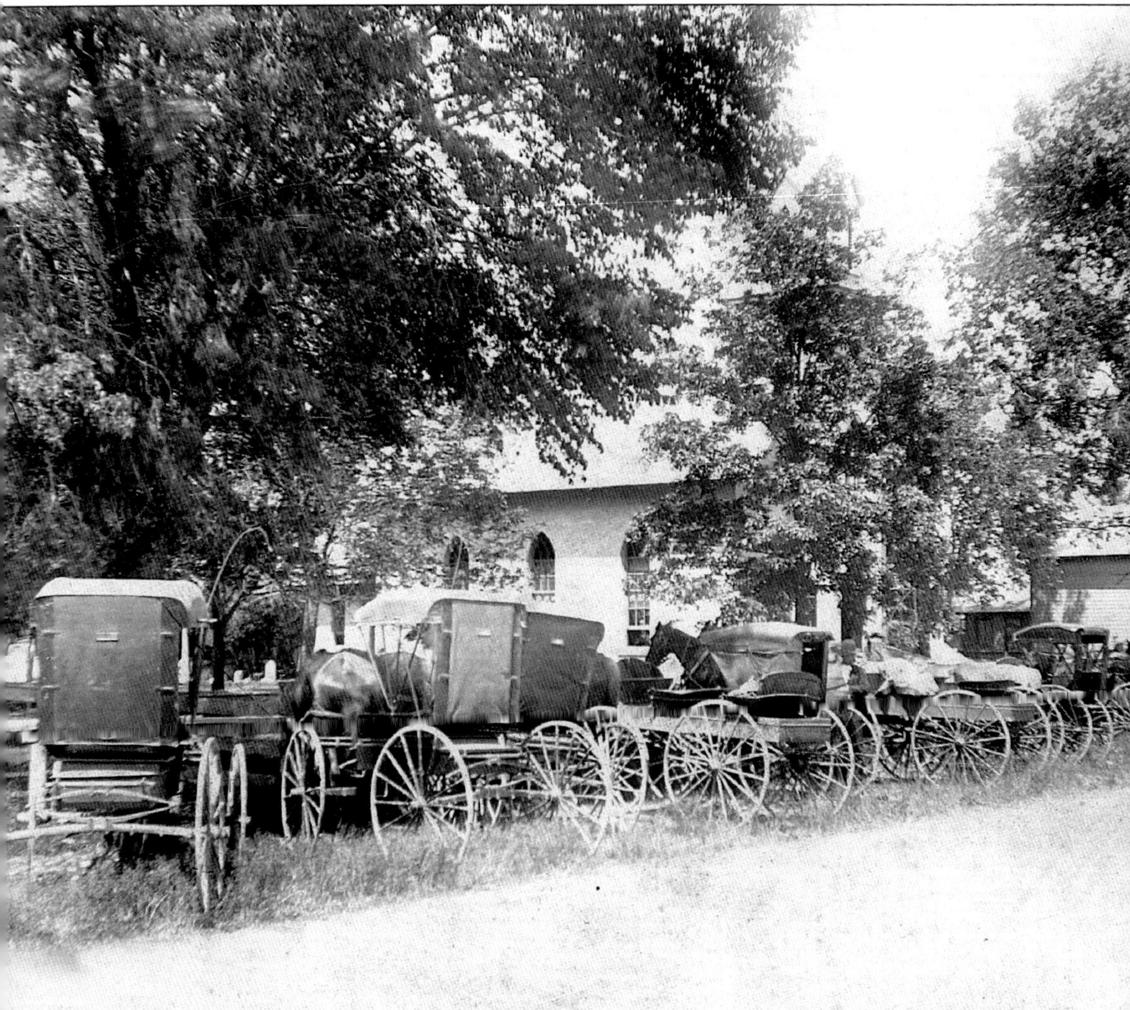

Those rural churches are a few miles north of Elkhorn, but many of the city's residents drive out there for services. Years ago, buggies used to fill the parking lots. The lots have been enlarged to make room for automobiles today.

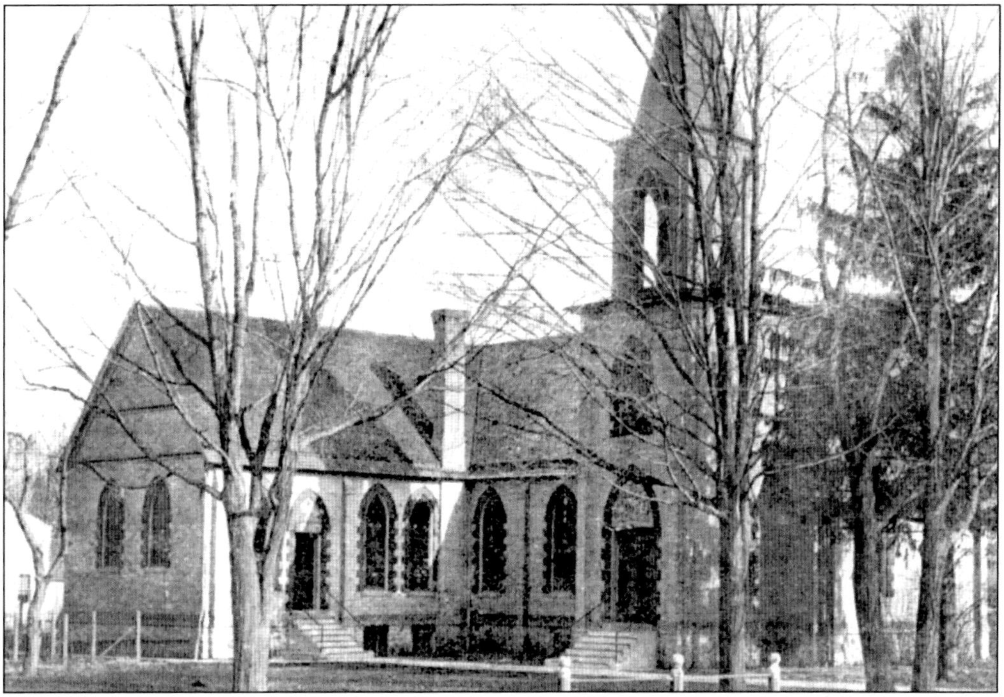

In the city of Elkhorn, the religious settlers held services in their homes and in public buildings at first. As soon as possible, modest churches were put up. They were replaced by larger, more elaborate buildings when the membership increased. The first church established in Elkhorn was the Episcopalian Church, St. John's in the Wilderness.

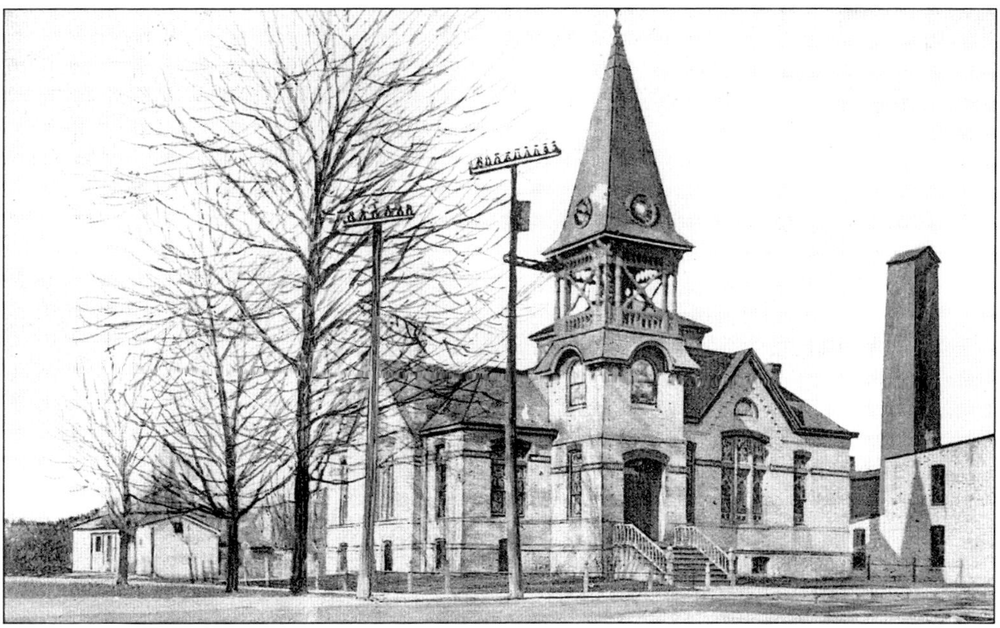

The Congregational Church also had its start early in the city's history. The present brick church was built in 1882. For a while, high school graduation services were held in it. Just recently, the pointed steeple has been returned to the top of the bell tower.

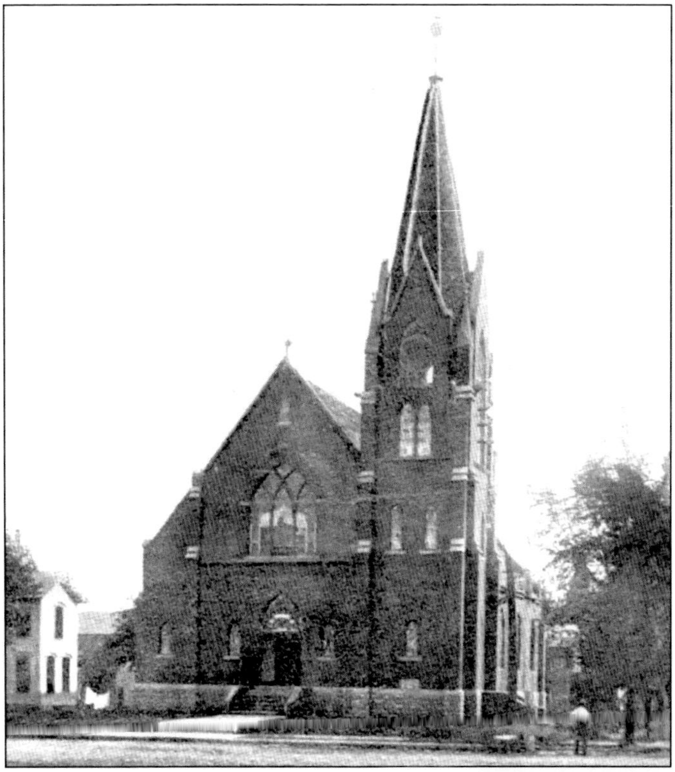

Other denominations followed. The Catholics built the tall spired St. Patrick's Church on a corner opposite the downtown square.

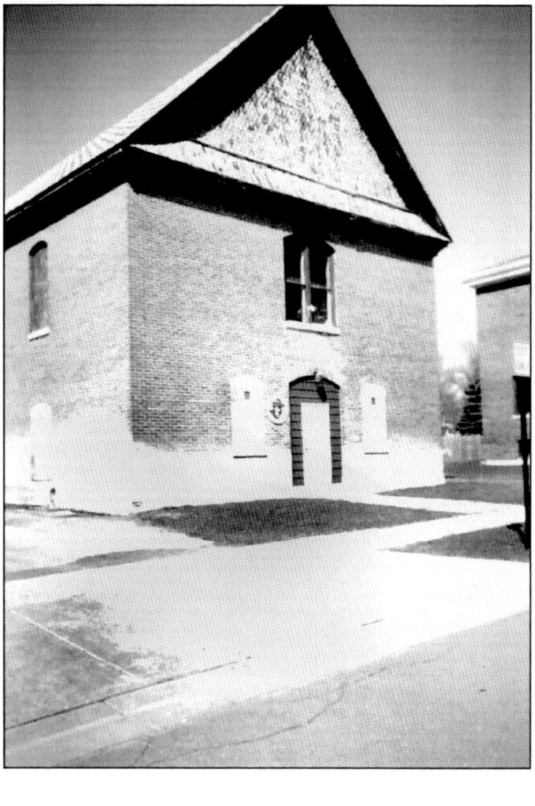

A parsonage was built next to it and at the far side of the parking lot stood Columbus Hall. The hall was the scene of many community events.

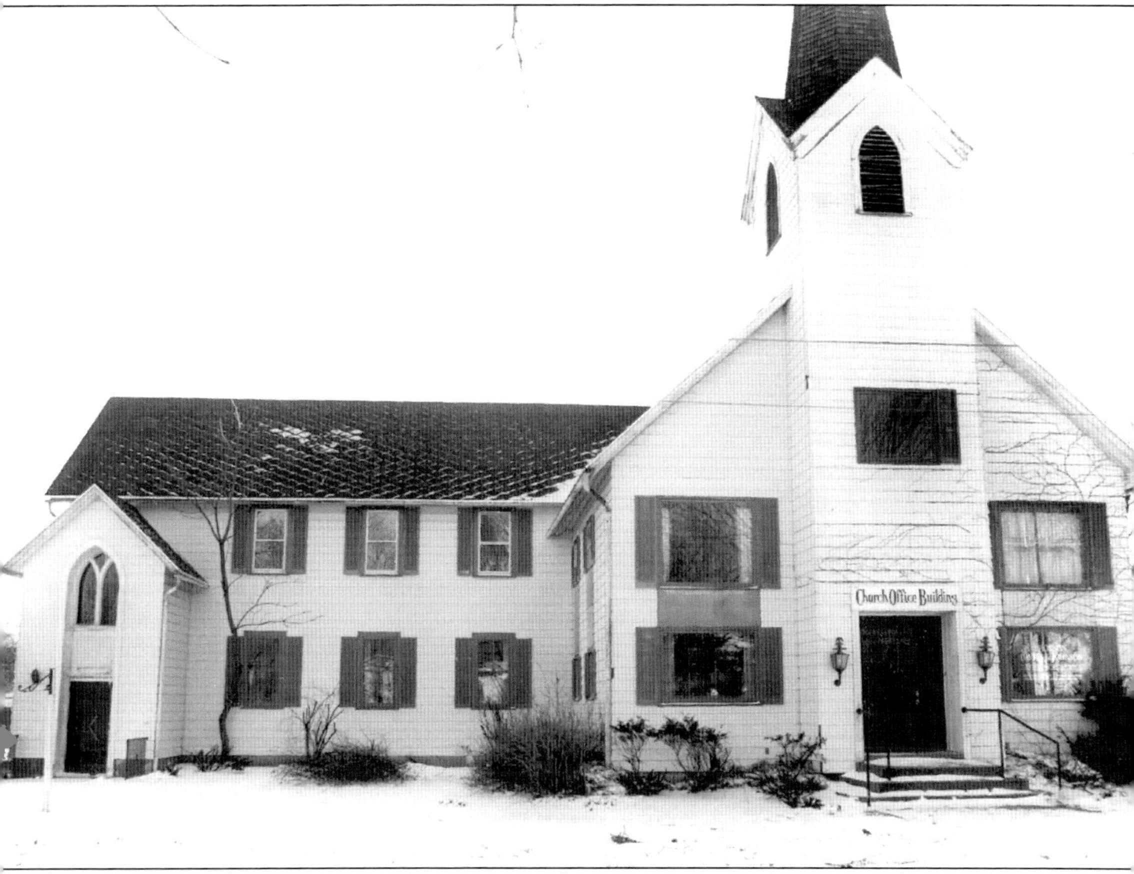

The Lutheran Church began as a German language church. There was a dispute among members later and the congregation split. Part of them remained in the first building and the others built a church next door. The first frame church is now an office, appropriately called the Church Office Building. The congregation now has a much larger church on the southeast side of Elkhorn.

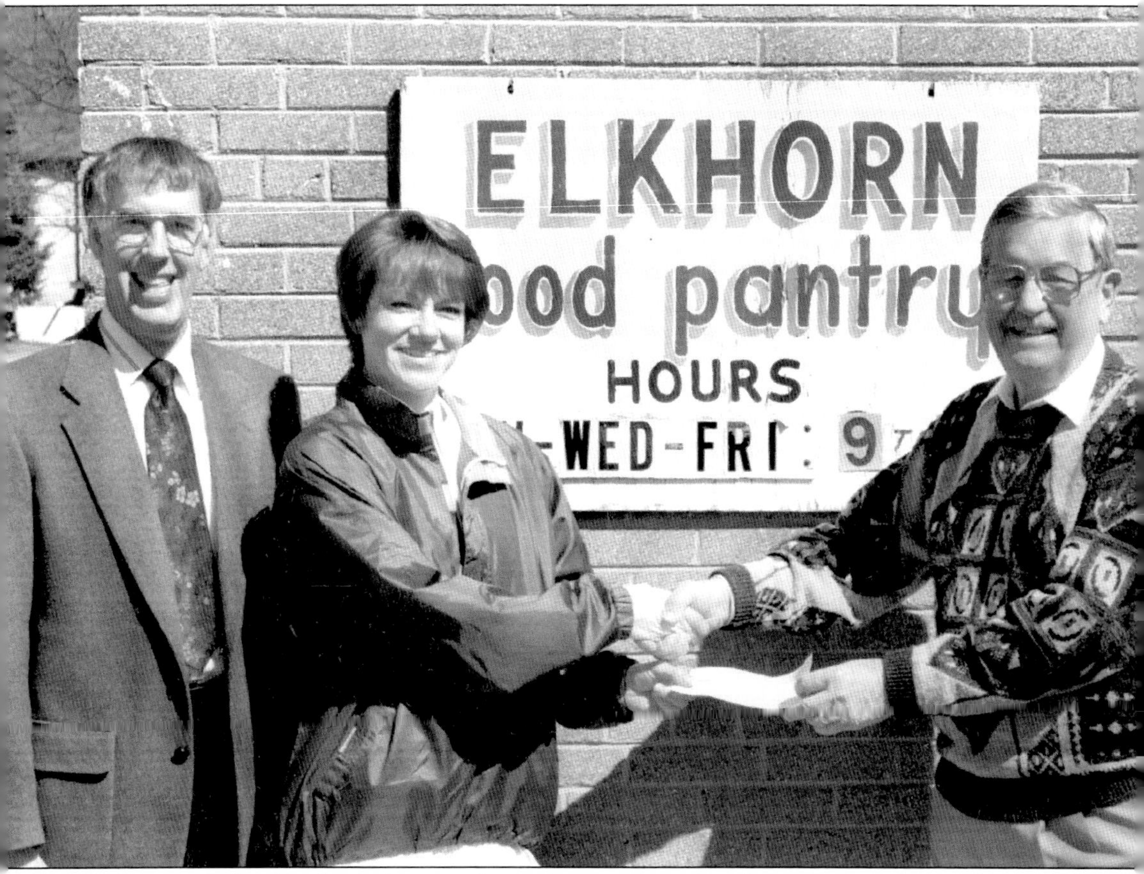

The very old churches, along with the many new ones that have come into being since those pioneer days, have always been eager to loan their space for charitable purposes. The ELCA Lutherans have had the Elkhorn Food Pantry on its premises for many years. Most of the churches in town are on the pantry's board of directors. Frank Grunseth, retired school principal, is its president.

Five

Education for the Children

Once the family had a roof over their heads, the education of the children became important. Little classes were held in homes at first. Mothers who had some basic knowledge of reading and math skills taught their own children and those of their neighbors.

Land was set aside for a school when the village of Elkhorn was platted and in 1840 a small frame school was built. It was merely 20 ft. x 20 ft. in size. In 10 years, it was outgrown and a larger two-story brick school house was constructed in 1850. Like other important buildings, it was located across from the downtown square.

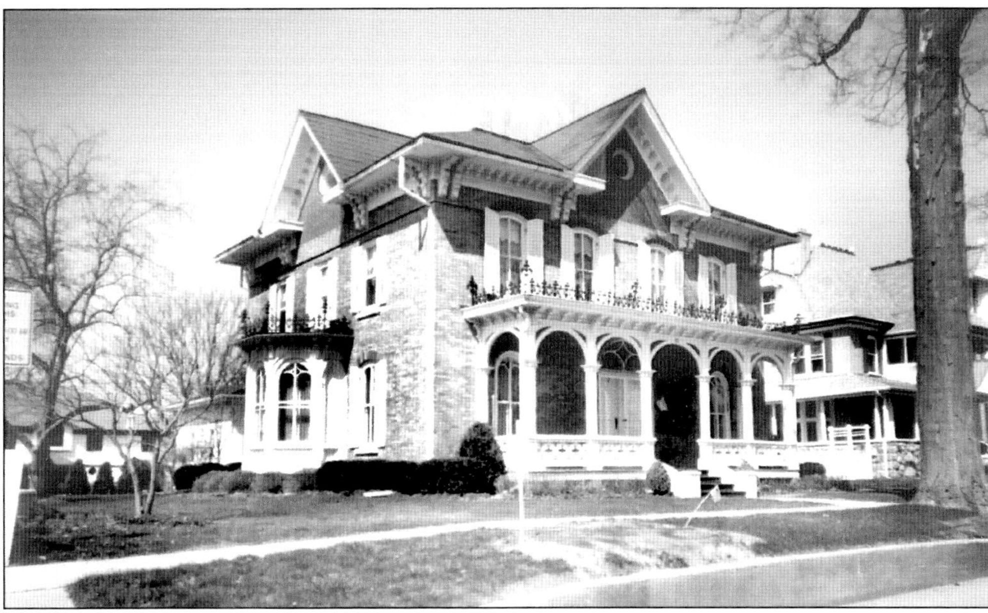

As soon as a much larger school was built in 1857, this first brick one was purchased by Dr. Benoni Reynolds and it became his residence. On the National Register, it is known today as the Reynolds-Weed house.

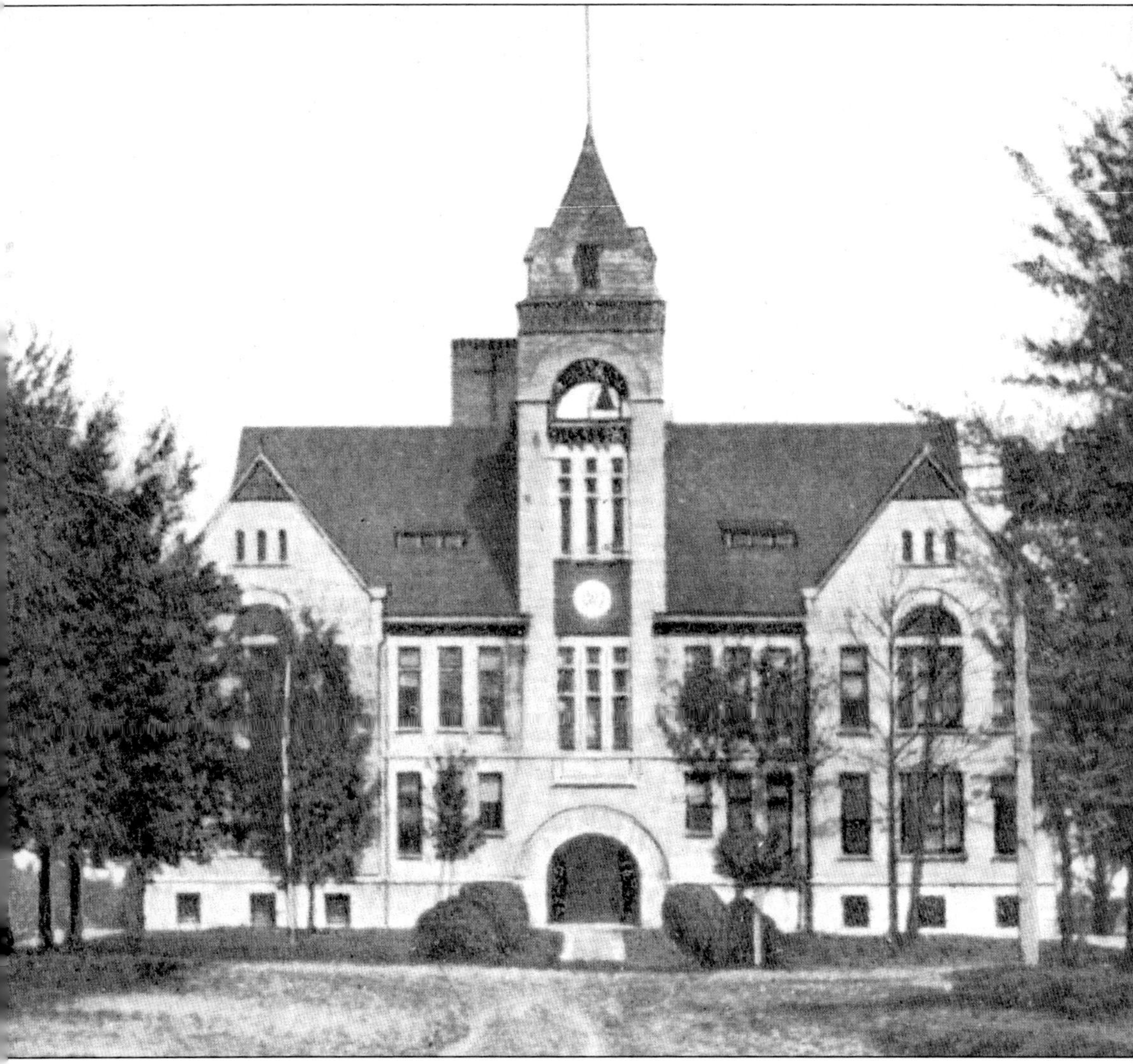

The 1857 school had four classrooms. Two on the first floor were for primary and intermediate students. The two on the top floor were for the high school. This building burned down in 1886. It was replaced by a large brick structure, which is still there at the end of a boulevard today. Until 1906, all grades from first through twelfth met in that one building.

There were 14 high school graduates in 1897. The graduation exercises were then held in the new Sprague Opera House, so that there would be room for all the parents, teachers, and friends. The class motto in 1897 was "Not drifting, but rowing." E.H. Sprague, president of the board of education, presented the diplomas.

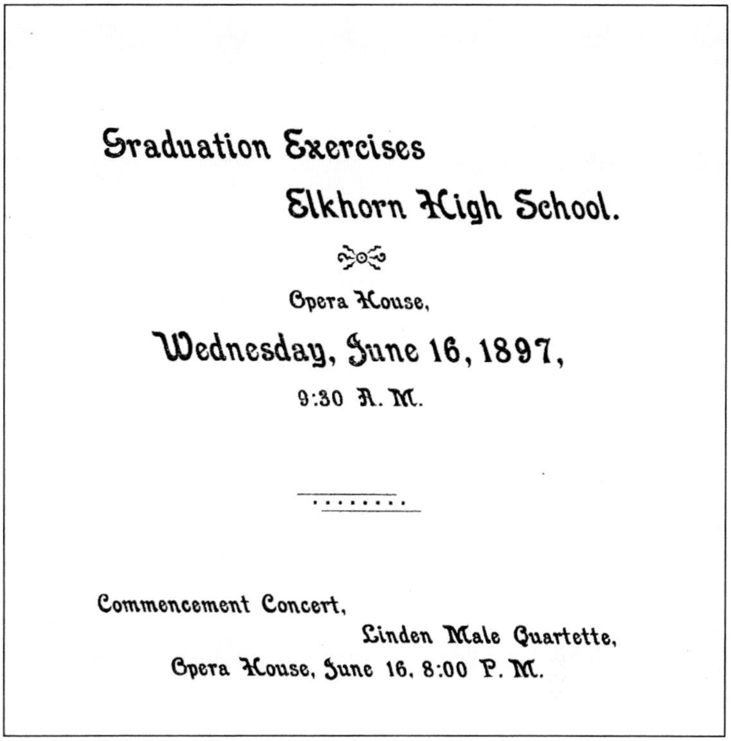

Graduation Exercises

Elkhorn High School.

Opera House,

Wednesday, June 16, 1897,

9:30 A. M.

Commencement Concert,

Linden Male Quartette,

Opera House, June 16, 8:00 P. M.

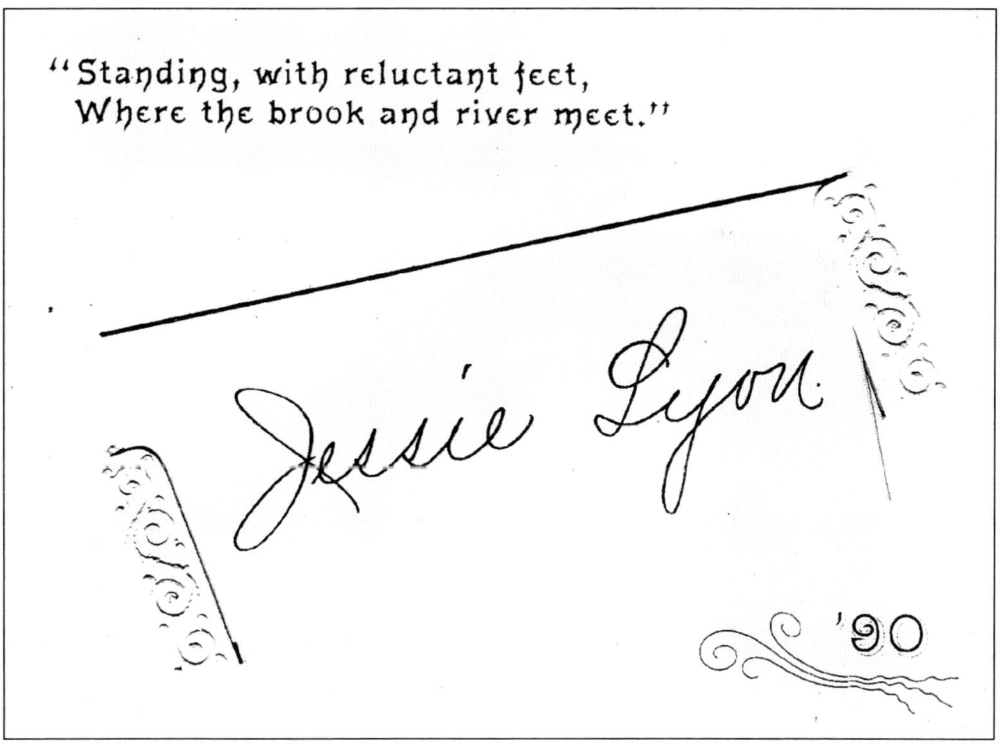

Calling cards for the graduating ladies and gentlemen were part of the ritual of that important stage of life. Jessie Lyon saved one of her cards for many years. She was in the class of 1890.

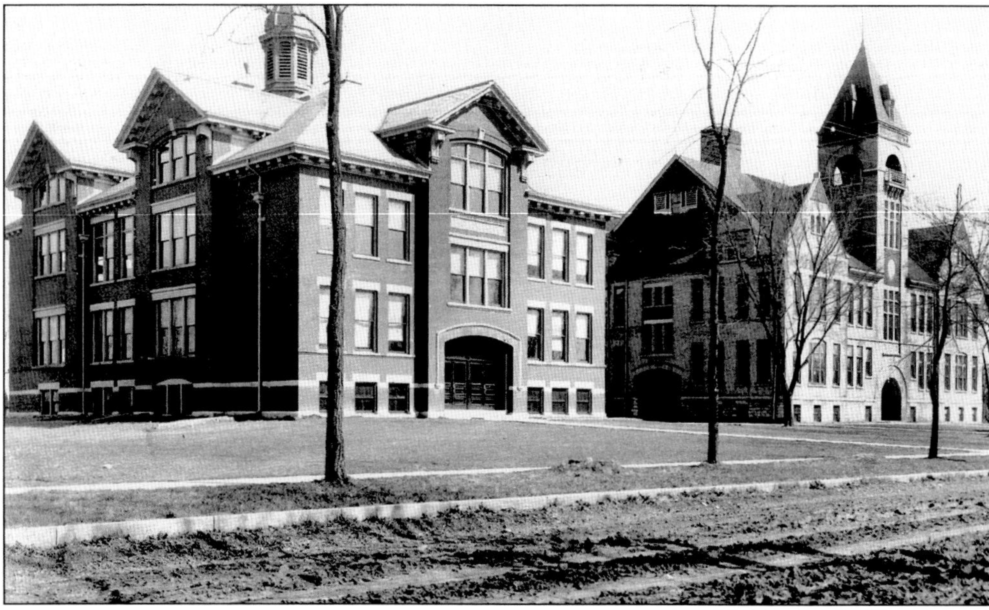

By 1906, it was evident that more classrooms were needed for the expanding school-age population. Therefore, a separate high school was built next to the 1887 school.

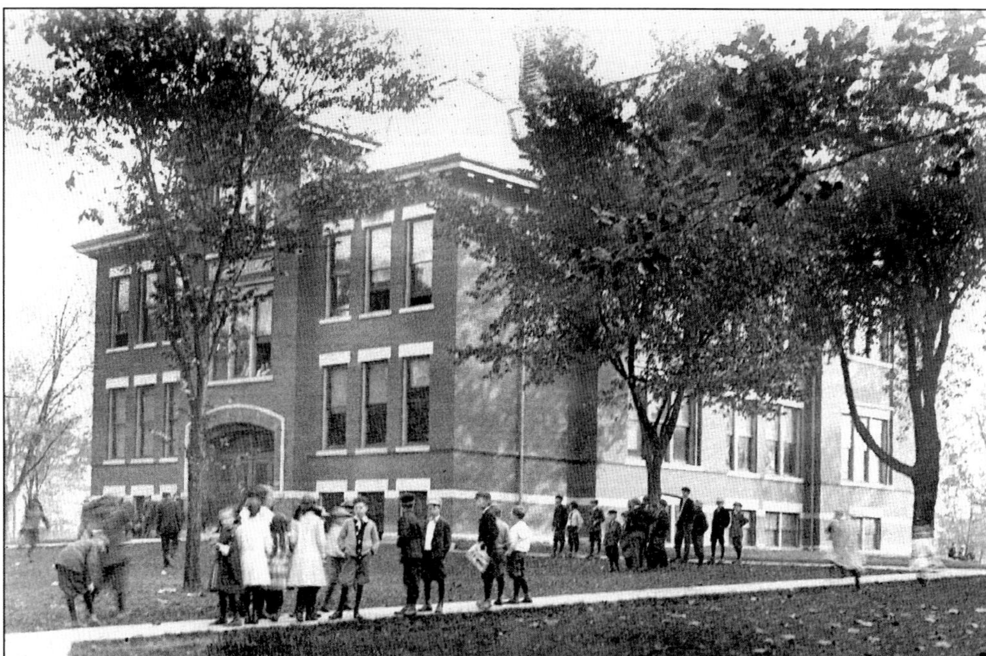

Boys wearing knickers and girls with long black stockings were excited to have a high school separate from the lower grades for the first time.

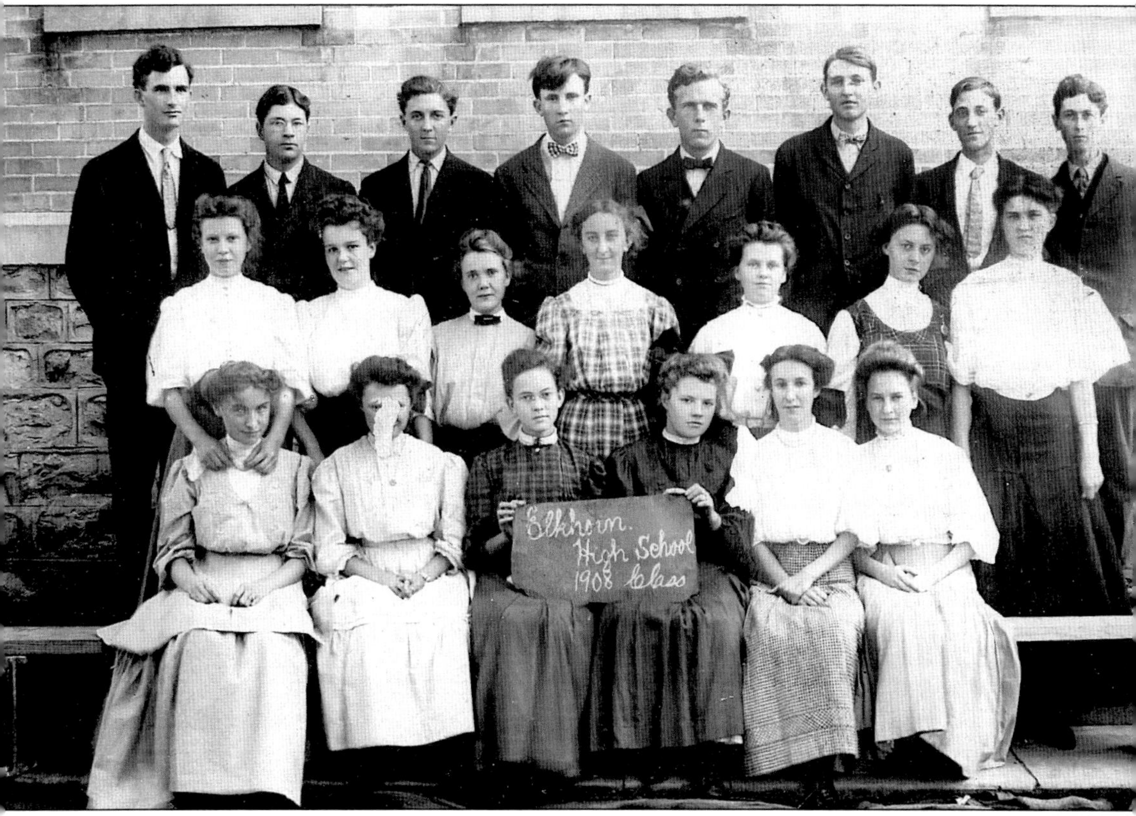

The Elkhorn High Class of 1908 posed in front of the new high school. Many of them came from rural areas and rode to high school on horseback or found a place to room and board within walking distance of the school.

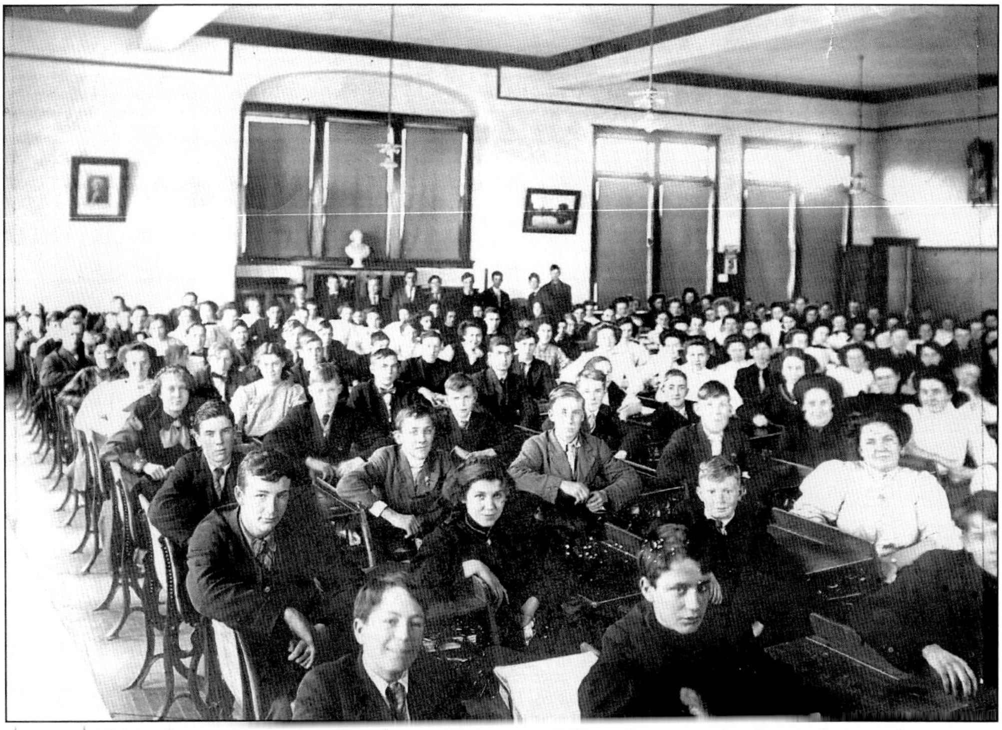

Around 1910, the entire high school population could be photographed together as they sat at the desks in the "main room" of the 1906 building.

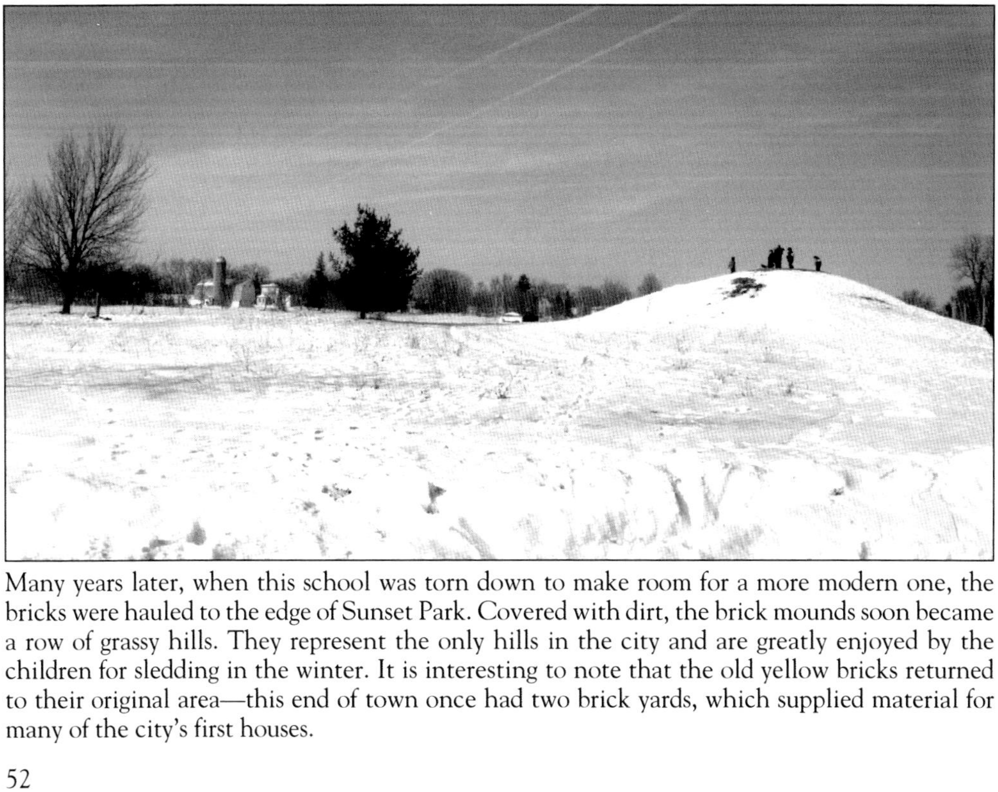

Many years later, when this school was torn down to make room for a more modern one, the bricks were hauled to the edge of Sunset Park. Covered with dirt, the brick mounds soon became a row of grassy hills. They represent the only hills in the city and are greatly enjoyed by the children for sledding in the winter. It is interesting to note that the old yellow bricks returned to their original area—this end of town once had two brick yards, which supplied material for many of the city's first houses.

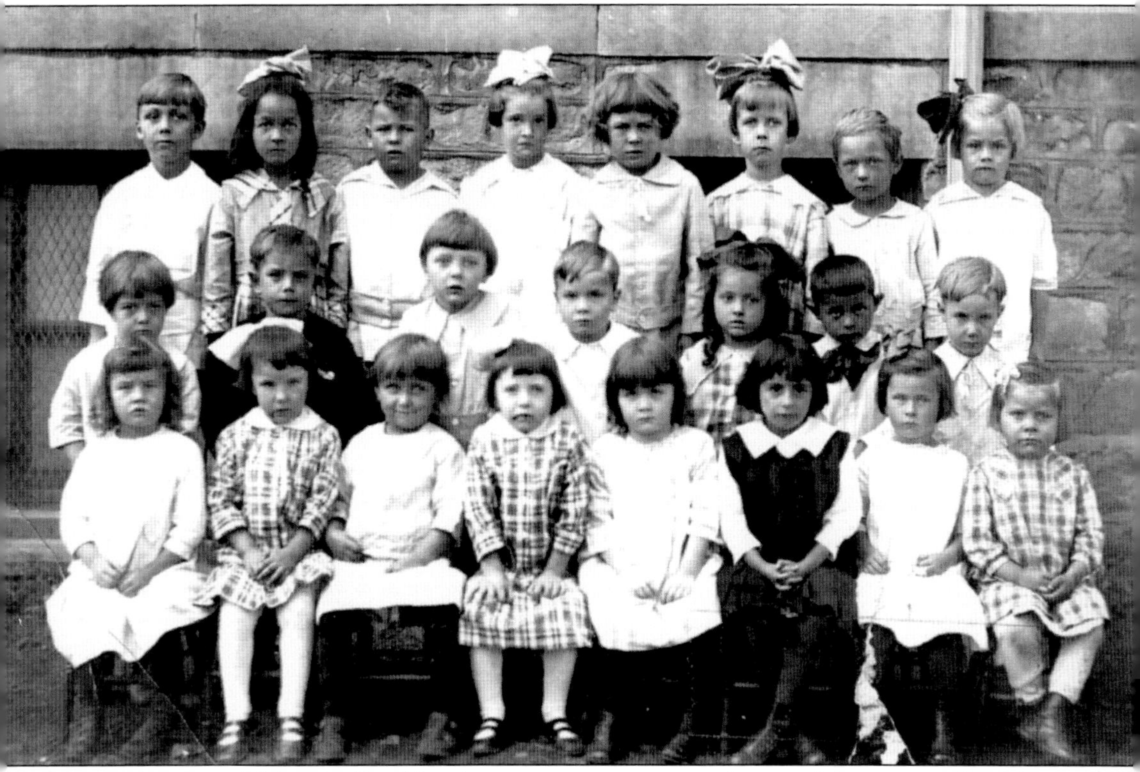

From early times, Elkhorn offered kindergarten instruction to four- and five-year-olds. The first kindergarten in the United States was established in Watertown, Wisconsin, less than a hundred miles away. This may have influenced people here to want early education for their children. The 23 children in Mrs. Florence Norton's kindergarten had their picture taken in front of the 1887 building where all the grade school children went to class.

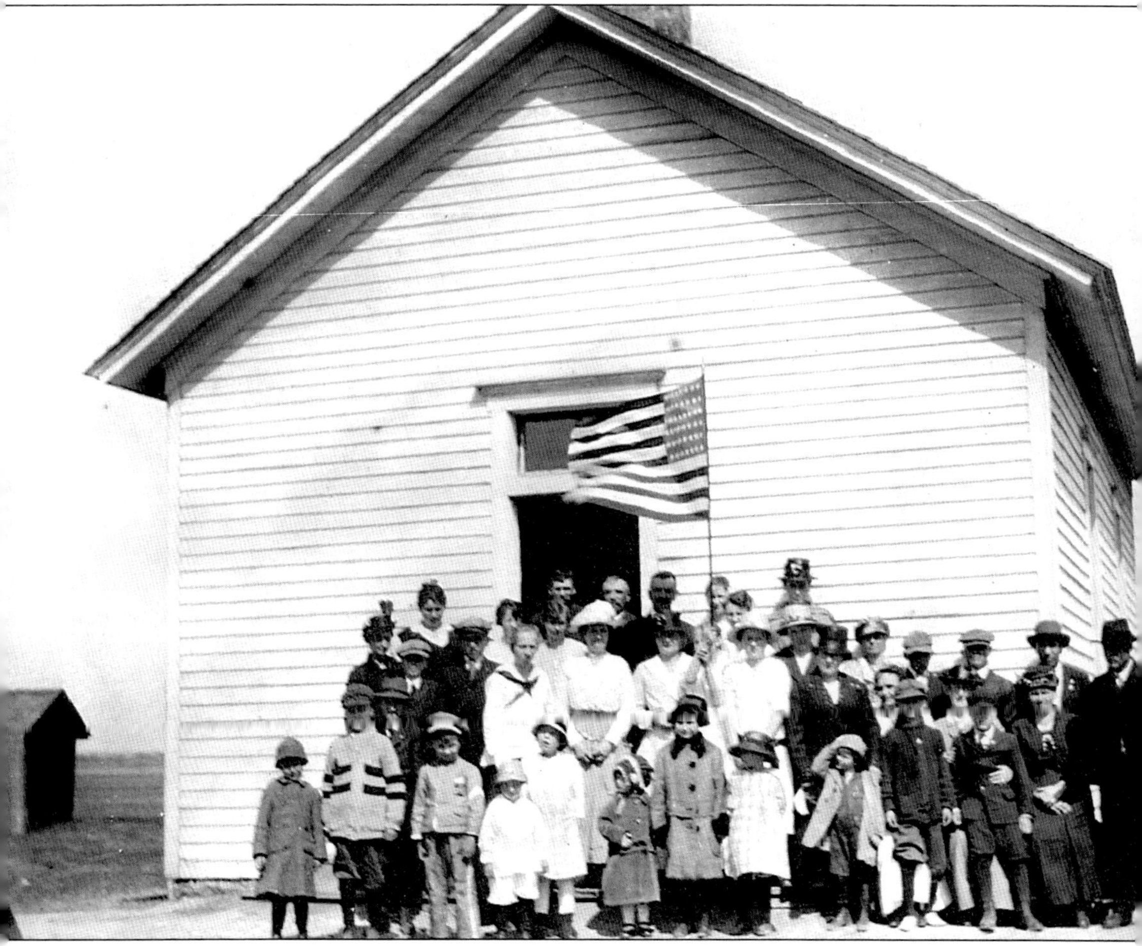

Until the mid-1950s, most children in the rural areas around Elkhorn received their early education in one-room school houses. One teacher might have 35 or 40 students, ranging in grade level from one to eight. Parents, children, and teacher posed for a picture outside a typical rural school. Water had to be carried from some nearby farm and on the left an "out house" took care of the sanitary needs of the children.

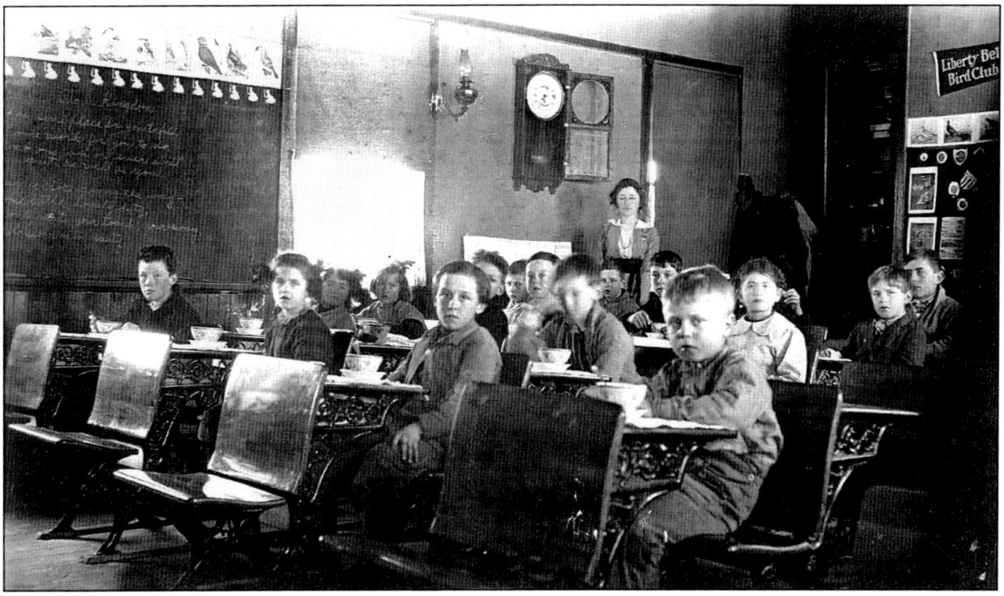

With the teacher standing in back, children sat at their desks in a one-room school. Note a kerosene lamp near the window, which tried to furnish a bit more light in the room. Some rural schools, with the help of nearby parents, attempted to provide hot soup. This was a healthy addition to the sandwich brought from home in a tin lunch box.

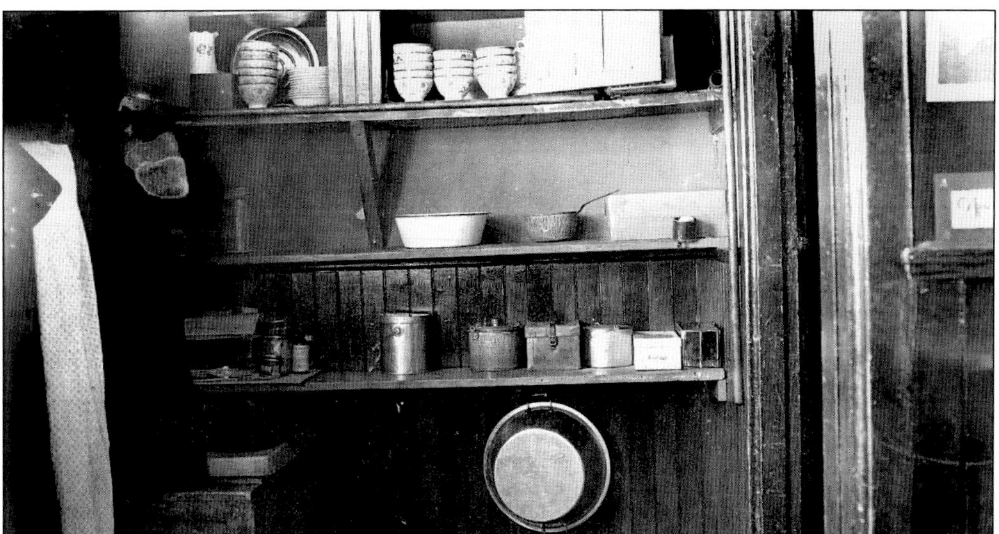

If the school district allowed it, a crude pantry held the necessary utensils for the school lunch program of those days.

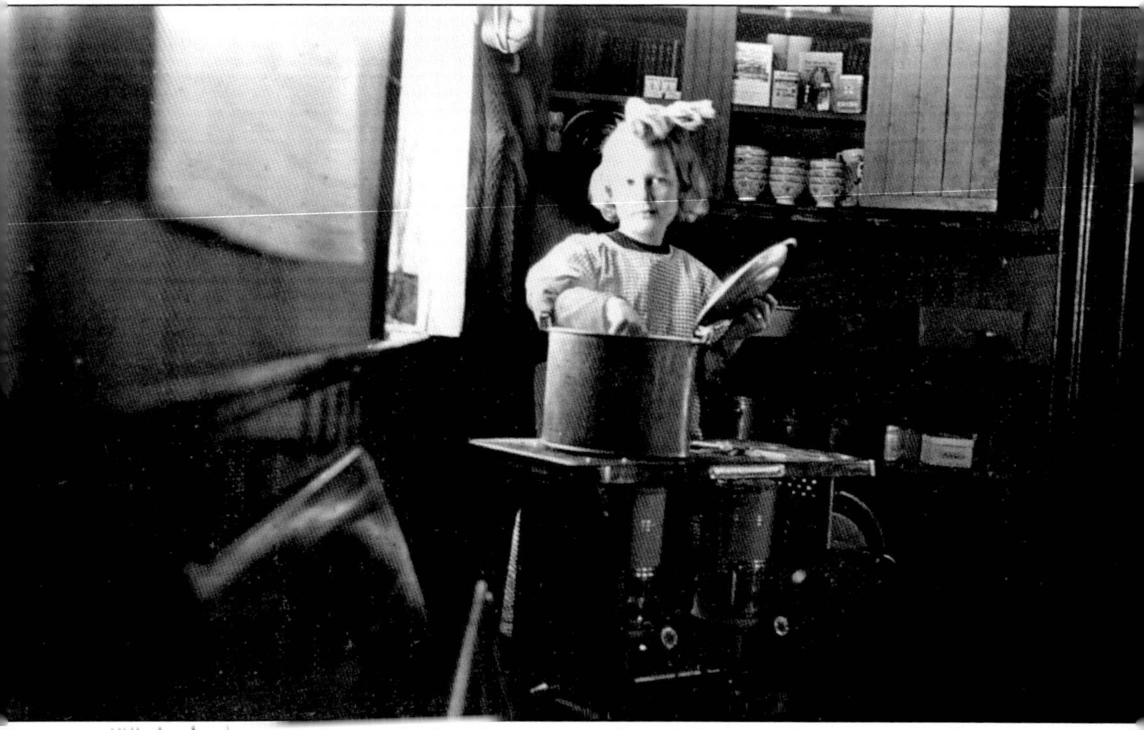

While the busy teacher worked with many pupils at different achievement levels, responsible children were sometimes allowed to help stir the soup which was the "hot" part of the school lunch. A kerosene stove furnished the heat.

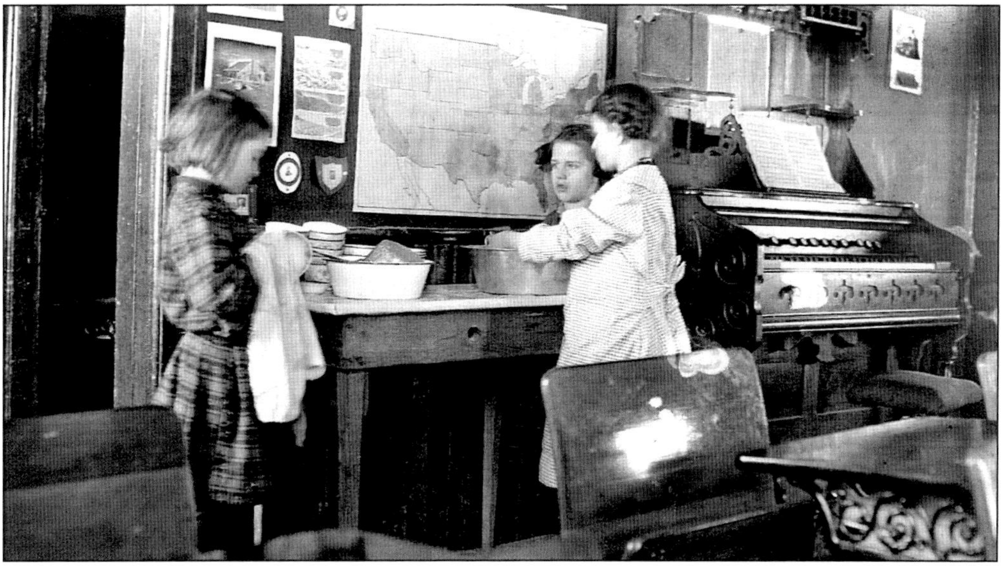

Girls and boys helped at clean up time, washing and wiping the dishes. There was an organ in the corner ready for the teacher to accompany the class during music time.

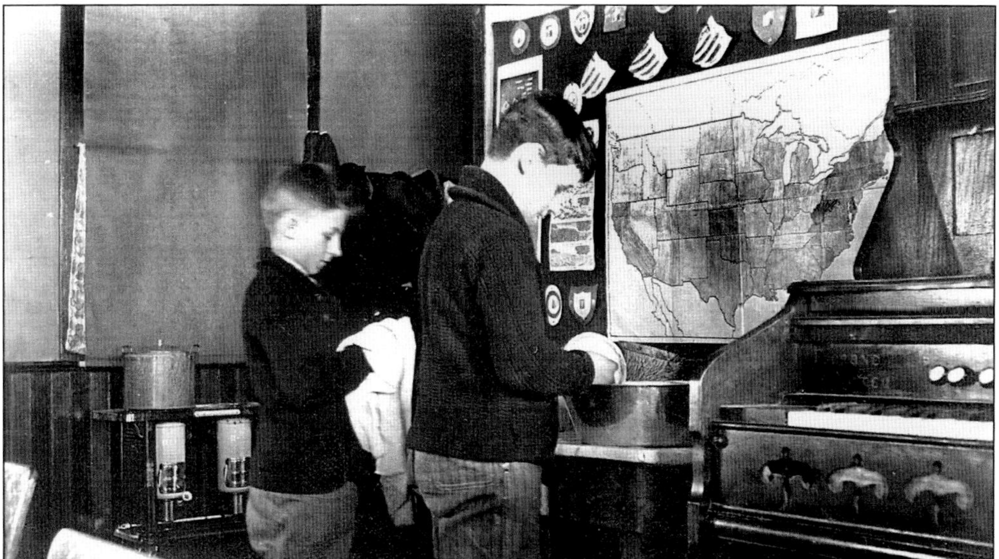

Those doing the dishes had to be careful not to splatter the large map of the United States. The map did not yet include the new states of Alaska and Hawaii.

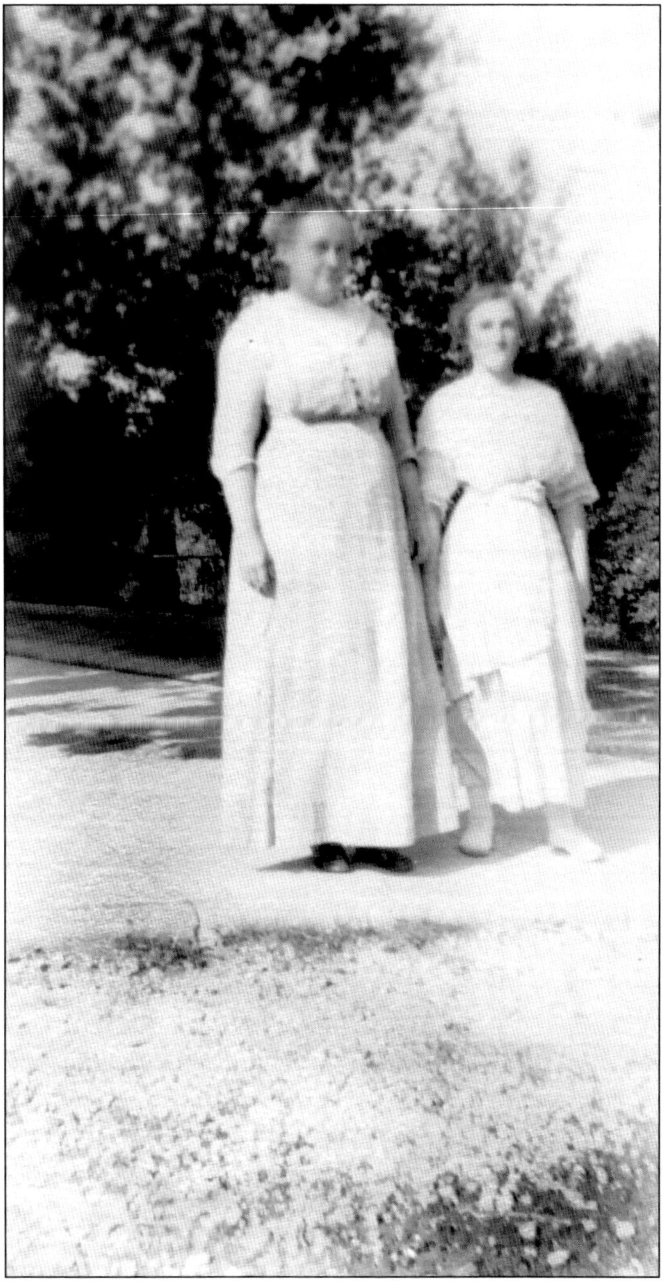

Helen Martin, pictured on the left in this old snapshot, was a legendary county superintendent. She was elected to office in an age when only men were allowed to vote—yet she won.

She drove her horse and buggy from one country school to another. Her job was to oversee the education in rural schools, to give advice to teachers and to recommend any changes which would be beneficial for the schools. One of her recommendations was to have a hitching post at each school so she did not have to worry about her horse getting loose. Her most lasting recommendation was to change school names from a mere number to more descriptive terms. After that, children attended classes in schools named Blooming Prairie, Island, Prairie View, and Sugar Creek.

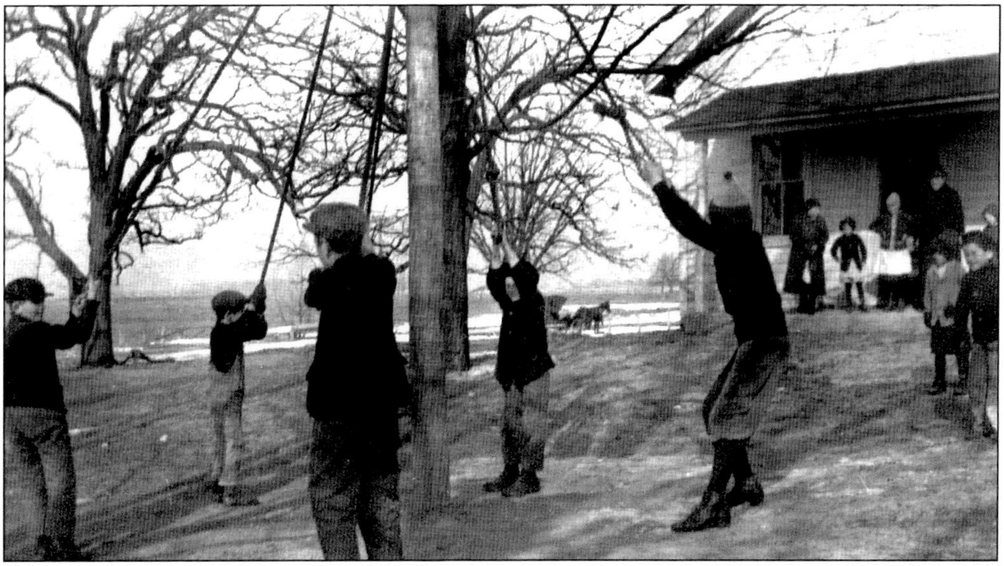

At recess time and noon hour, children enjoyed exercise on the playground equipment. This piece of equipment was known as the high flyer.

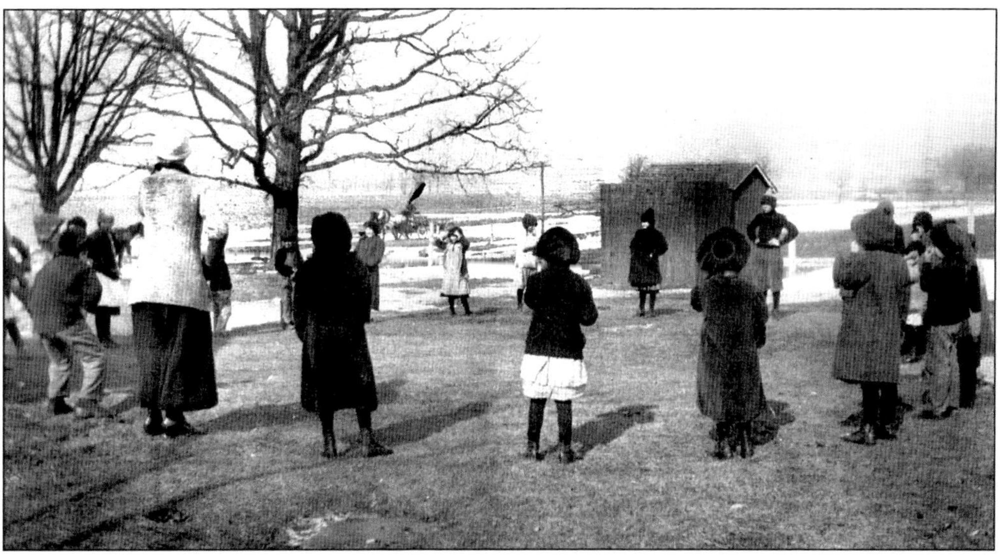

Circle games like Drop the Handkerchief and Duck, Duck, Goose were popular. The teacher usually joined right in with the children in playing games.

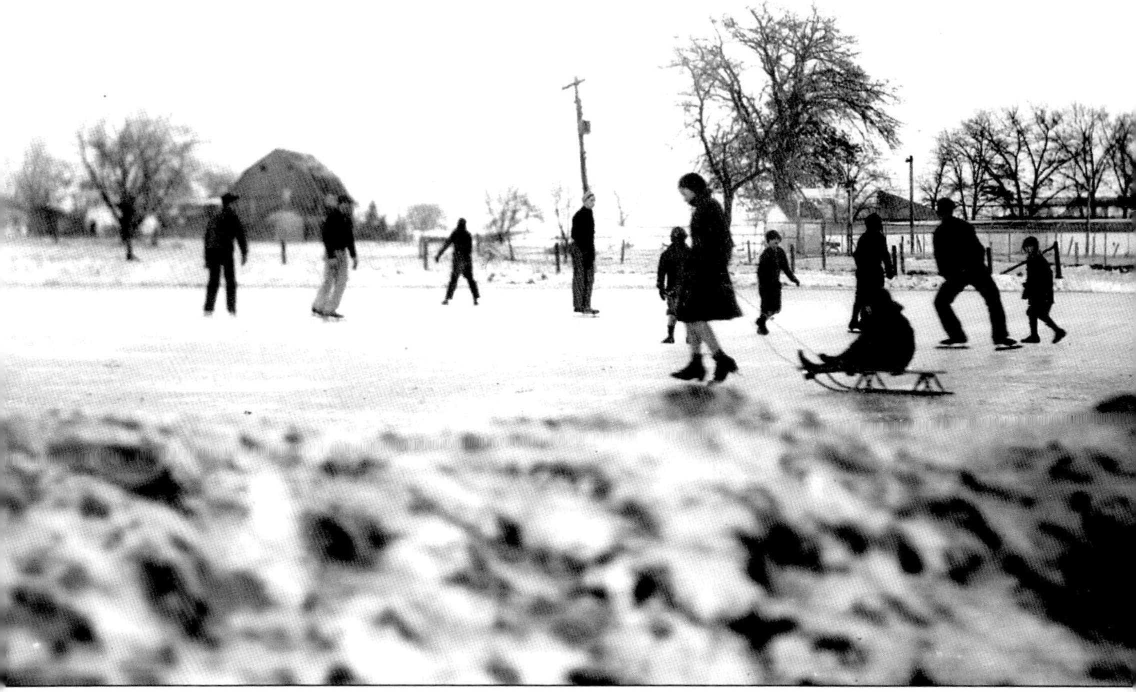

Children brought skates from home on winter days and a nearby pond became a skating rink.

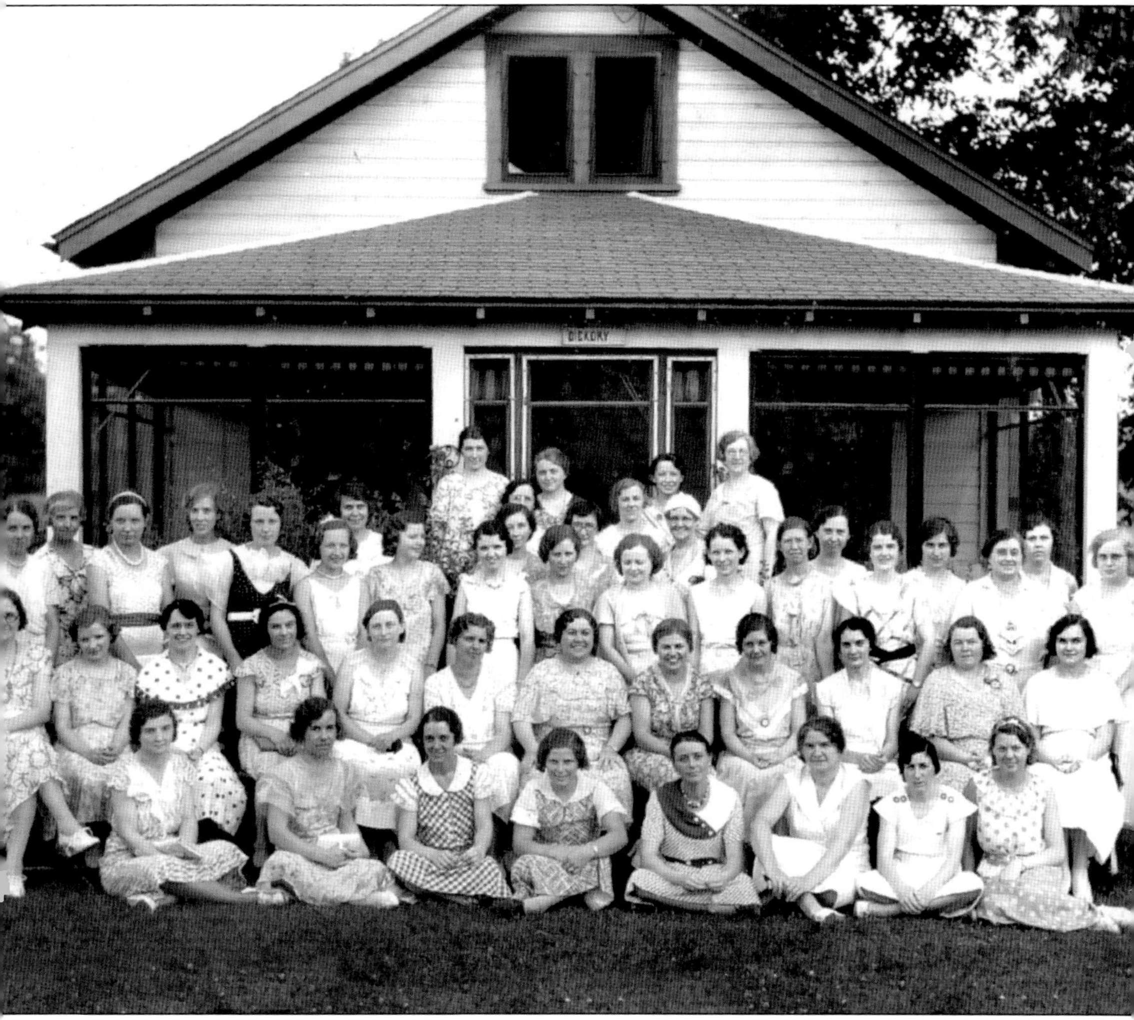

A teacher's life was quite restricted years ago. They were bound by rules about how to dress and how to act. They were banned from smoking, drinking any alcohol, and keeping late hours. Nevertheless most of the teachers managed to have good times within the rules. Here the Teachers' Choral Club enjoyed a picnic at a lake cottage in 1935.

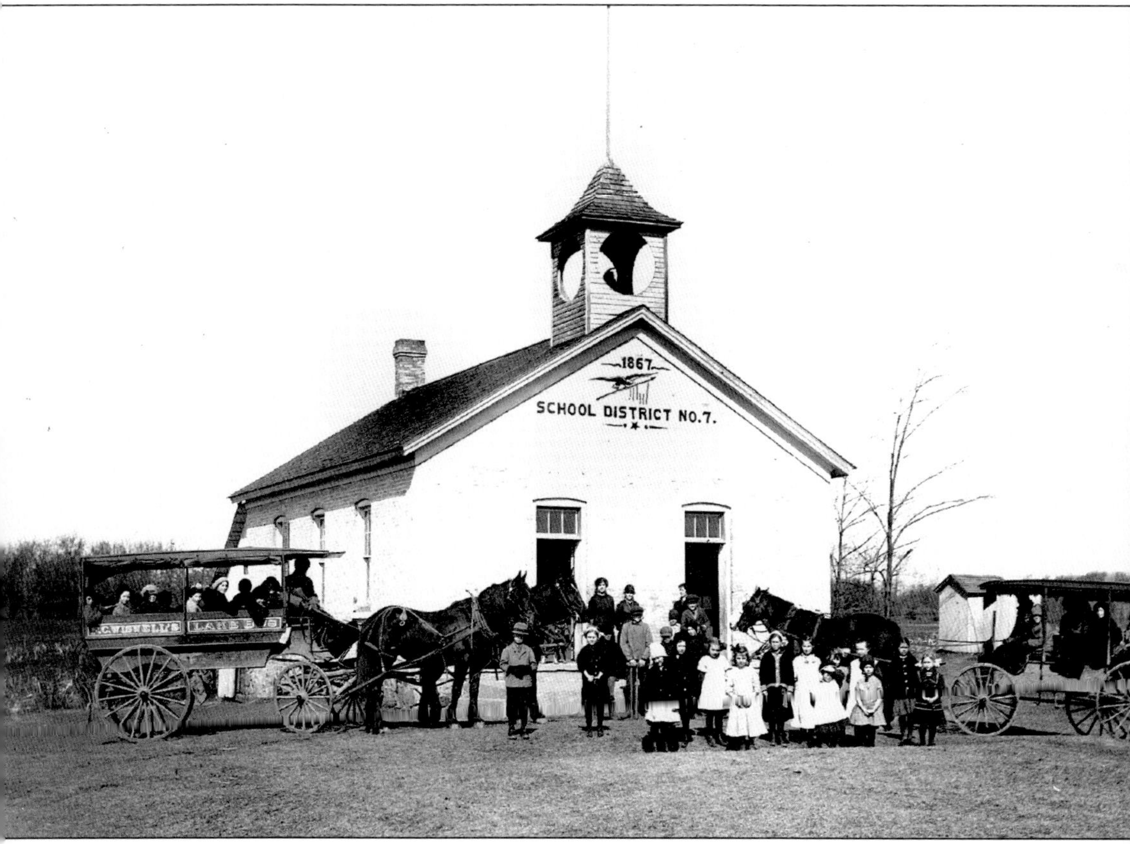

Sometimes the one-room schools held a play day and children from one school would visit another. It was a gala occasion and parents enjoyed the day along with their children. Here, Wiswell's Lake bus, drawn by a team of horses, has brought a group for play day. Wiswell had a livery stable in town.

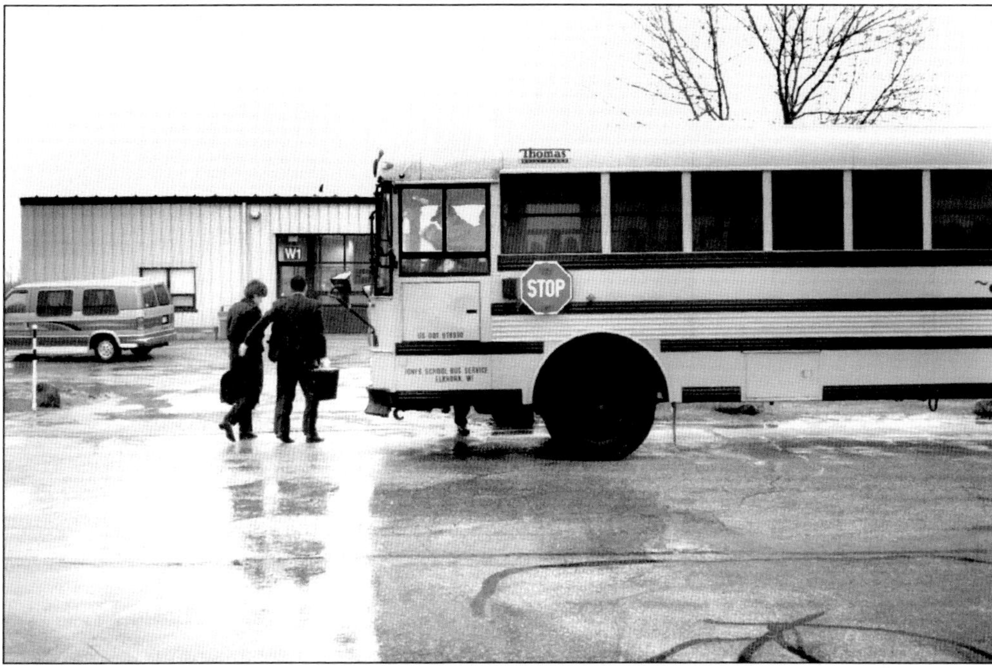

Today, fleets of yellow school buses carry children to and from school and home, to extra events, and from rural areas to the central educational centers. This all began in the 1950s and 1960s when one-room schools closed and children began coming into Elkhorn for their education.

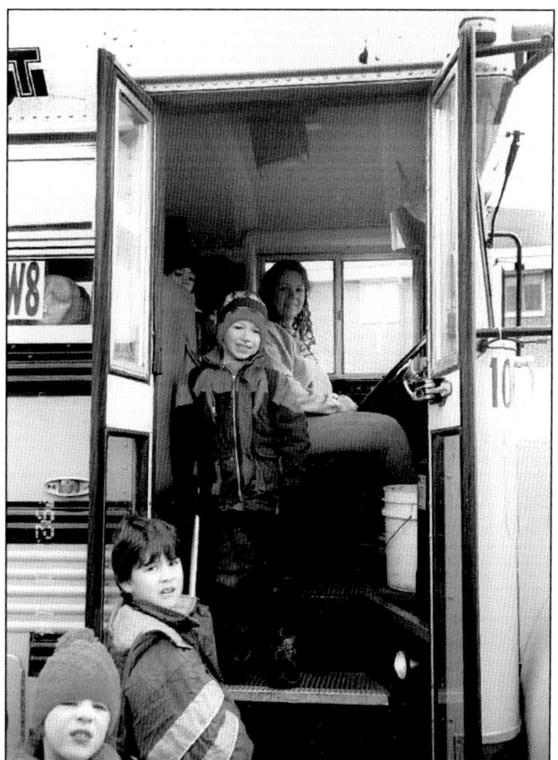

Sometimes the first bus ride is scary for the kindergarteners, but in a short time they learn the ropes and have fun.

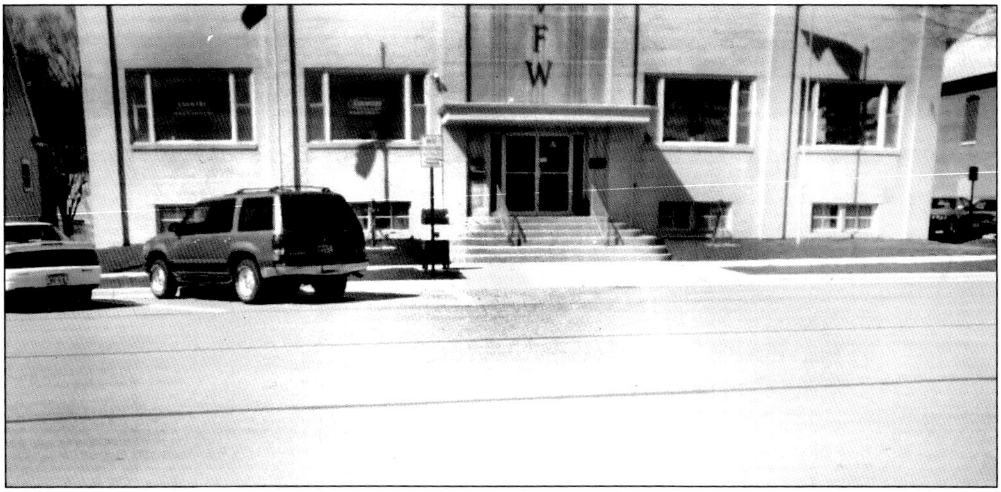

A first was chalked up when the county opened a school for the mentally and physically handicapped children in Elkhorn. Most small towns did not have facilities for such children and many of them did not even attend any school as a result. It began in 1950 with 15 pupils attending class in the VFW building. Miss Ruth Curran was the teacher and her outstanding work was recognized in 1953 when she received national honor as "Teacher of the Year."

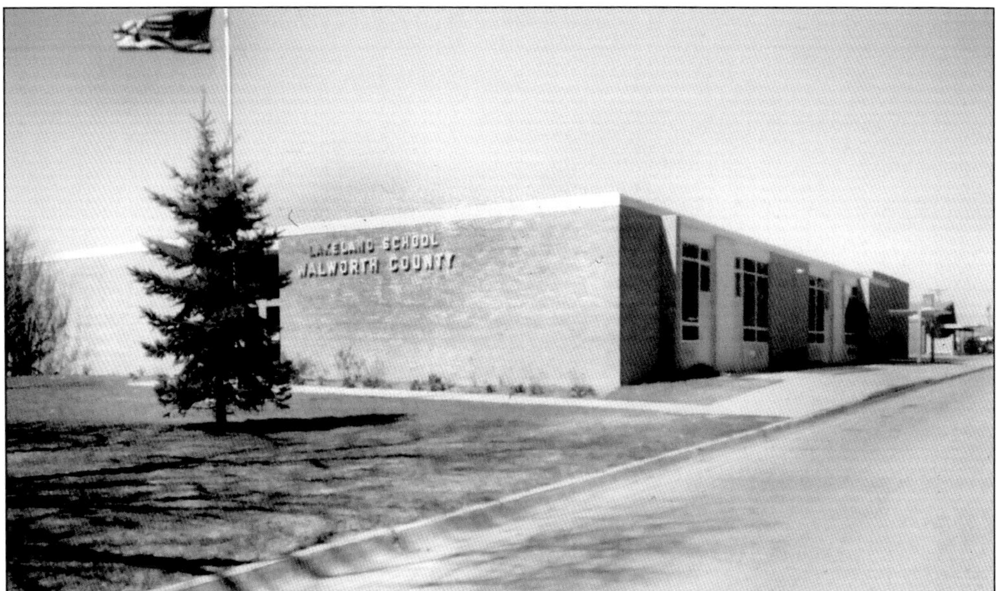

In 1955, a new school building was constructed in Elkhorn and children came from all over Walworth County to take advantage of the educational opportunities available. From the start, it was known as the "Special School." For many years it was the only school in Elkhorn which had a swimming pool.

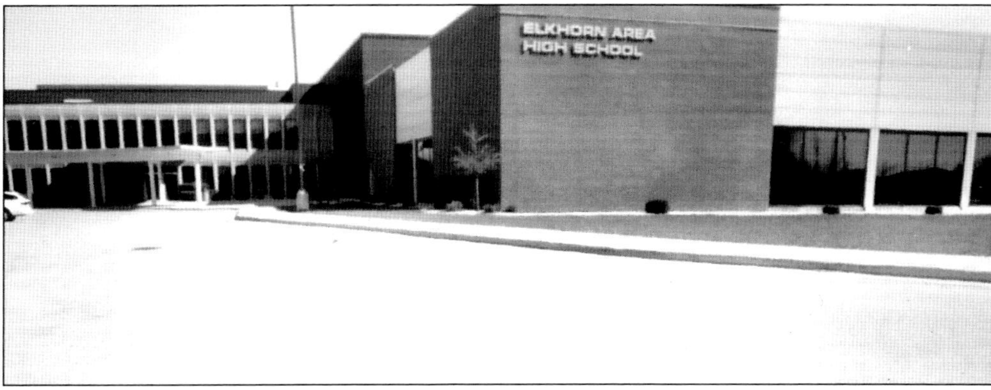

Elkhorn has now embarked on a huge school building program. A new high school has been completed and an alternative high school proffers education to high school boys and girls who have difficulty working in regular school situations.

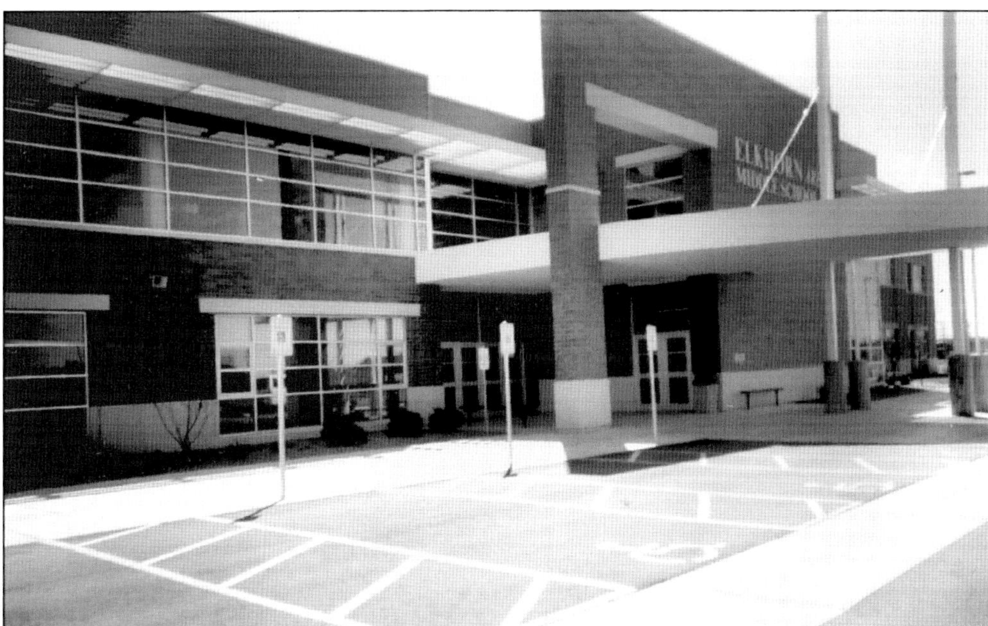

A new middle school, Jackson, just opened in 2003. The old middle school is being rebuilt as an elementary school.

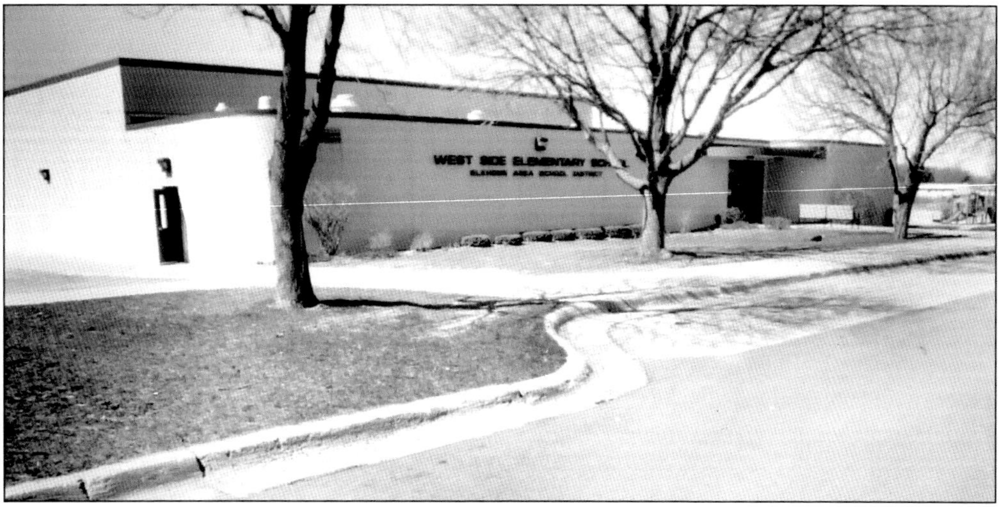

Above is West Side Elementary School, which was constructed during the building boom of the 1960s. It has been considerably enlarged since then. Tibbets Elementary School was constructed in those same years. There are also two private schools—St. Patrick's and the Lutheran school.

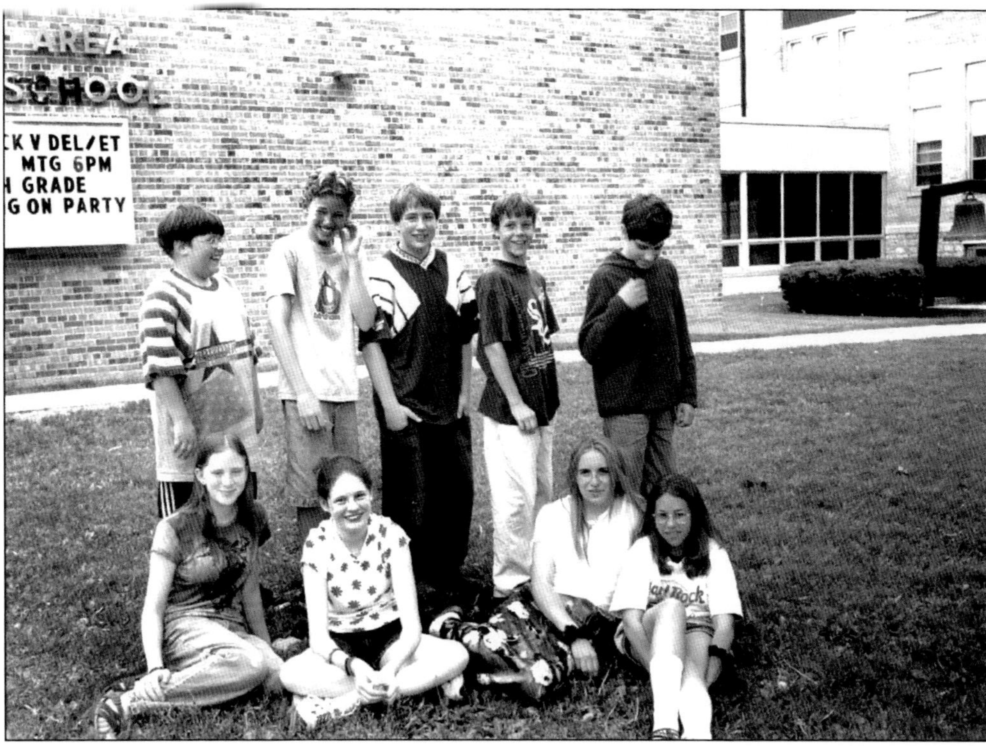

In this photo, middle-school students were photographed on the lawn in front of their school, which will soon be the new elementary building. The school bell at the right side of the photo once hung in the cupola of the 1887 building.

Six

MUSIC, MUSIC EVERYWHERE

Almost from the beginning, music has been important to Elkhorn. A band was formed as soon as there were enough men in the village who could play an instrument and enough women and children to make up an audience. The Elkhorn Band was one of those that played at Lincoln's funeral in Springfield, Illinois.

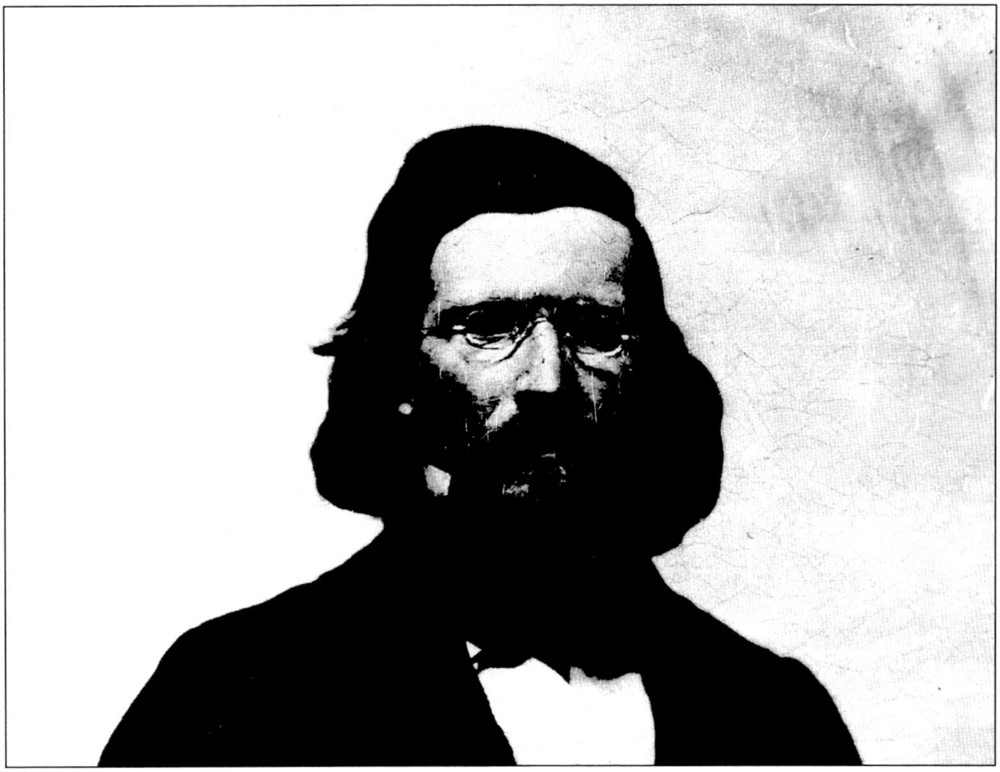

Music in Elkhorn rose to a crescendo when Joseph Philbrick Webster moved to the city in 1857. He purchased Rockwell's building, which had been moved to East Rockwell Street after being on the square in the center of town since 1837.

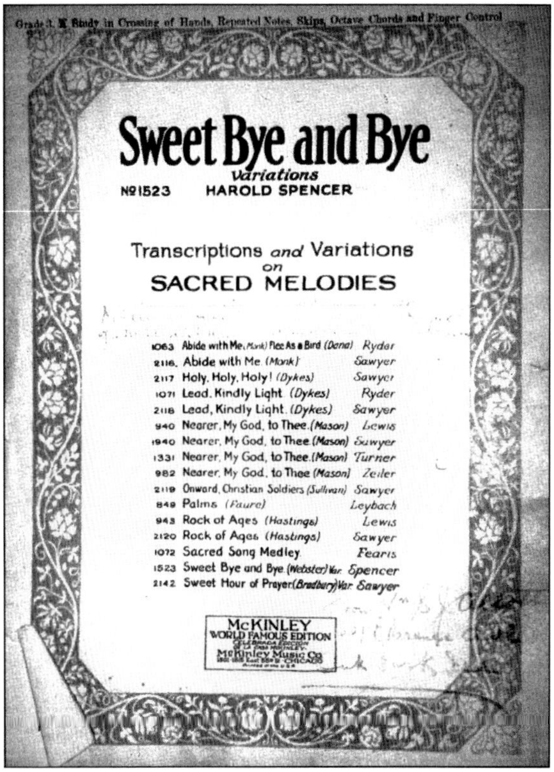

Webster was called the "composer of the west" in those days because Wisconsin was the west as far as most people were concerned. He wrote more than a thousand pieces of music during his lifetime. "Lorena," the hit song of the Civil War, was composed in 1857, the year he moved to Elkhorn. About 10 years later, he wrote the music for "Sweet By and By." Both of these songs are still played today.

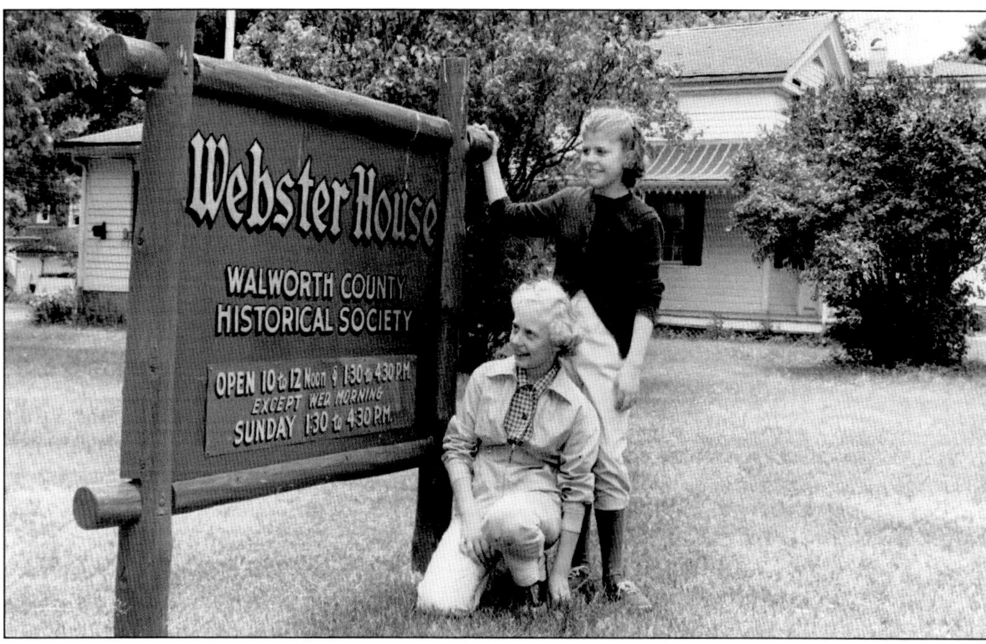

The house Webster lived in from 1857 until his death in 1875 is now a museum operated by the Walworth County Historical Society.

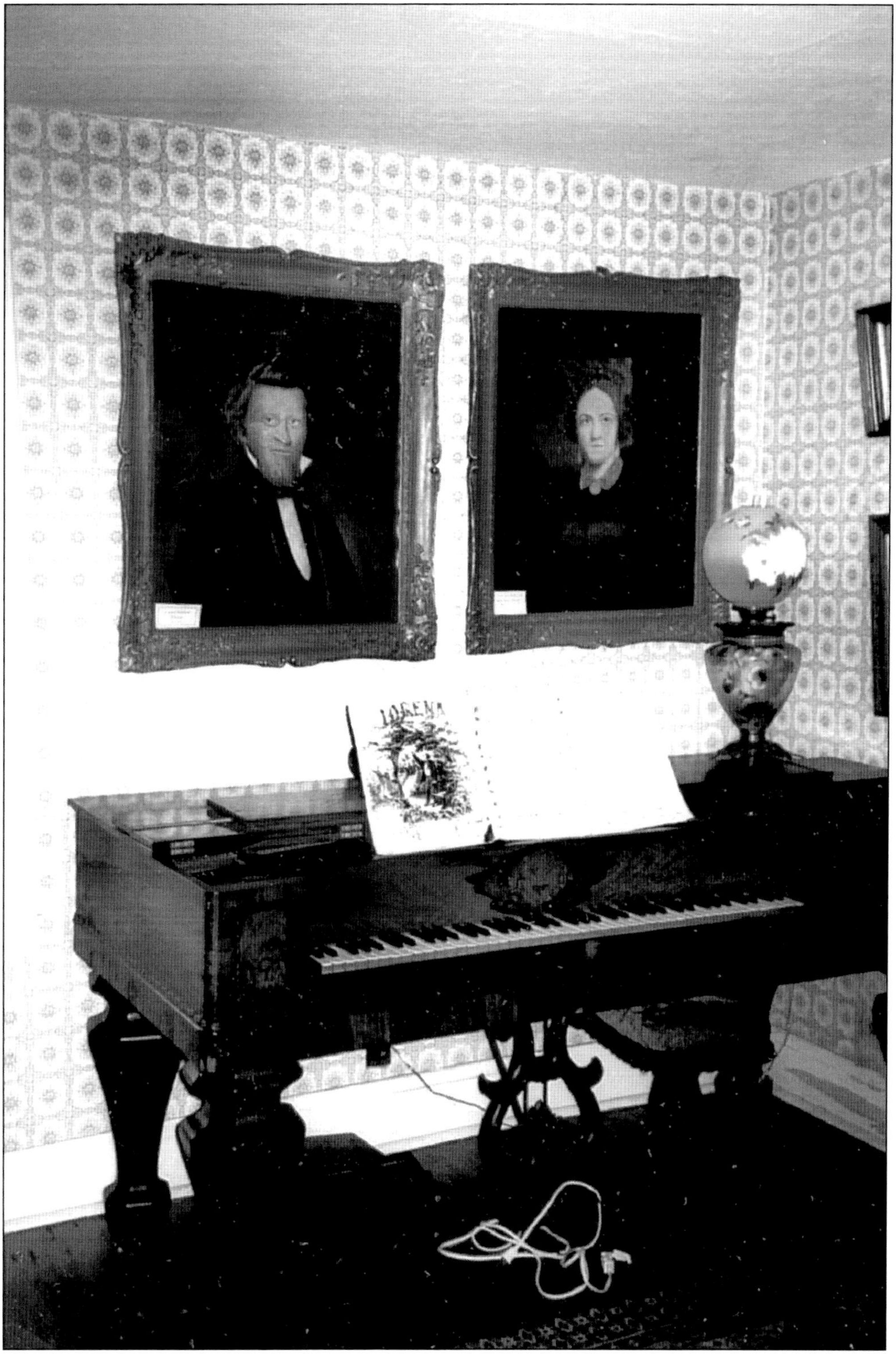

Webster's heavy square piano stands in the music room, on view to those who visit the museum.

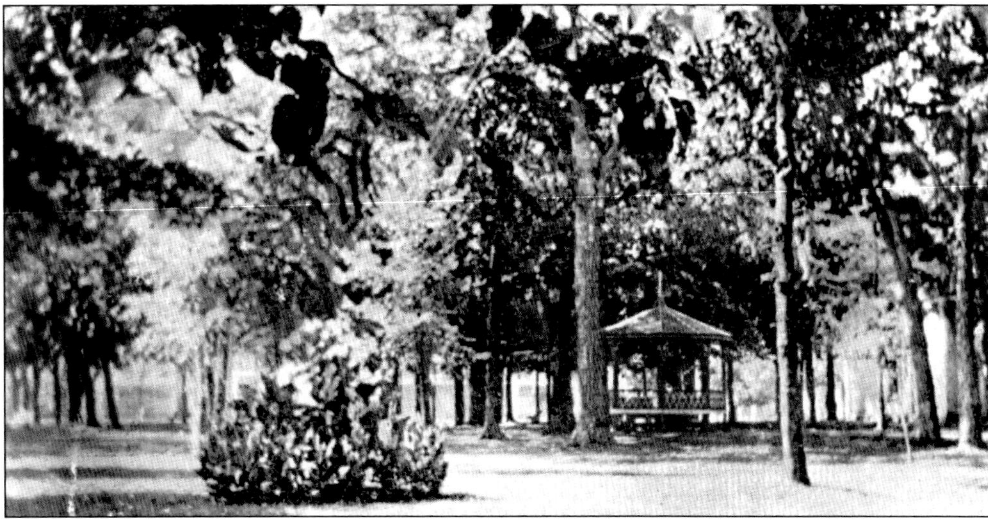

Almost as soon as the first courthouse was built on the public square downtown, band concerts were given there. A small round band shell was erected so that the musicians had a special area where they could perform.

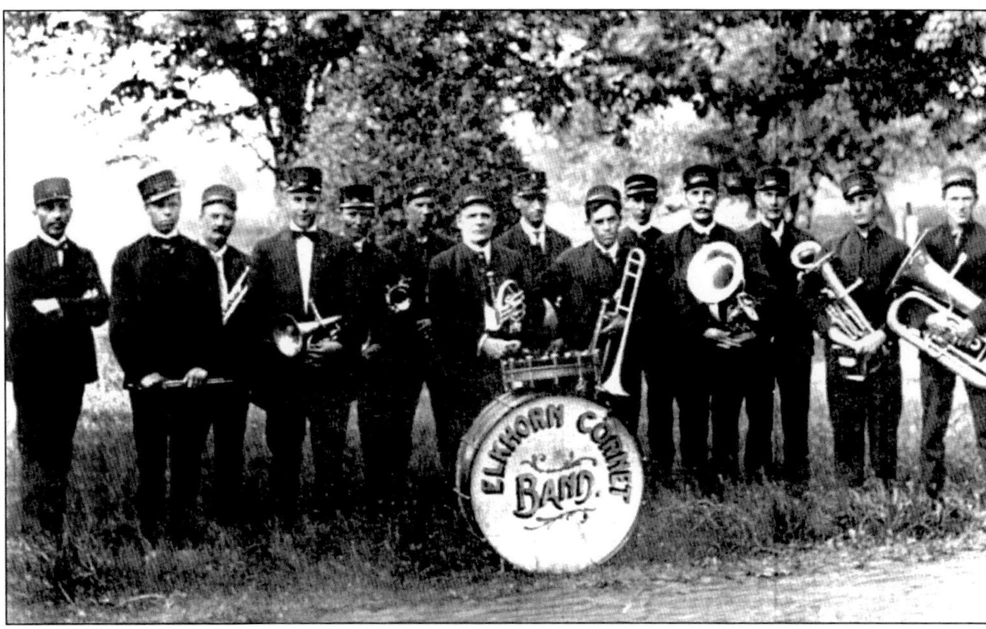

The Elkhorn Cornet Band was very prominent and came to the attention of a music instrument manufacturer in Chicago, Illinois, partly because they consistently purchased a goodly number of horns from him.

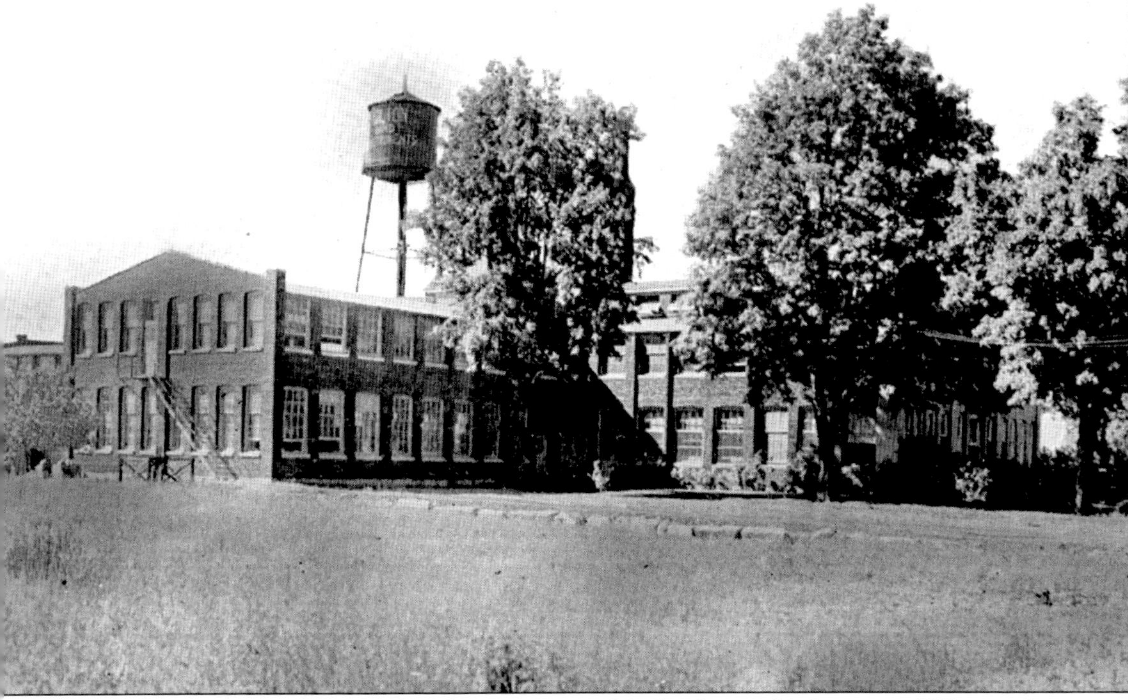

Strange as it may seem, the city's bands were responsible for the establishment in Elkhorn of one of its main industries, The Frank Holton Band Instrument Co. Holton suggested to the city that it build him a factory so he could move his company to Elkhorn. The city of Elkhorn agreed and soon the new home of Holton's company was on the north side of Elkhorn.

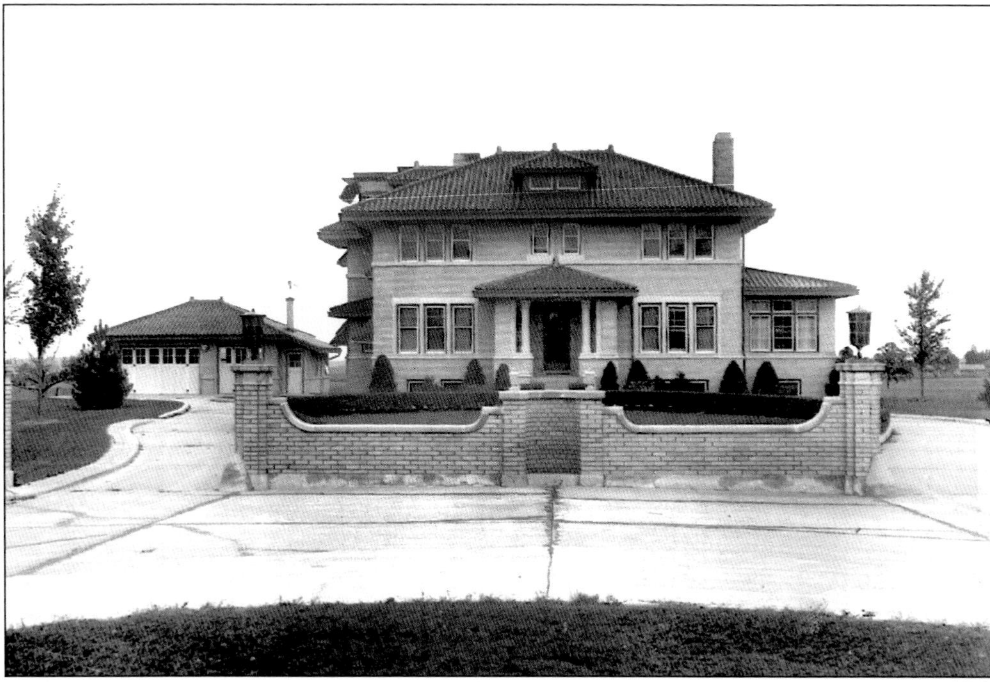

This industry employed many workers, which brought increased prosperity. On the 10th anniversary of the move to Elkhorn, Holton used silver dollars to pay his workers' wages. When Elkhorn's merchants saw their cash registers filled with silver dollars, they vividly realized what the coming of the music factory meant to the city. Above is the beautiful brick house at the end of Broad Street Boulevard where Frank Holton lived.

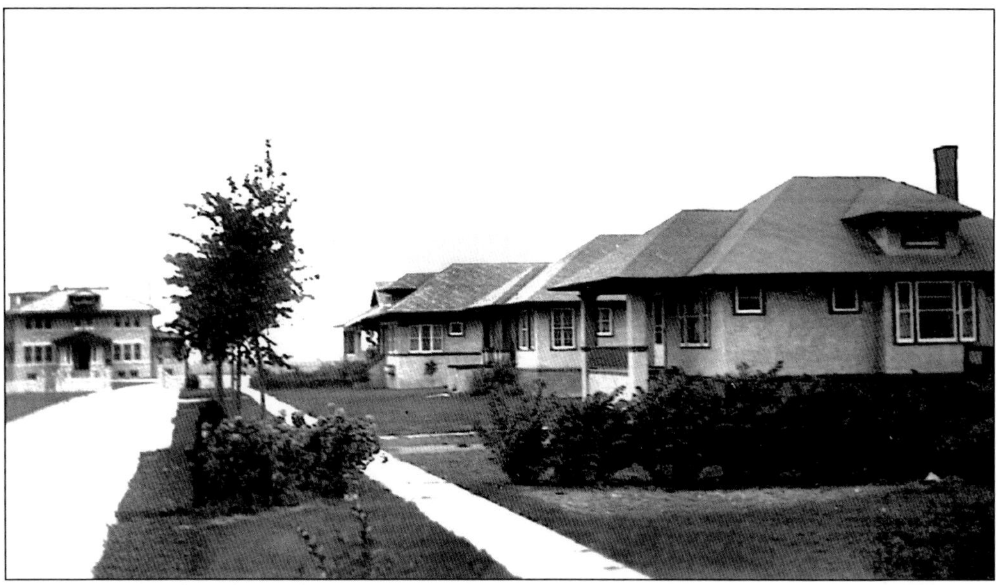

The hundreds of workers who came to make horns needed homes, and so an entirely new subdivision was developed for them. It was called Holton Heights and several blocks of bungalows were built within easy walking distance of the band instrument factory. Holton's own house stands at the end of a block of workers' houses.

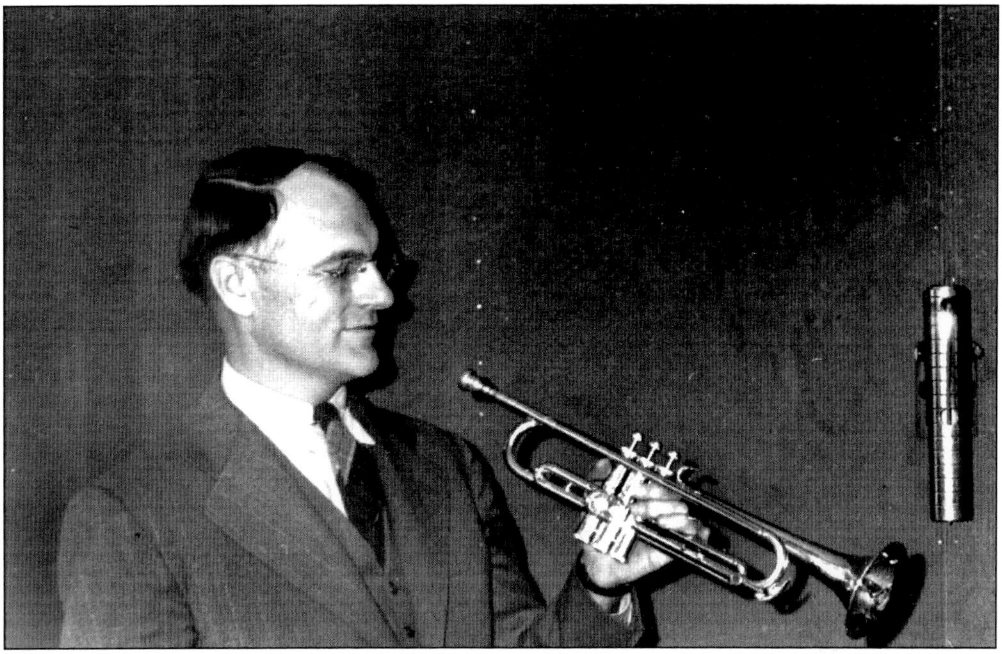

Elliott Kehl, long-time plant superintendent, proudly displayed one of the special horns that were manufactured at the Holton factory. Residents became accustomed to seeing famous musicians in town to pick up their specially designed instruments.

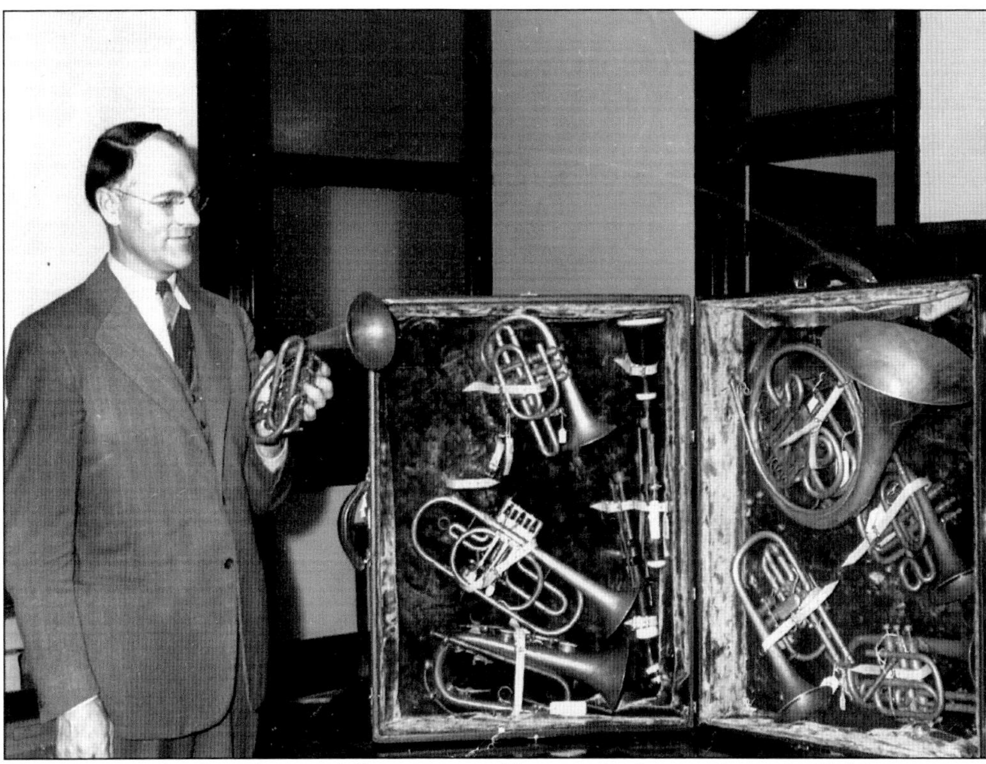

The company developed many different types of horns, which were shown by Kehl.

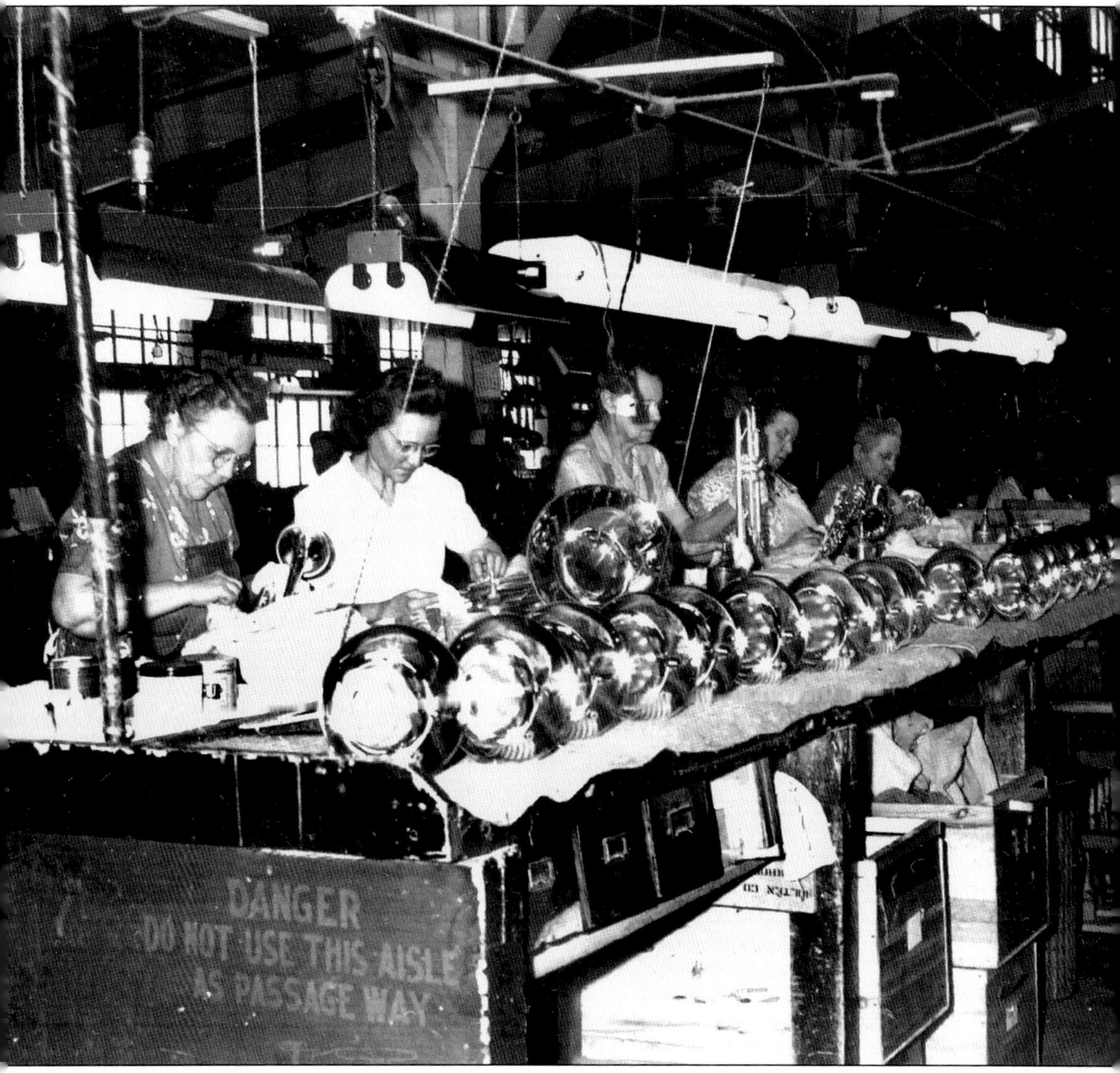

The factory employed women as well as men to produce the horns distributed and sold all over the nation. Holton Company is now part of the LeBlanc Corporation of Kenosha, Wisconsin.

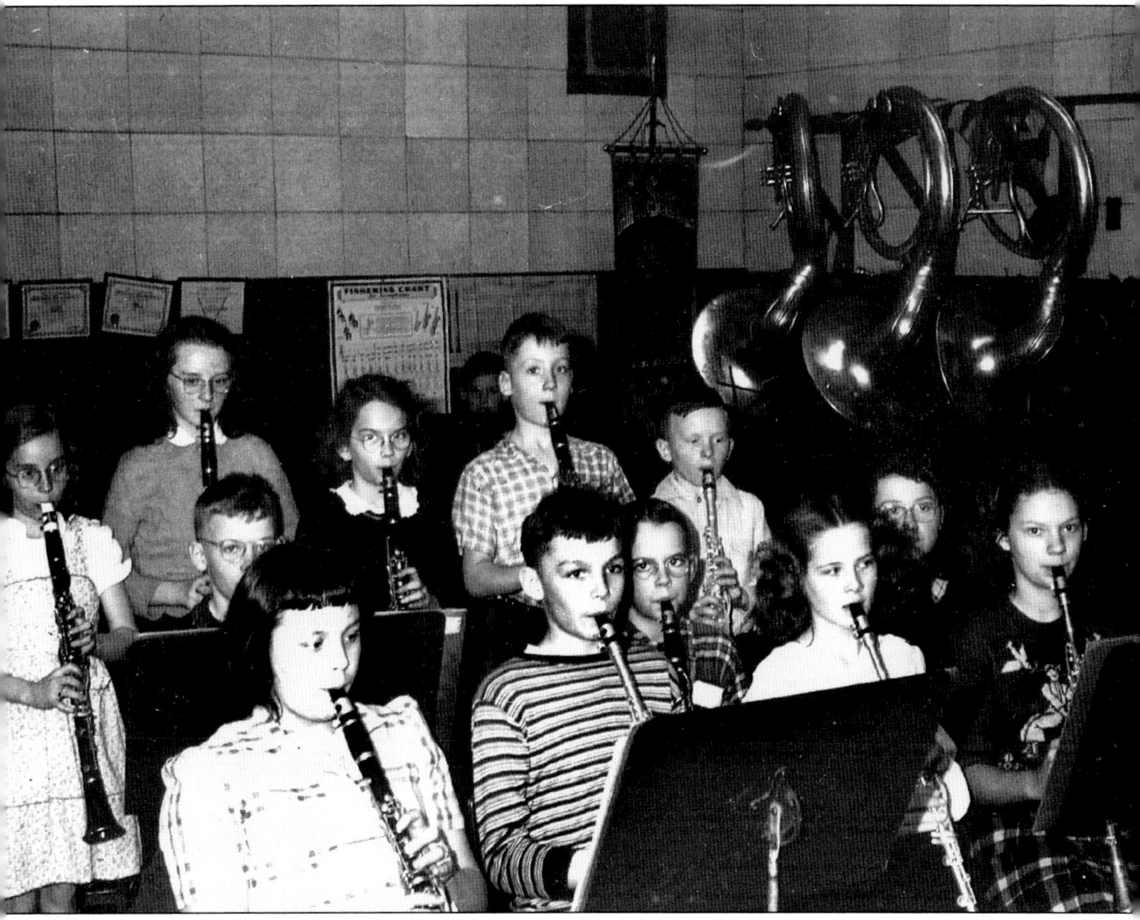

Pictured here is the clarinet section of the middle school band. Kehl said that Elkhorn's "horn-tooters" start young.

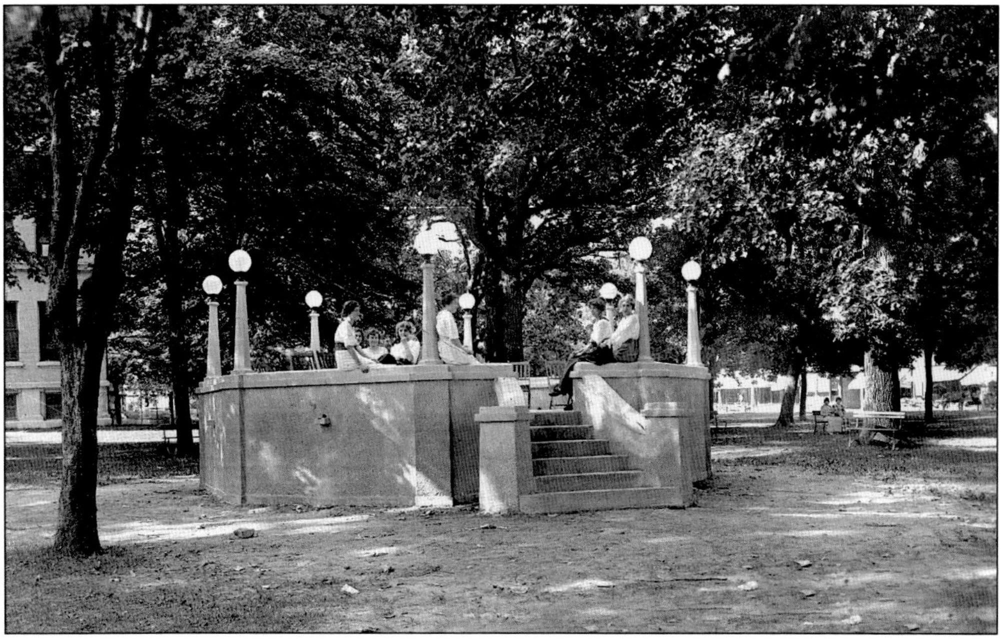

Young band students in Elkhorn dreamed of the time when they could join the city band and perform in the bandstand in the park. This concrete bandstand was erected soon after lights were installed downtown.

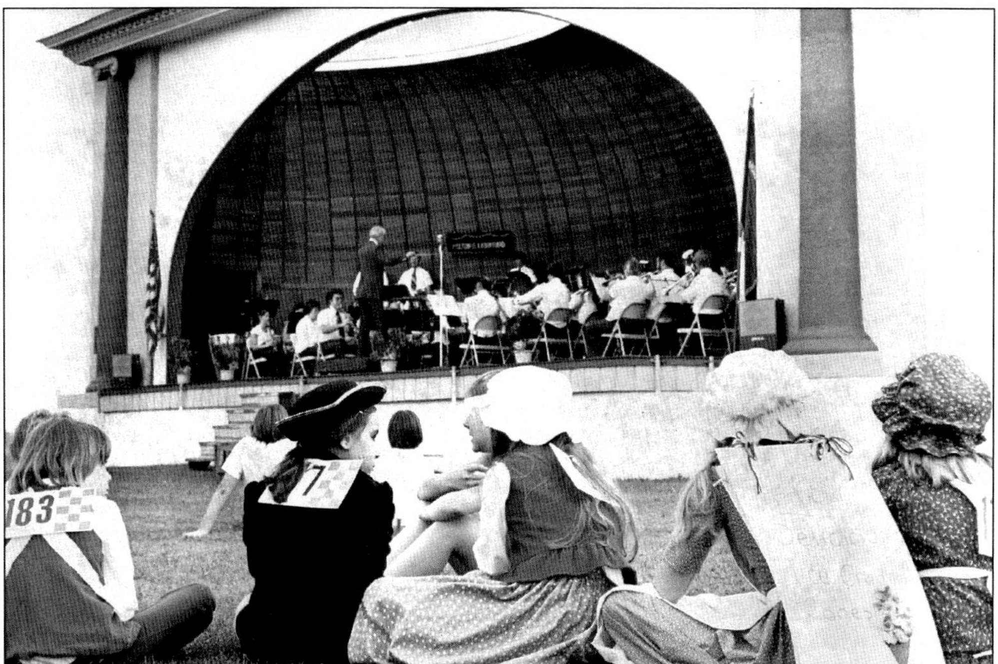

Some years later, their dreams centered around a larger stand, which had much better acoustics. This bandstand was also in the park.

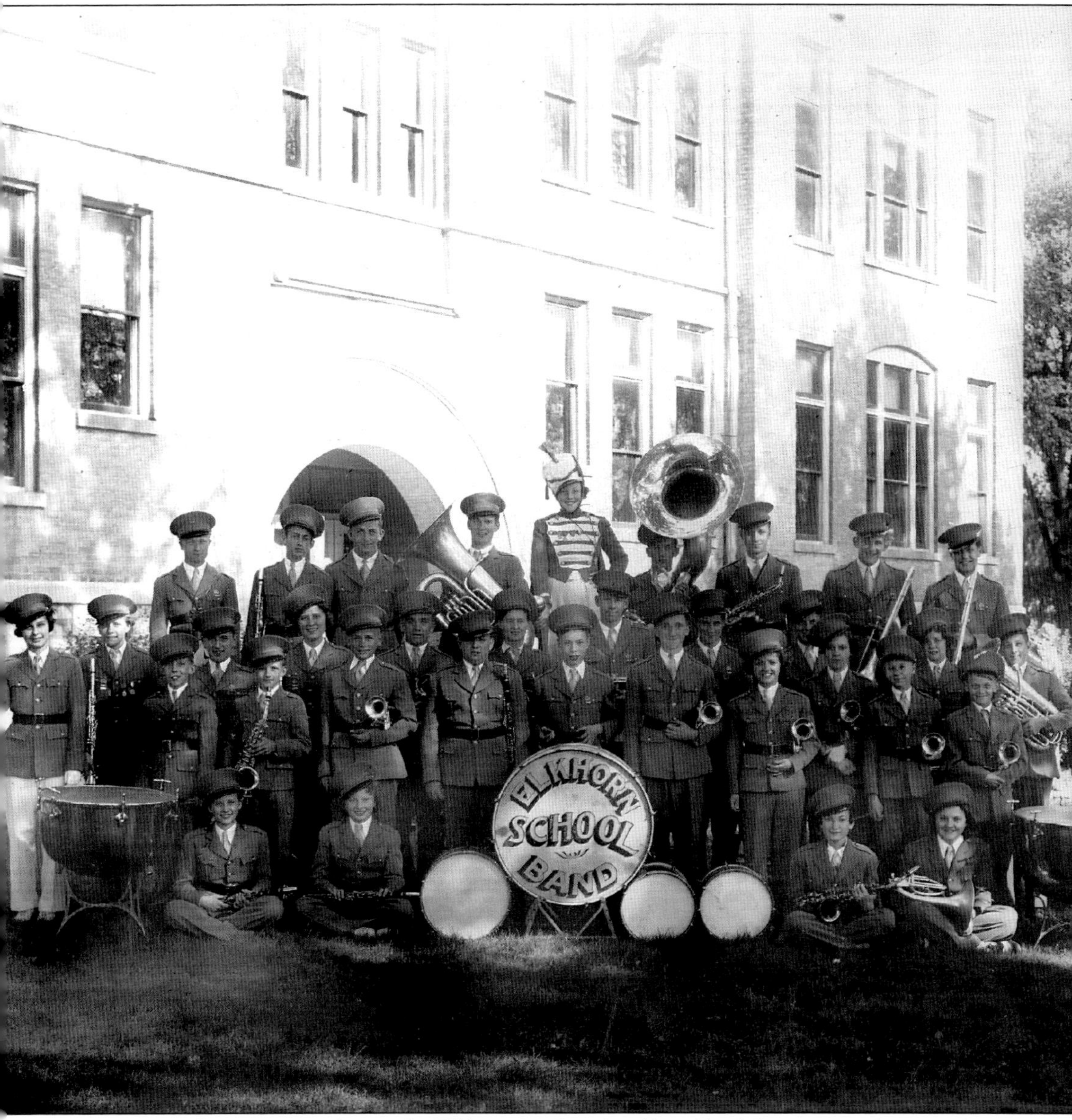

Dressed in their fancy new uniforms, the Elkhorn High School band had their group photograph taken in front of the 1887 grade school. They are all ready to march down the street and join the Memorial Day parade of 1934.

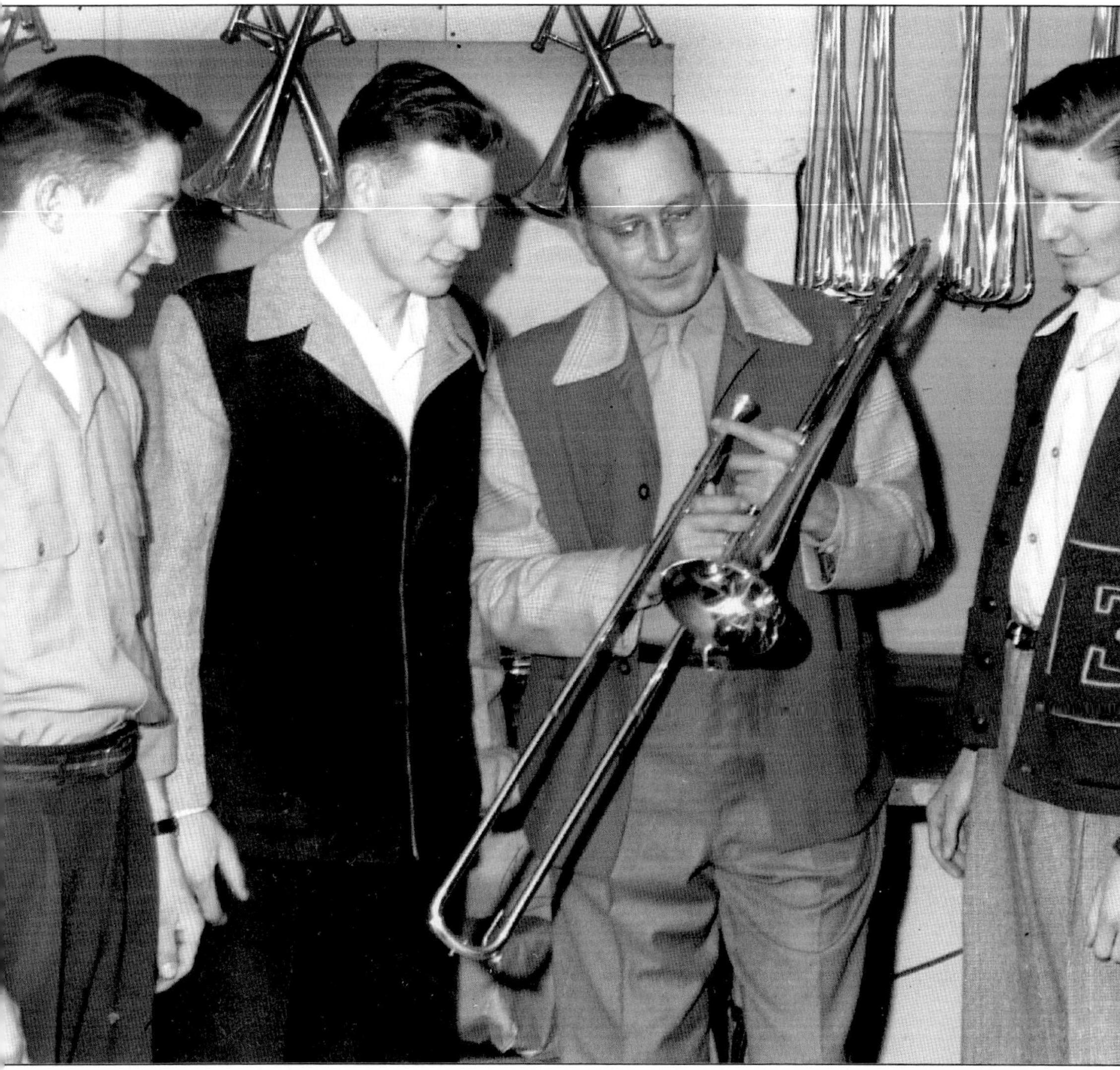

It wasn't long before music was coming from the south side of town also. Tony Getzen, who received his training at the Holton factory, established his own business in 1939. His sons, Robert, Donald, and William joined him in it. This photo shows the sons at a very young age examining a trombone with their father. Pictured, from left to right, are Robert, Donald, Tony, and William.

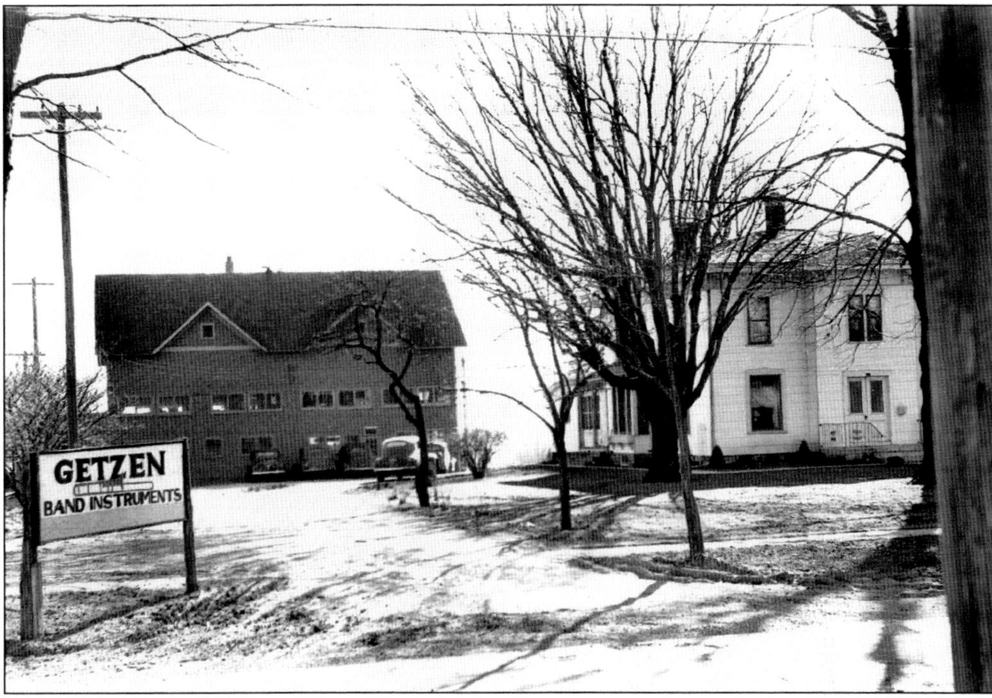

Getzen's first instrument plant was in an old building that had been a barn. He manufactured trumpets, French horns, cornets, and tubas.

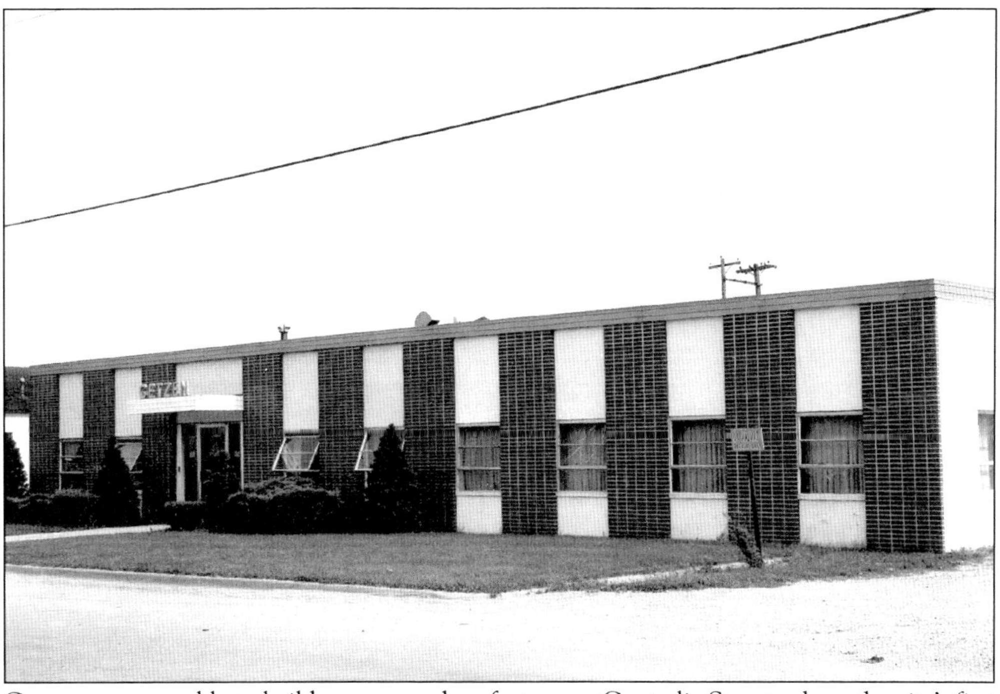

Getzen was soon able to build a more modern factory on Centralia Street, where the city's first industrial area was located. The well-known trumpet player, Doc Severinsen, joined the firm as research director.

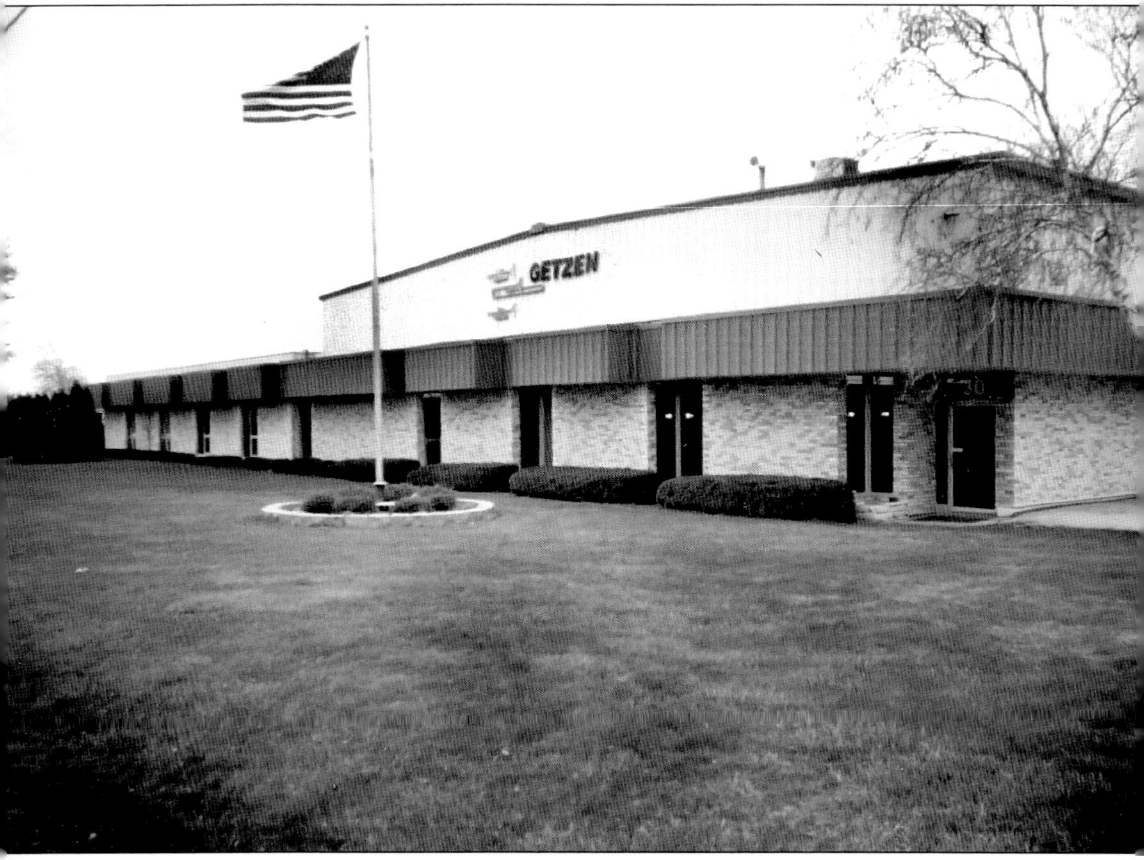

The latest Getzen building is situated near Elkhorn's new industrial park. Tom Getzen is the owner of the company now. He also is the head of Allied Supply Corporation, which offers instrument repair.

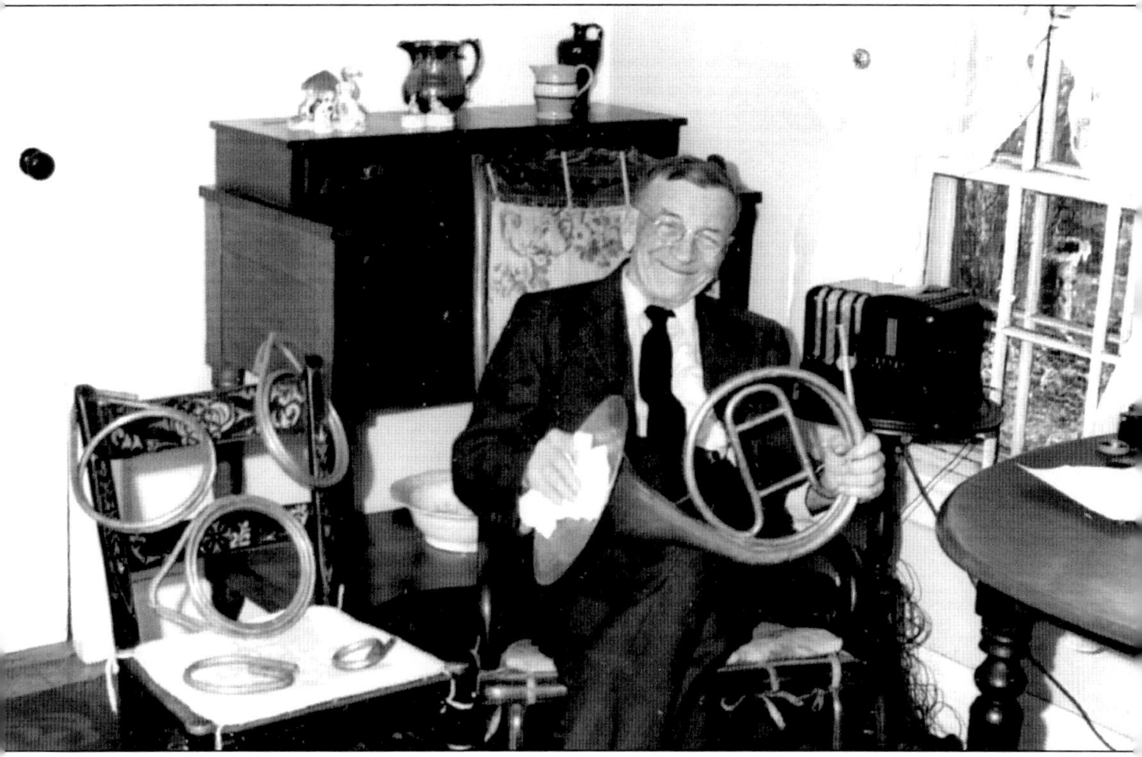

Earlier horns were much different from those being produced in instrument factories today. Frederick Webster, the youngest son of Joseph Webster (a famous 19th century composer), was photographed displaying a French horn that was used in Elkhorn's first band. There were no valves. The notes were played by wrapping a handkerchief around the musician's fist and inserting it into the horn in different positions and depth. This method of playing was called "fisting."

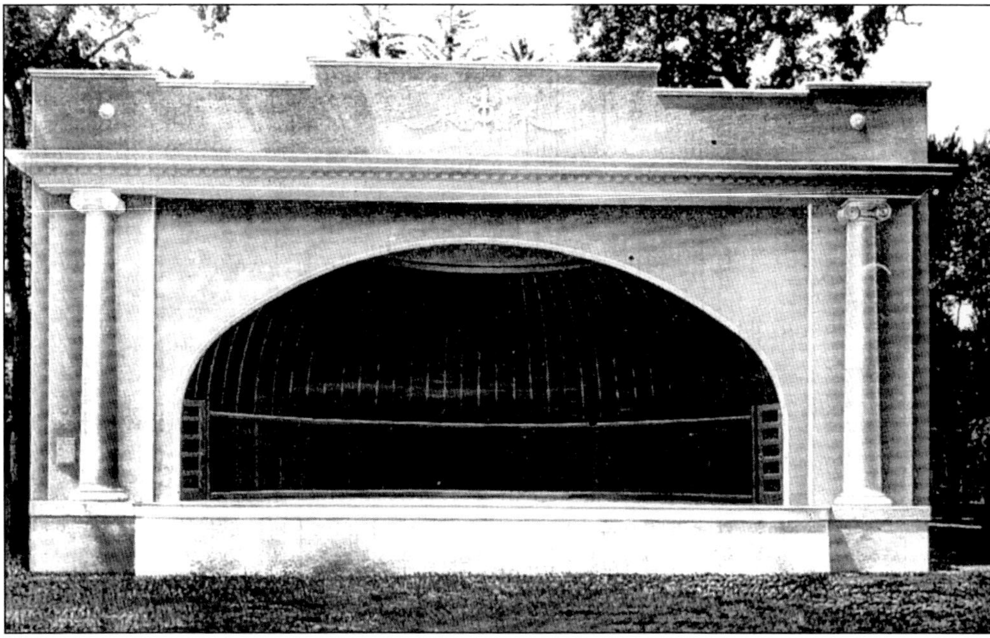

By 1926, it was agreed that Elkhorn's band needed a better band shell, since the summer concerts were drawing increasing crowds to the city. A new shell was designed by G. Pheby of Phoenix, Arizona. His invention of a special background for the performers resulted in great acoustics. The first concert in the band shell downtown was attended by 4,000 music lovers.

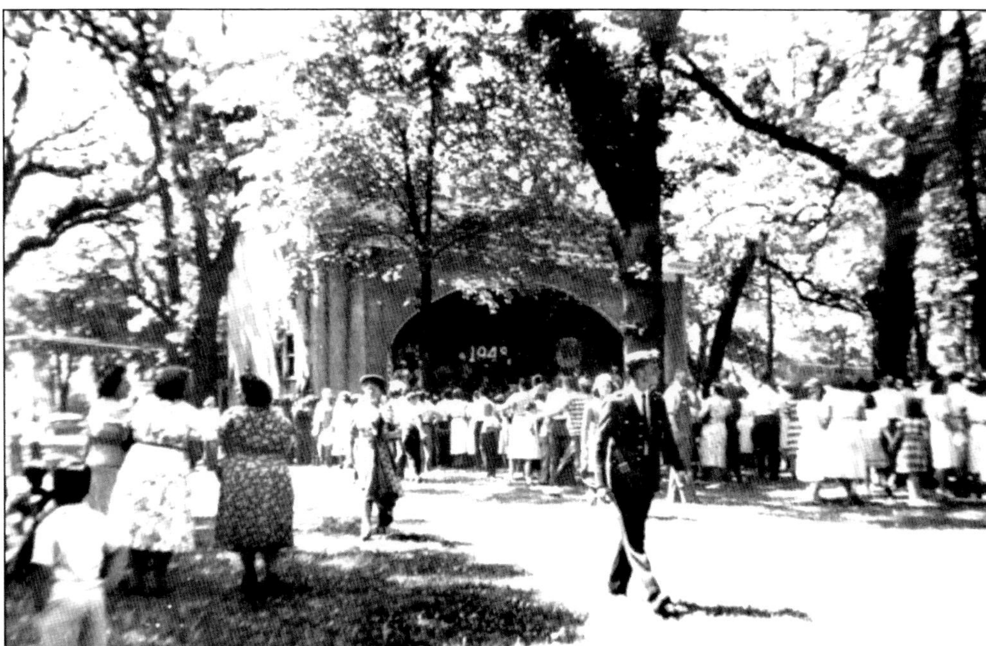

The building was moved to Sunset Park later and is still the scene of summer concerts. There is time during intermission to talk to friends and look for refreshments.

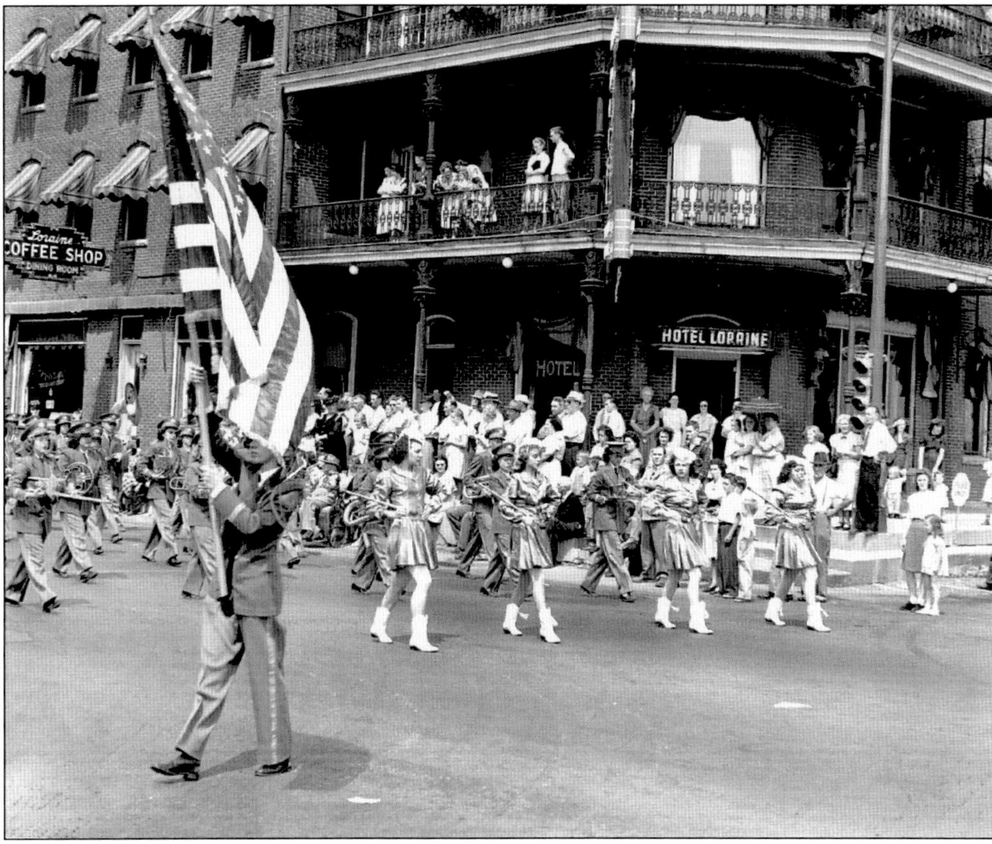

Capably playing instruments manufactured by Elkhorn's two band instrument factories, the high school band marched down the main street in a parade, as residents watched. The building in the background is the 1893 Elkhorn House Hotel. It had undergone a name change and became the Loraine Hotel. Today it is Moy's restaurant.

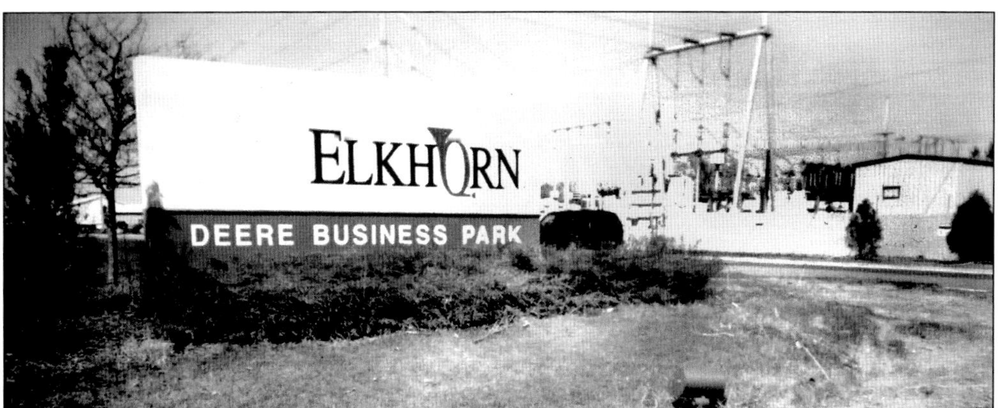

The city recognizes the importance of music in its past, present, and future by inserting a horn in place of the letter "O" in its welcome signs.

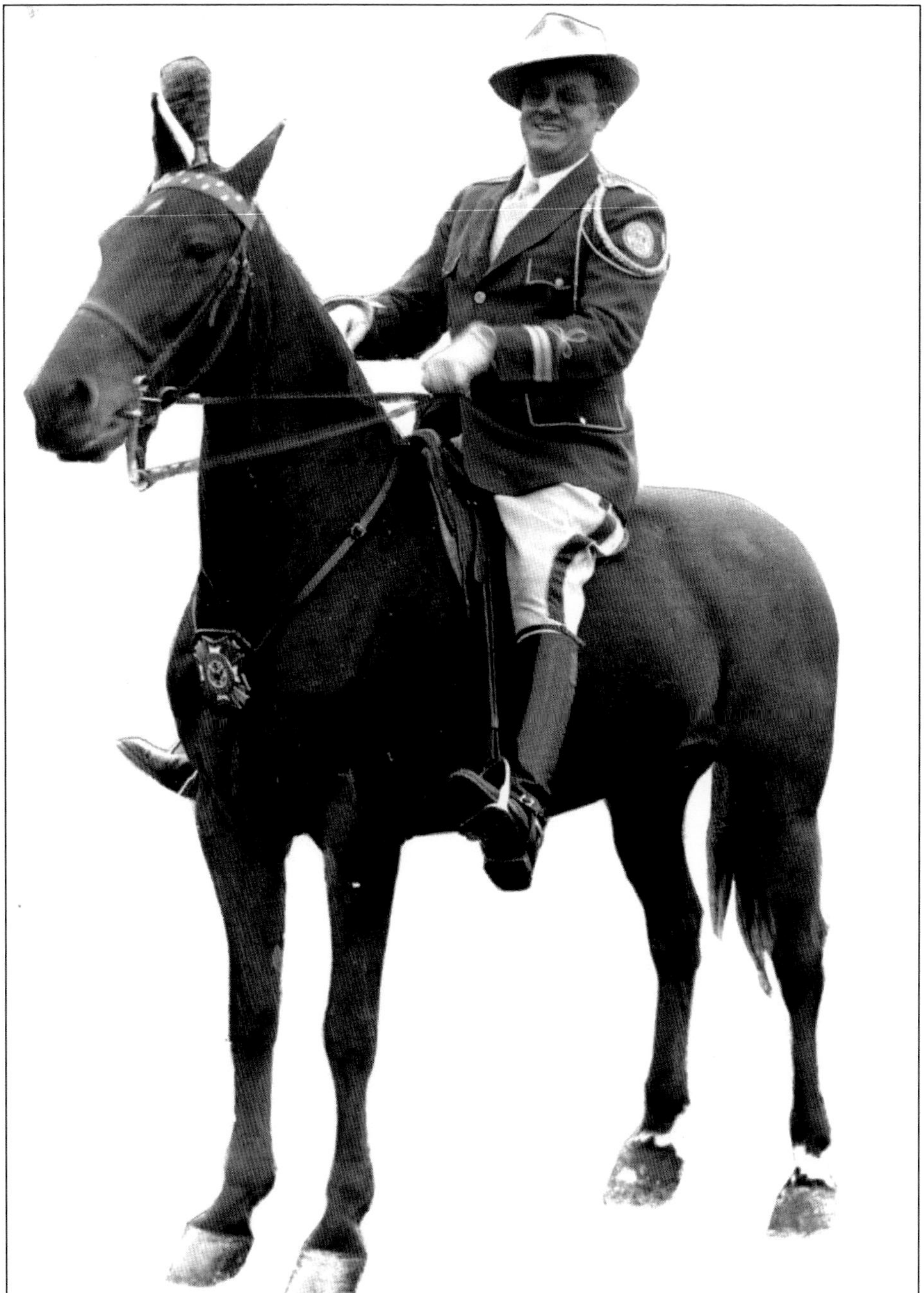

Once upon a time, Elkhorn even had a musical horse, Lady. She belonged to Fred Platts, co-owner of the hardware store. Platts was very interested in the local drum and bugle corps and offered to head it, astride his bay mare. It seemed like a good idea.

It turned out that, unknown to Platts, the horse loved music. Once the corps started to play, Lady began to prance and dance. Platts and Lady were the unexpected stars of the parade and from then on they appeared at every performance.

They even went to Washington, D.C., to lead the Wisconsin contingent in President Eisenhower's inaugural parade.

Seven

Fun and Relaxation

Before radio and television, life was much simpler. Many happy hours were spent just reading books and writing letters. Ladies had their "at home" days when it was known that they were available to have visitors. The stereoscope pictures, placed one at a time in the viewer, provided entertainment for everyone. Those three-dimensional pictures were considered educational as well.

The younger set found fun with a taffy pull in the kitchen, and it might even be considered "a date." Neighborhood children played games together outside after supper until darkness set in and it was time to go home. Hide and Go Seek and Red Rover were favorite games. Pitching horse shoes was popular too, for all age groups.

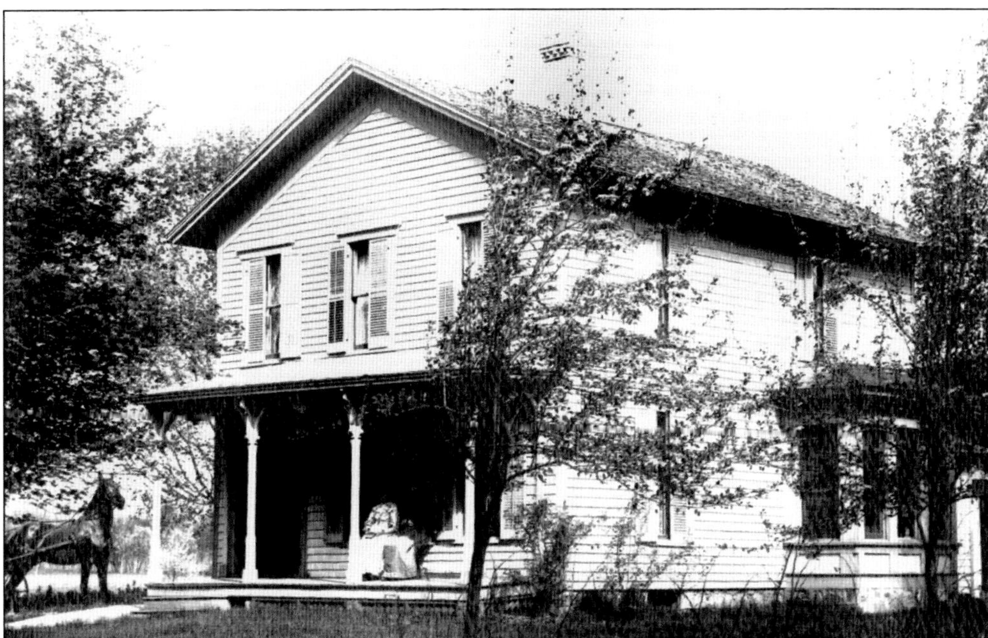

Just sitting on the front porch on a warm summer afternoon was a form of recreation. It was the ideal location to view passers by and a pleasant place when waiting for visitors to arrive. For some unexplained reason, there did not seem to be so many mosquitoes in those days. A screened porch was almost unheard of.

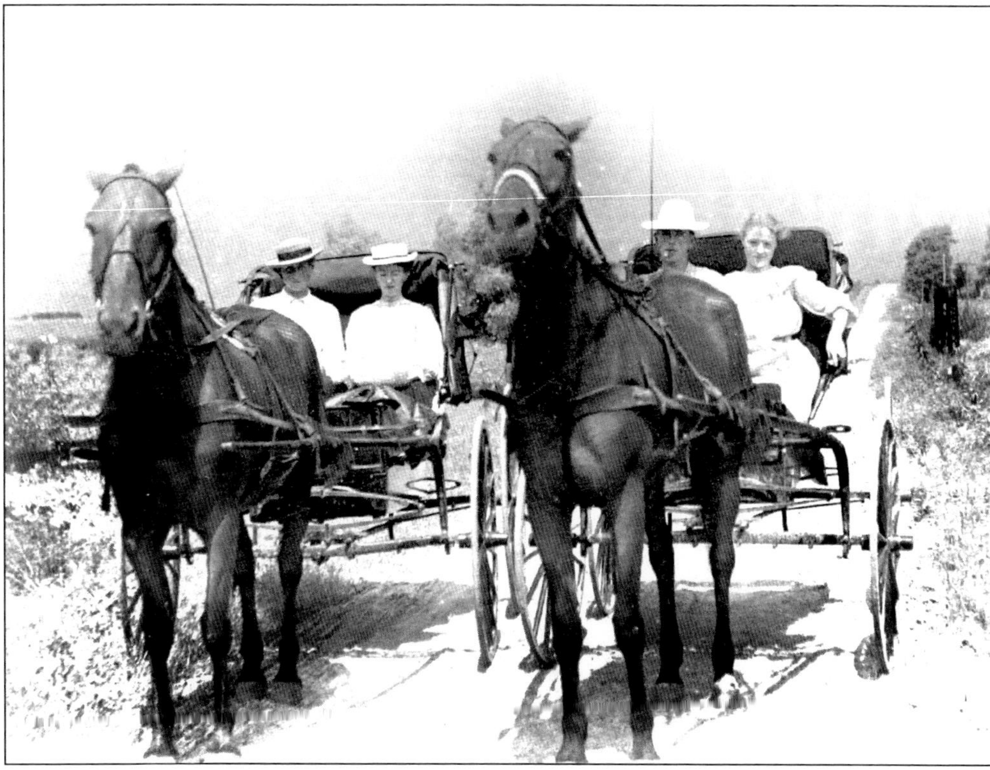

If one didn't care to sit every afternoon on the front porch, a buggy ride was just the thing. Quiet rural roads were often the scene of impromptu races since a fast, high stepping horse was much desired. However, the livery stable advertised that it had horses gentle enough for a lady to drive.

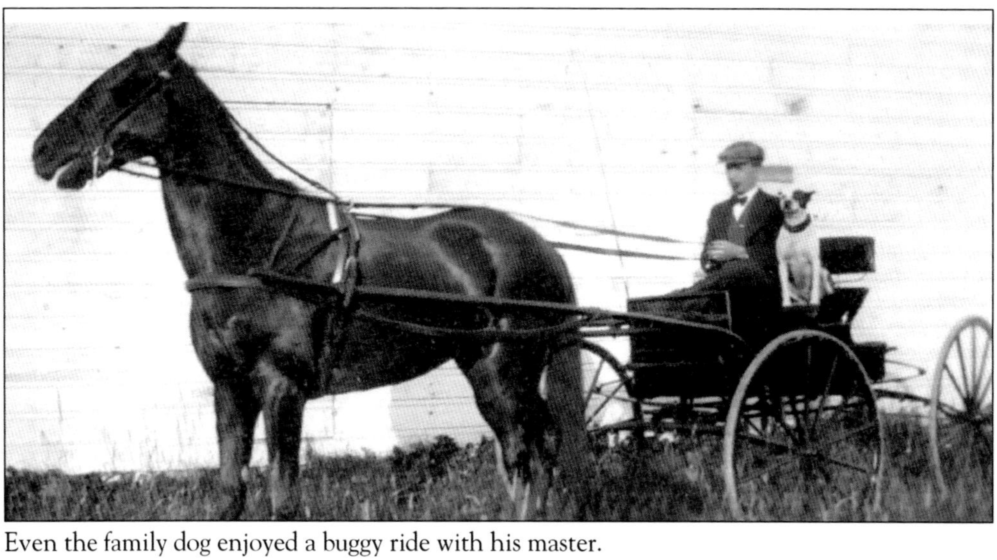

Even the family dog enjoyed a buggy ride with his master.

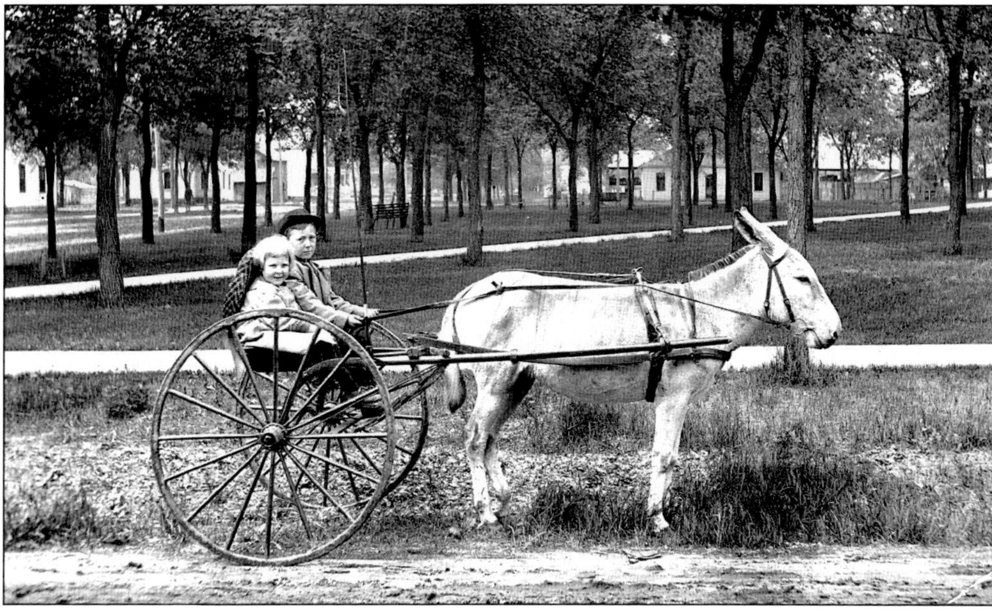

Some children were fortunate enough to have a little cart of their own. These young ones have a patient donkey to pull their two-wheeled cart. Goats were also kept as pets and trained to pull a cart.

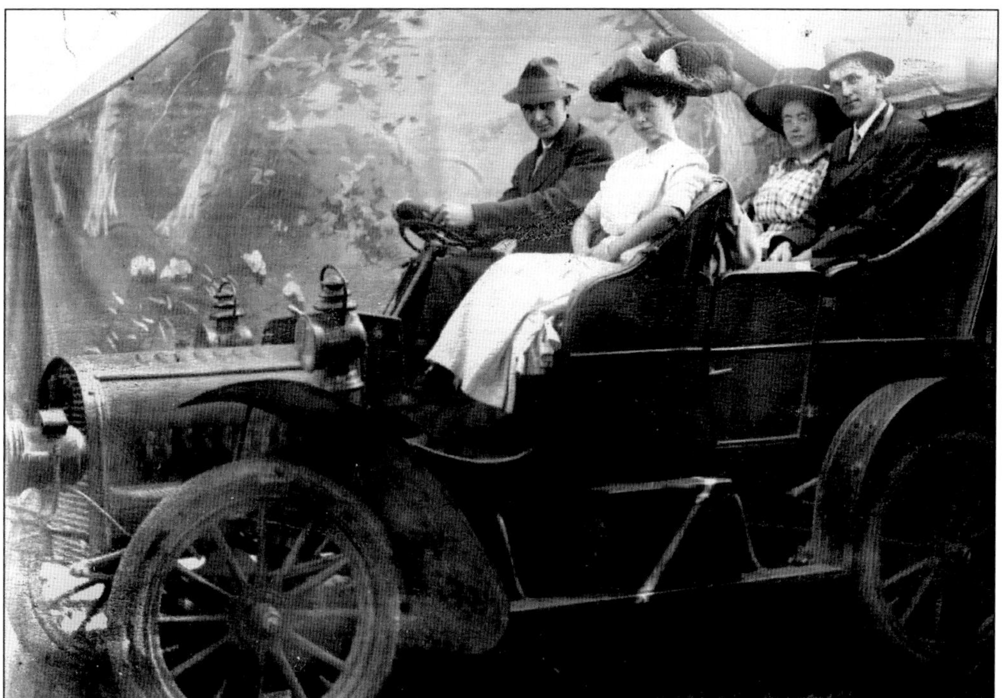

When automobiles began to appear, very few people had the money or the daring to buy one. However, it was fun to go to the photographer's studio and pose for a picture in one. Here two couples were all dressed up and no place to go, but the picture looked very real when sent to distant friends.

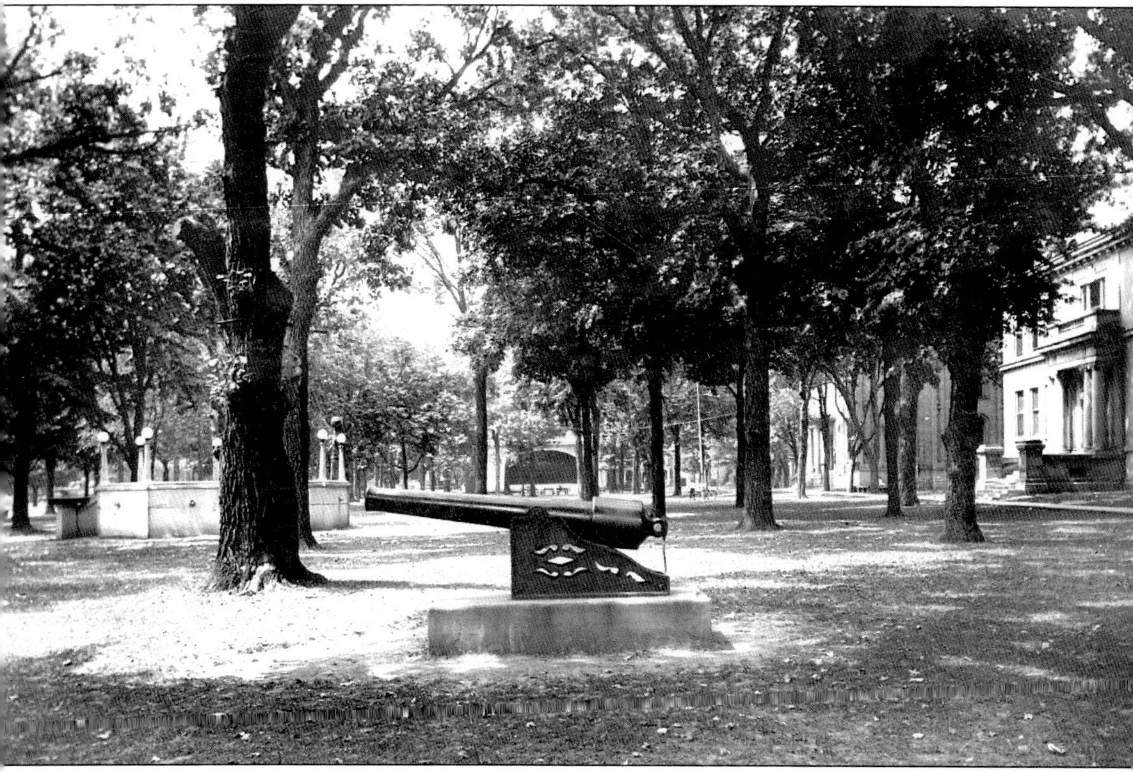

Just strolling in the downtown park, past the government buildings, made for a nice walk to pass the time. A Civil War cannon was interesting to look at. If children came along they had fun climbing on it or running around the cement bandstand seen in the background. The majestic burr oak trees, which had been there from Elkhorn's beginning, provided cool shade for pedestrians.

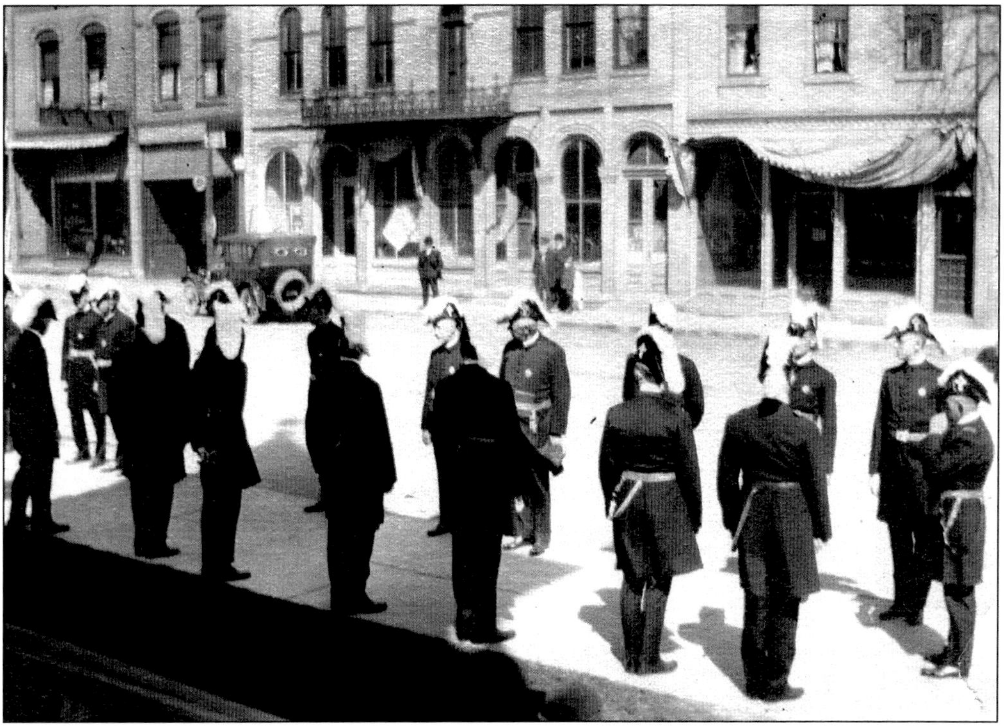

Fraternal organizations thrived in that long ago era before television, video, and computer games. The Knights Templar drilled on South Wisconsin Street downtown on Easter, 1919. They had previously attended services at the nearby church.

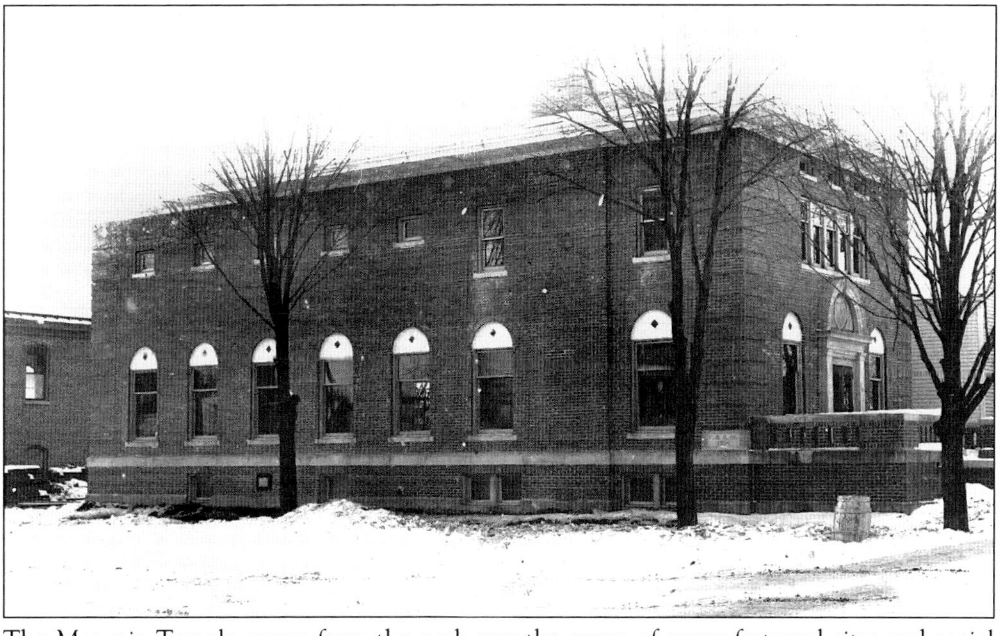

The Masonic Temple across from the park was the scene of many fraternal rites and social events too. Many of Elkhorn's leading citizens belonged to it. Recently, the building was sold and now contains offices.

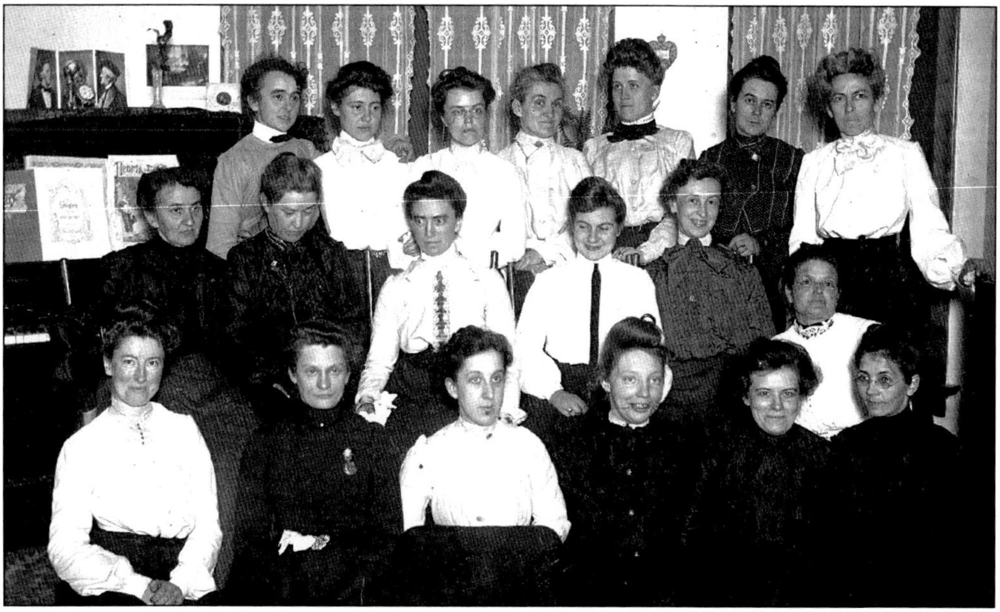

Women's clubs flourished in the early days too. The Elkhorn History Club started in 1893 and lasted for a hundred years. Its membership was limited to 25 so that meetings could be held in homes. The ladies had their picture taken at the annual party. Pictured from left to right are; (front row) Jessie Byington, Margaret Hurlbut, Edith Schmidt, Mabel Young Wiswell, Lutie Reed, and Lin Prisk; (second row) Bird Cain, Ruth Wales Isham, Helen Tubbs, Emma Sprague, Sarah Grancis, and Mary Mills; (third row) Jessie Lyon Jones, Jessie Sprague, Irene Norton, Lucy Coman, Millie Johnson, Mamie Hoffman, and Carrie Medberry.

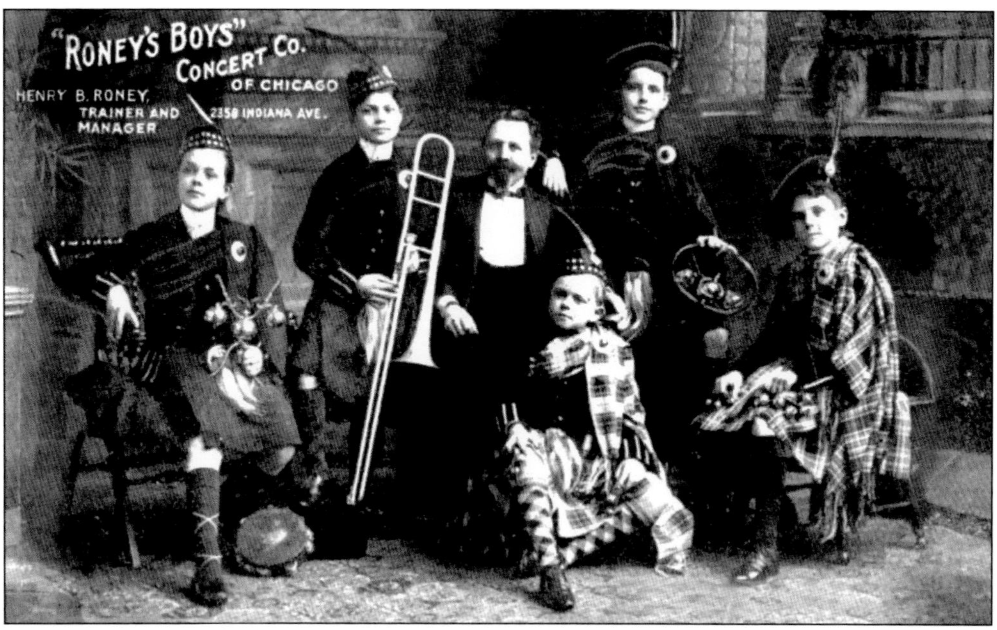

The Literary Club, which would become the Women's Club, was prominent too. Both of these groups endeavored to bring "culture" to town by sponsoring lectures and concerts. Roney Boys Concert Company of Chicago was one such program.

Even in the fast-paced world of today, there are still organizations that band together to serve the community. One such organization is the Garden Club, which is shown here planting a tree on Arbor Day.

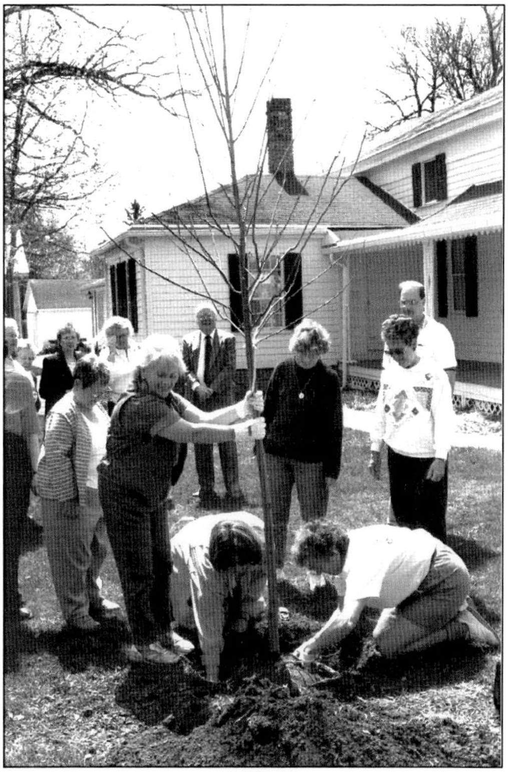

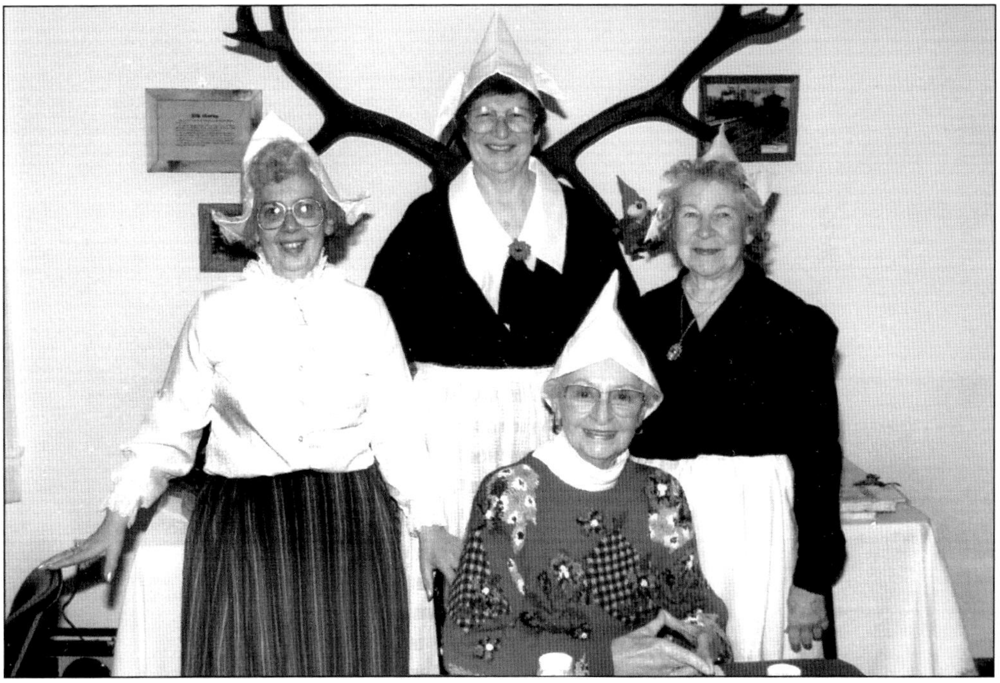

Ethnic groups enjoy getting together too. Here, the hostesses at Webster House Museum prepare to welcome guests to a Dutch program. Pictured, from left to right, are Merrybell Seeber, Lillian Magnus, Doris Reinke, and Harriet Llewellyn (seated).

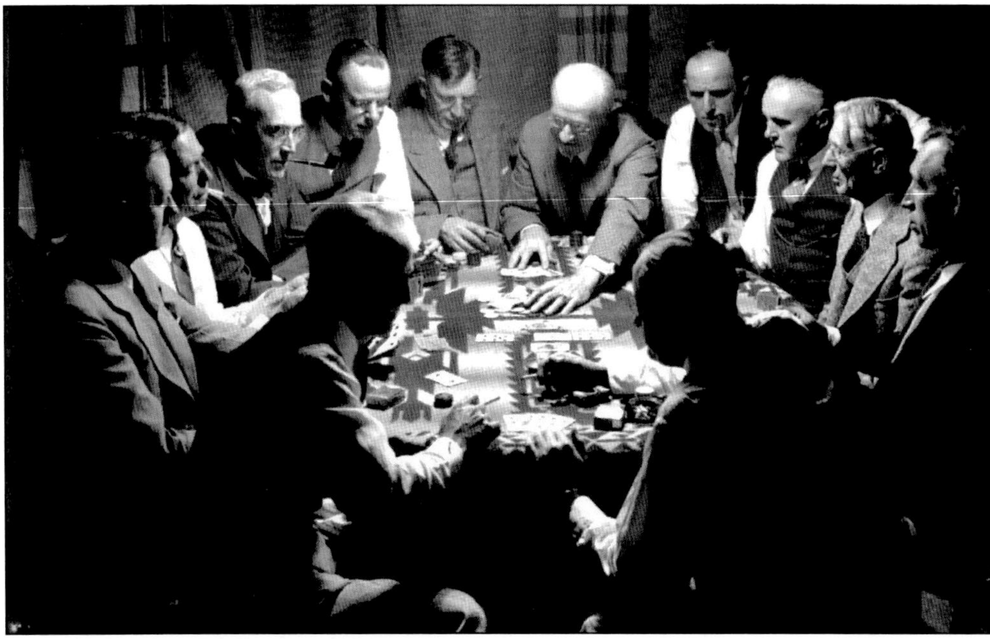

A friendly game of cards was a great way to spend a winter evening. A number of Elkhorn's most prominent men met regularly at each other's homes to play. Pictured in this group, from left to right, were Dan Kelliher, Art Desing, Weber Smith, Clarence Arp, Jim Harris, Judge Luce, Bill Brownlle, Bruce Harris, Harry Cain, Nick Carter, Lloyd Arp, and "Mud" Eames.

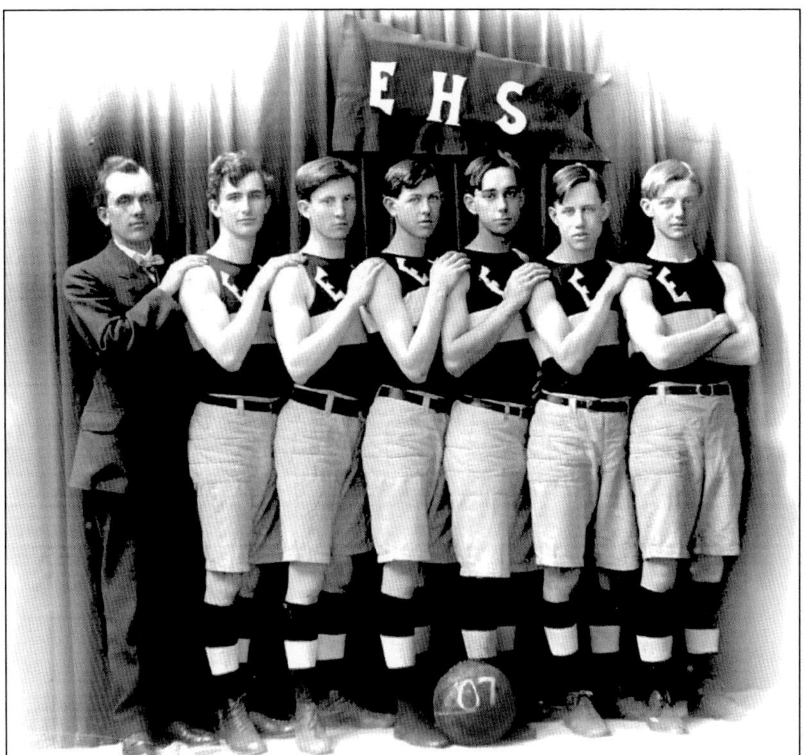

Attendance at local school sports events was a form of recreation too, whether those attending had children taking part or not. The basketball team of 1907 posed with their coach, W.C. Norton.

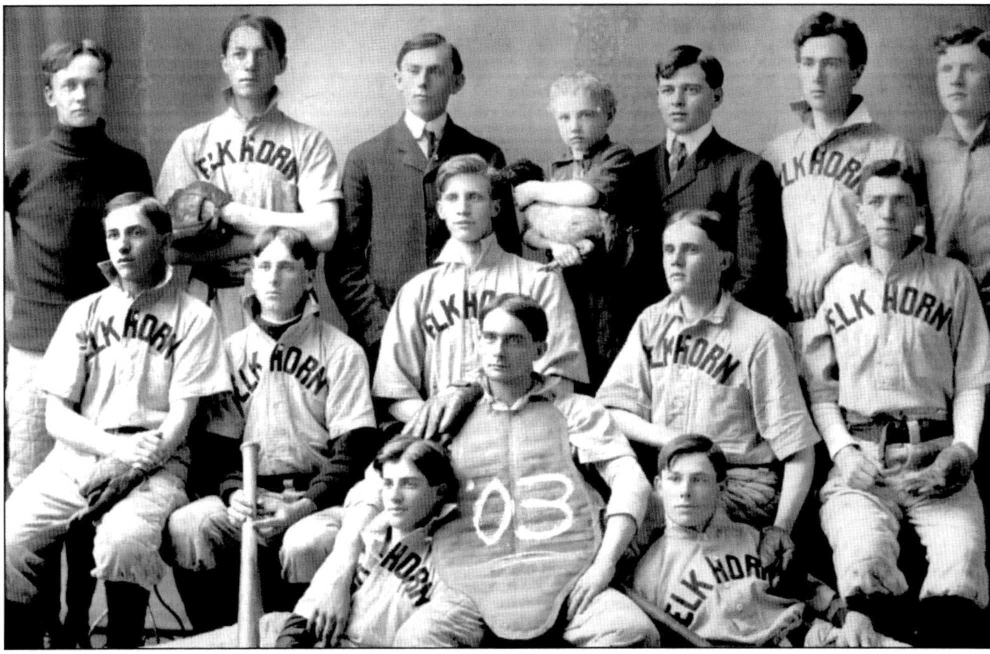

The 1903 high school baseball team had a young batboy who was photographed with them. He held the team mascot, a duck, firmly in his arms. Note that baseball was played with little more equipment than a few bats, balls, and fielding gloves. The catcher was the only one who wore any protective gear. Today's shin guards, batting gloves, and helmets with ear flaps were way in the future of the game.

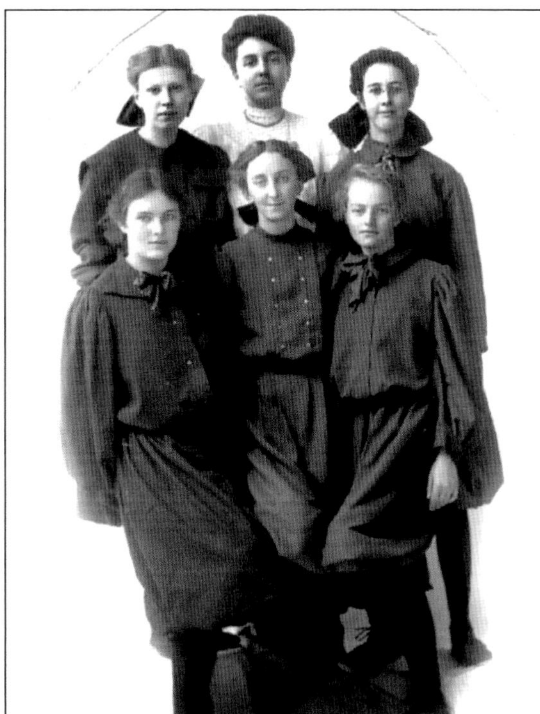

Contrary to popular belief, girls took part in high school athletics in long ago days. The members of the girls' basketball team wore knickers, which were proper attire then. Coach Florence Norton was an Elkhorn kindergarten teacher.

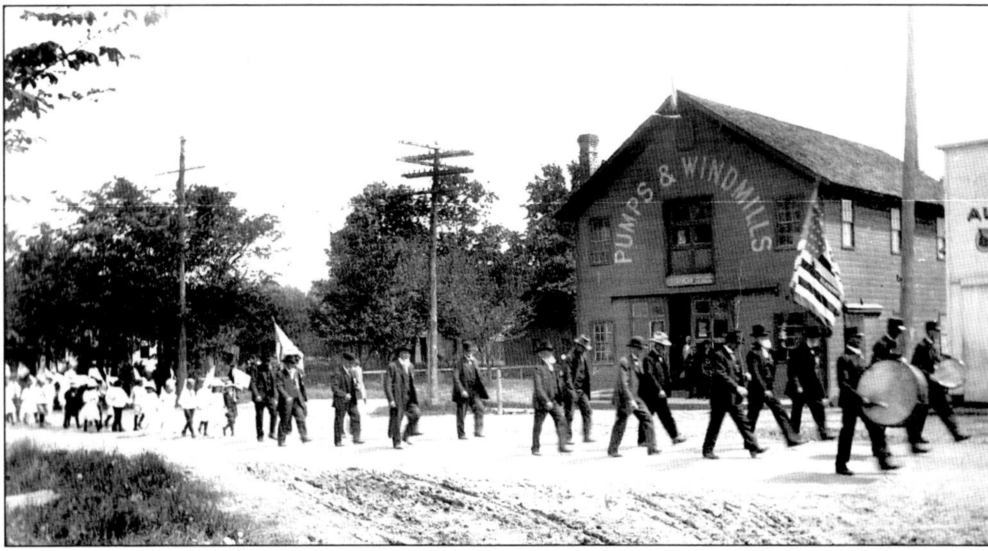

Like today, any kind of parade was recreation. Early parades were pretty simple affairs. In this photo, veterans and school children march from the school building to the downtown square on Memorial Day. The dusty, unpaved street did not detract from the enthusiasm of the marchers or the spectators.

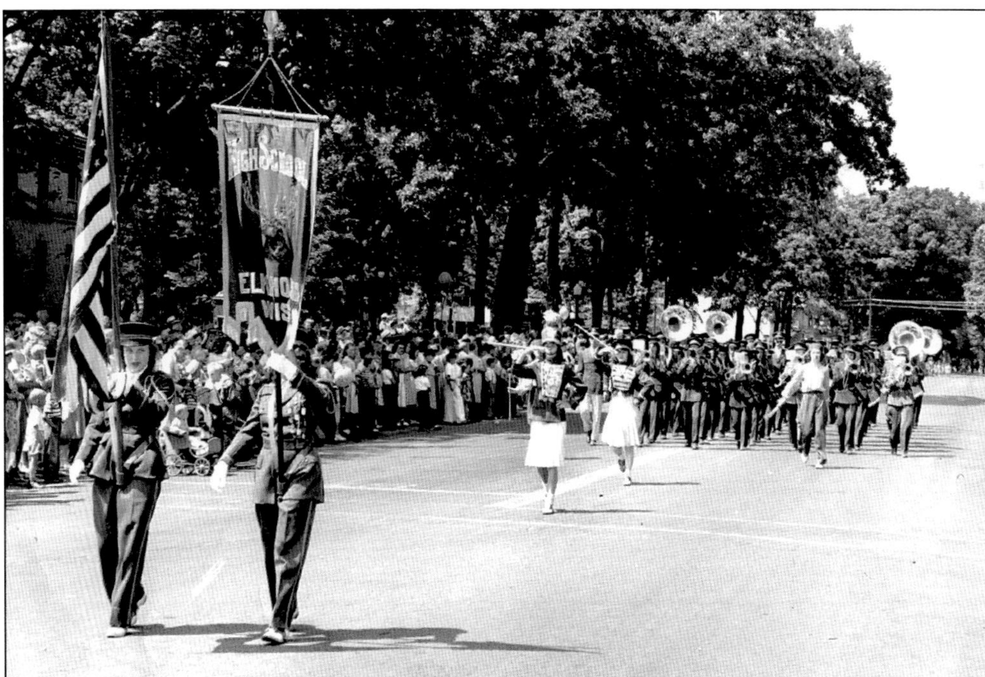

Many years later, the performers in the Memorial Day parade did not have to contend with a dirt road. The streets by then had been paved. The year was 1947.

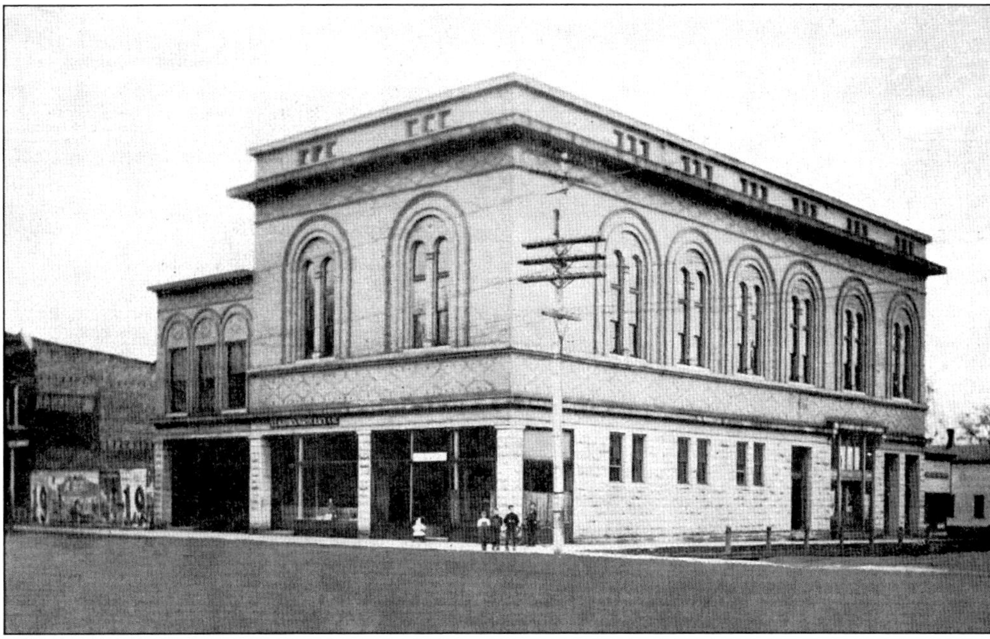

E.H. Sprague was a successful lawyer and owner of a brick yard. He erected a splendid building called the Sprague Opera House in 1901. It contained the post office, library, auditorium, variety store, and office space. It was the scene of plays, medicine shows, musical performances, and high school graduations. All this ended in 1925, when a disastrous fire consumed the building.

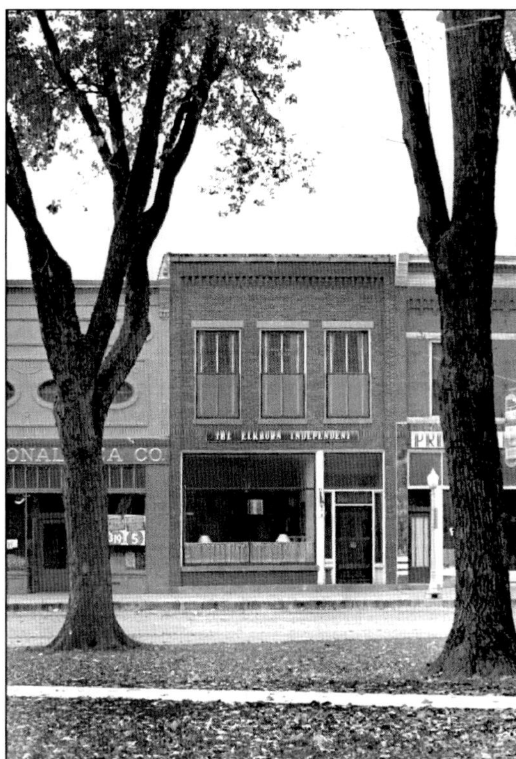

A newspaper is not exactly entertainment, but the early ones might be classified as such. They featured a chapter of a serial story in each issue. The *Elkhorn Independent* has been serving the community since 1853. In its 150 year history, it has covered the gold rush, the Civil War, the Titanic sinking, the rise of Hitler, and all the local news.

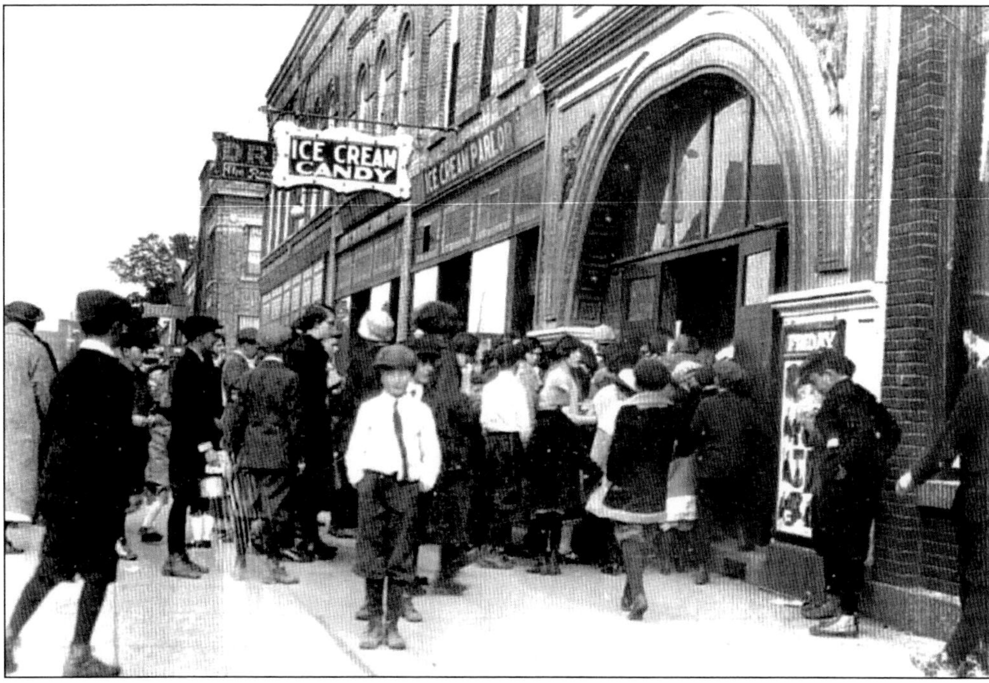

When motion pictures were invented, the people of Elkhorn lined up outside the Princess Theater to see this exciting phenomena. The movies were silent, of course, but the theater's pianist helped the audience interpret the mood of the story.

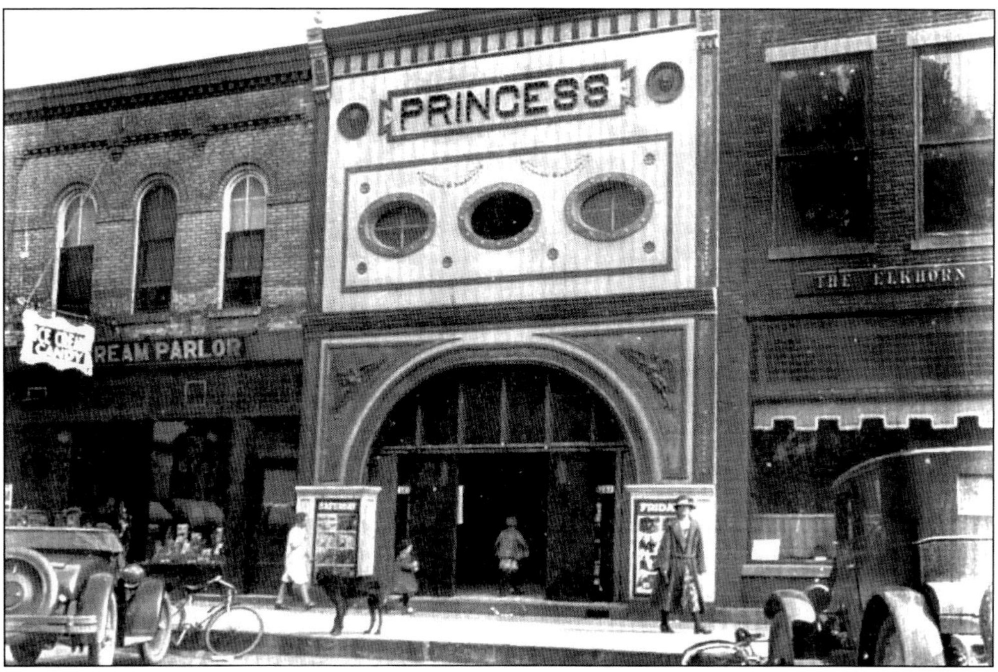

The ice cream parlor next door found that its business had more than doubled when the Princess began showing movies. Candy during the show and a dish of ice cream afterwards were part of movie tradition right from the start.

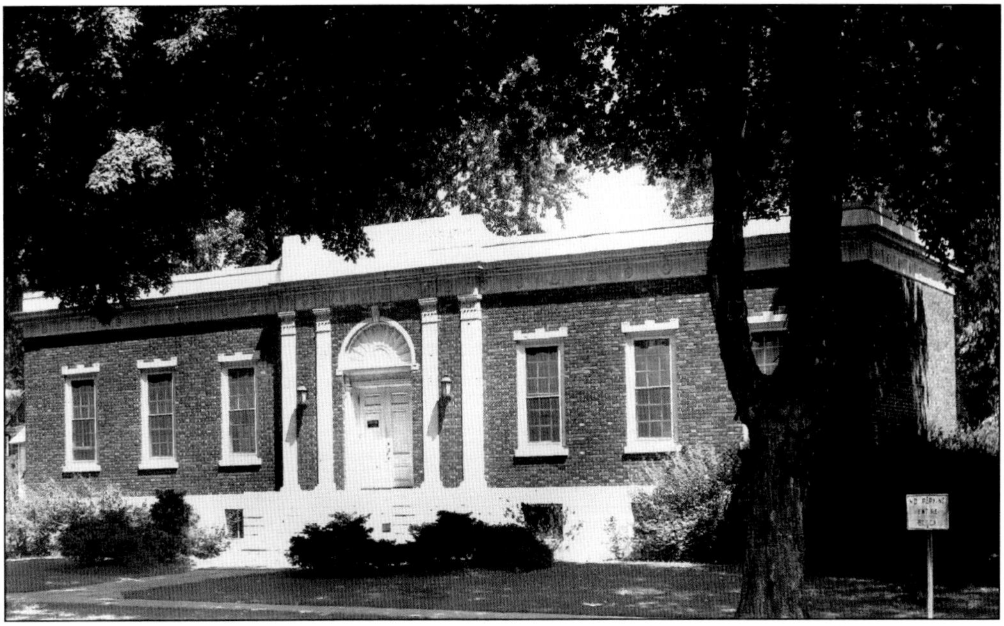

Elkhorn's present library was built in 1931 as a result of a large donation from William Matheson. He specified that it be constructed on a downtown corner where his family home had been. Consequently, the library was named the Matheson Memorial Library.

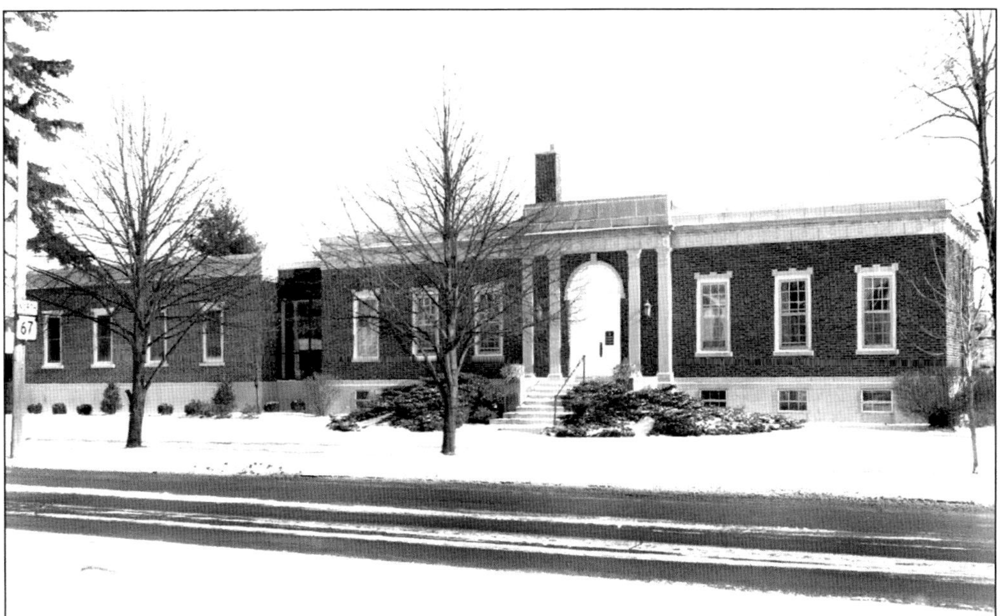

A wing was added some years later to give space for a children's book room, plus a section for videos and computers. A parking lot was also provided in the rear.

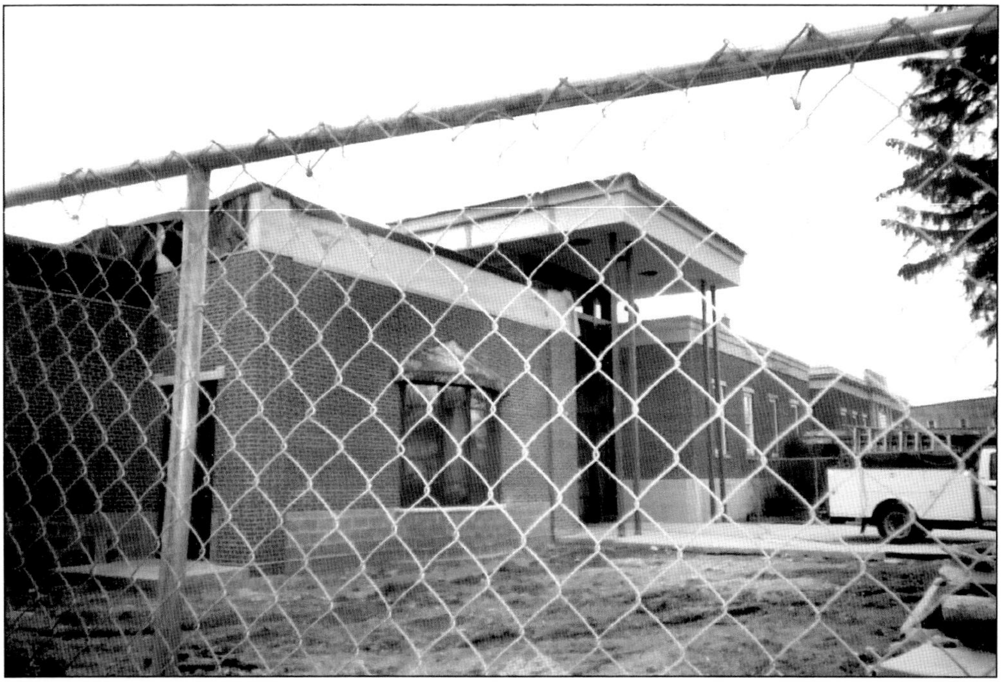

A civic center stood next to the library. In 2003, this center was torn down. In 2004, plans for a massive addition to the Matheson Library were underway. Attached to the library will be a new civic center.

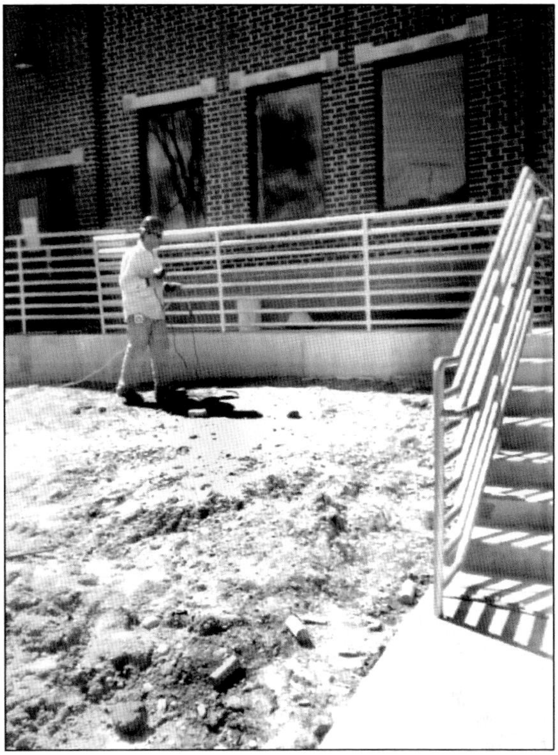

A workman is putting the finishing touches to one of the new entrances of the library. The new facility will open in 2004.

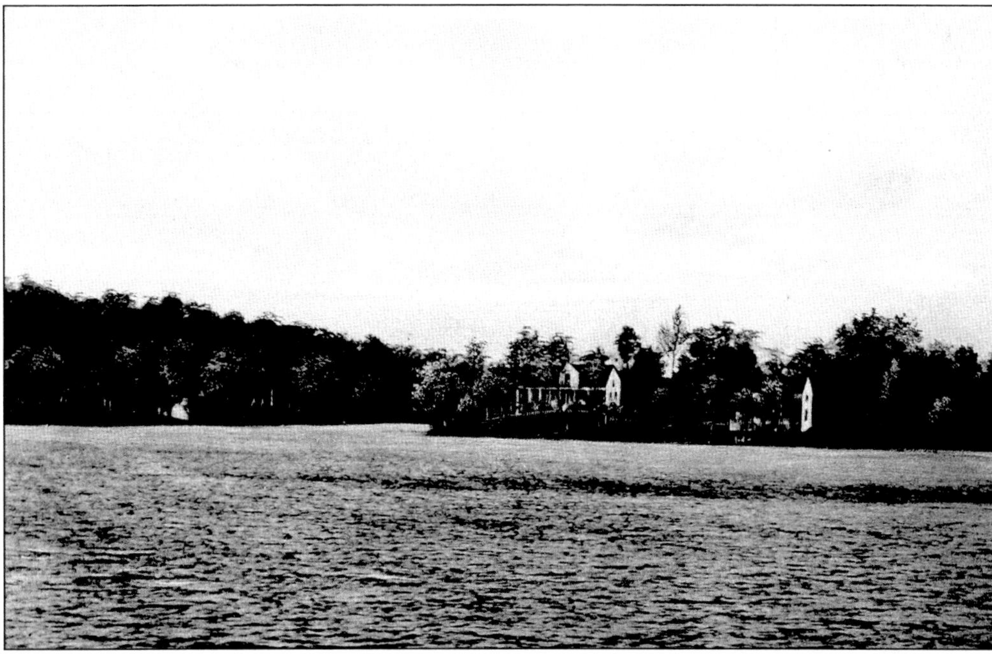

Although Elkhorn itself had no lake, there were two lakes a few miles north that the city's residents called their own. One of them was Lauderdale, which was actually a chain of three lakes—Green, Middle, and Mill. Many people from Elkhorn had cottages there and enjoyed fishing and boating.

Unlike luxurious Lake Geneva, a few miles south where millionaires built mansions, the Lauderdale cottages were modest and piers were short. Going to the lake was such a popular pastime that merchants in town observed "early closing" on Wednesday all summer. On that afternoon a good proportion of them were boating and fishing on Lauderdale. Here, a well-crafted wood boat is all ready for a fishing trip.

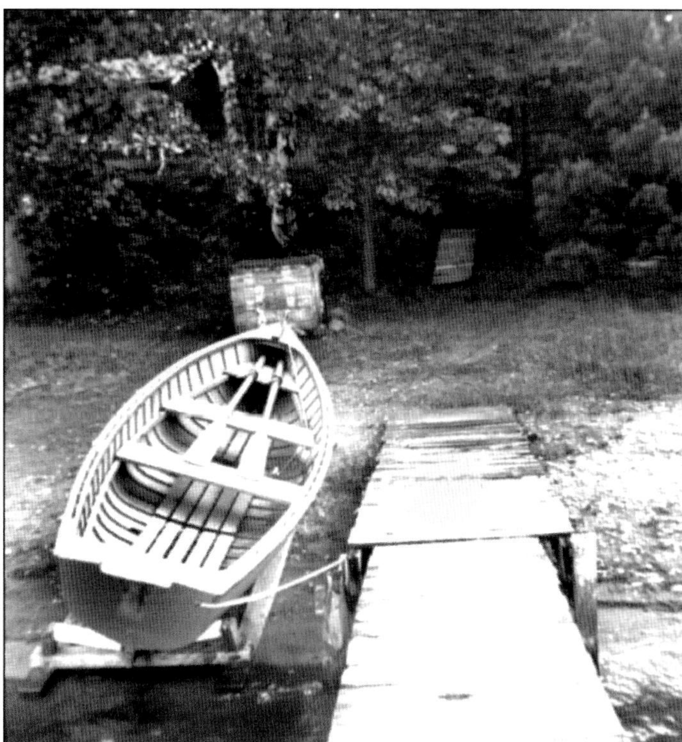

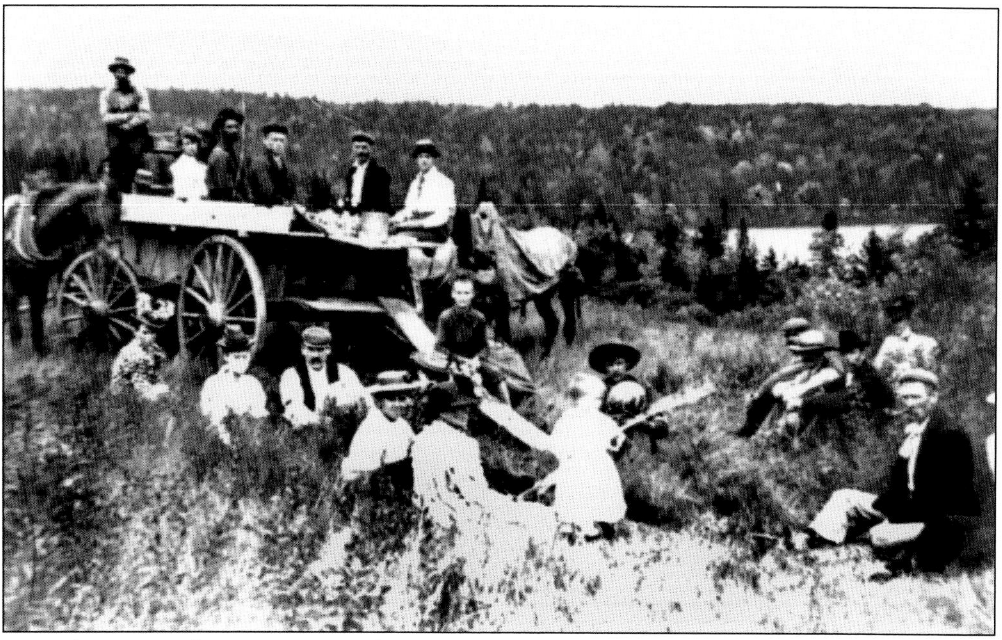

It was fun to crowd into a wagon and go to Lauderdale Lake for a picnic. People of all ages, right down to little babies, enjoyed an outing at the lake.

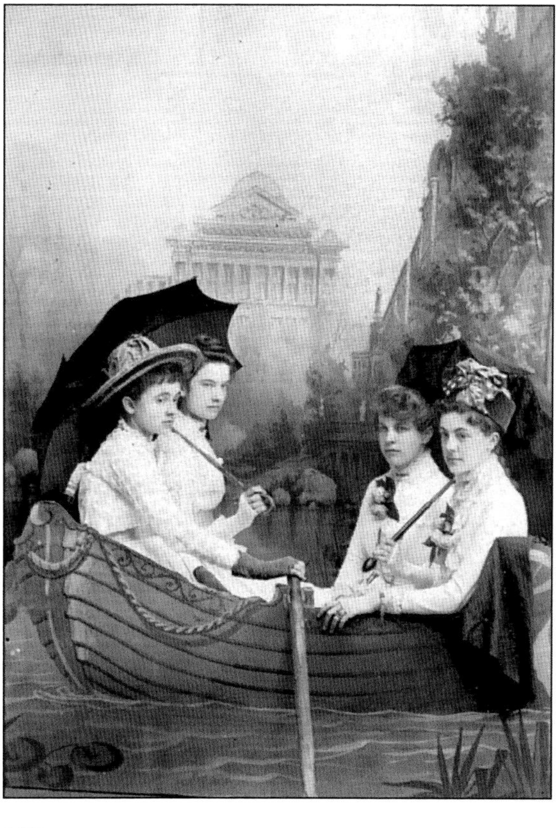

Often those who did not have a cottage at the lake or even a boat of their own went to the local photographer and had their picture taken in his make-believe boat. Here, four young Elkhorn ladies posed for a nautical portrait in 1886.

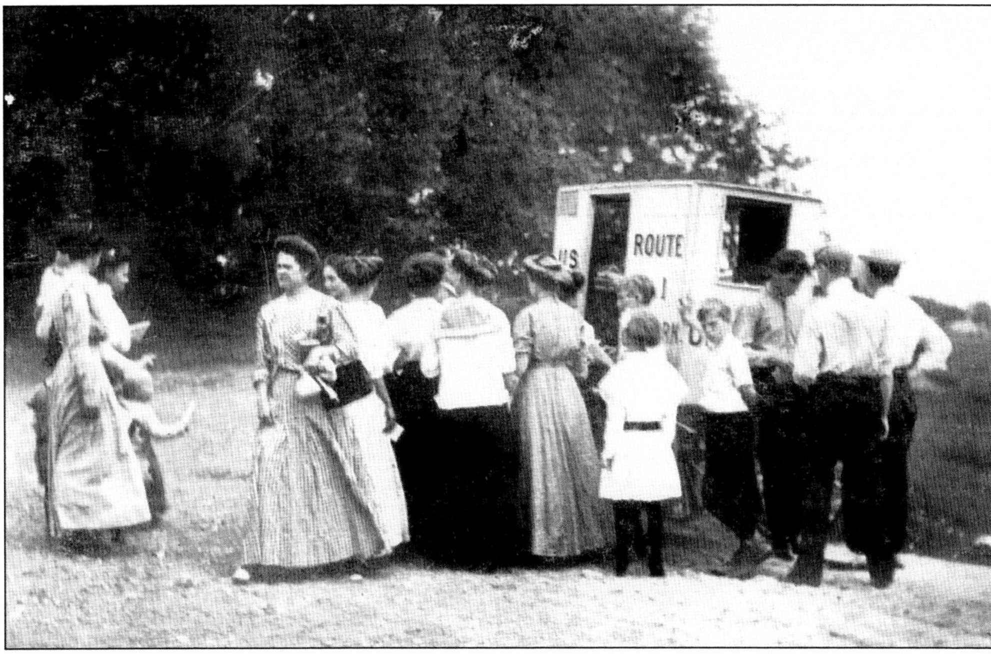

The people who had cottages on Lauderdale came to Sterlingworth Hotel to pick up their mail. This was before there were individual mail boxes. Those who lived in town had to go downtown to the post office for their letters also.

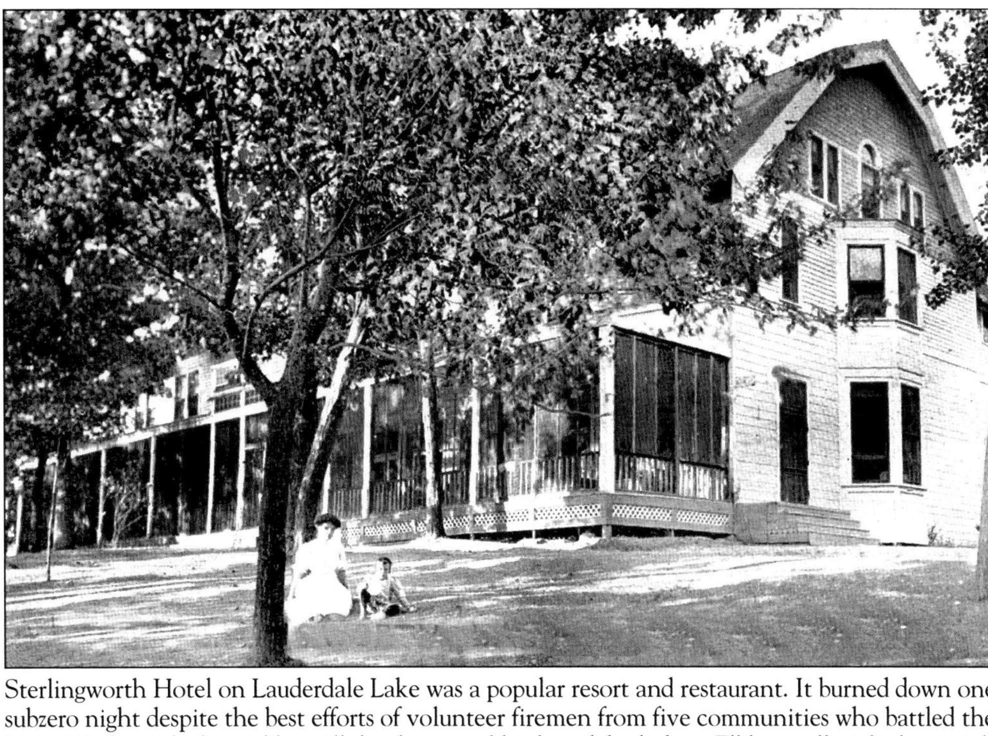

Sterlingworth Hotel on Lauderdale Lake was a popular resort and restaurant. It burned down one subzero night despite the best efforts of volunteer firemen from five communities who battled the blaze. Tank trucks loaned by milk haulers raced back and forth from Elkhorn all night long with additional water, but it was in vain. Sterlingworth has been rebuilt, but now is a condominium.

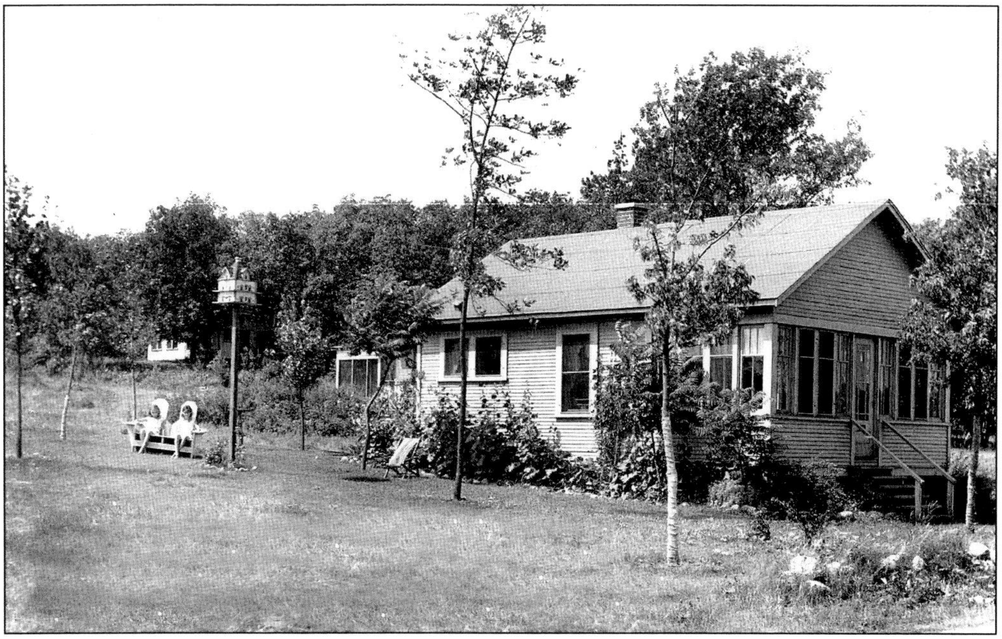

Wandawega was the other lake favored by Elkhorn people. When it was being developed, lots as small as twenty feet in width were being sold. Three or four lots had to be joined together to make room for a normal sized cottage and yard.

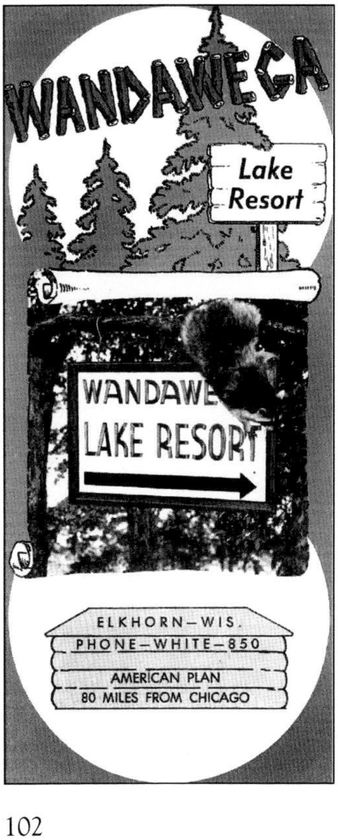

A small resort was built on Wandawega and its advertising stressed that the resort was rustic and restful. It had separate cottages as well as the hotel. Vacationing there was not too rustic, as electricity and running water were furnished.

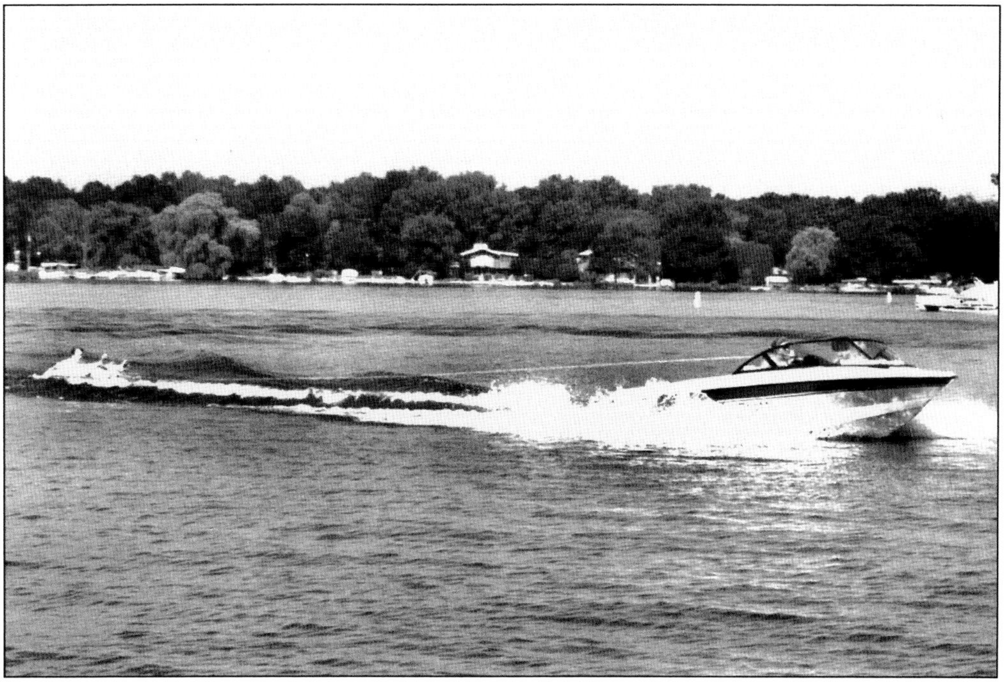

In modern times, things have speeded up a bit on the lakes. Much bigger boats now cruise the waters and powerful motors have replaced the pair of oars that once moved a boat. A popular sport that has developed is water skiing.

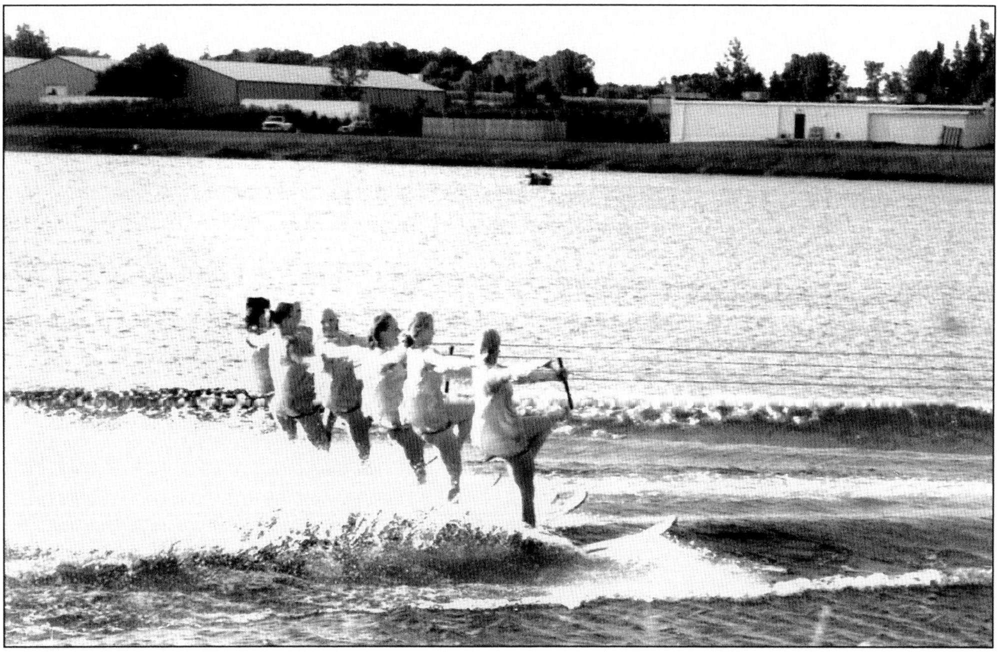

The Lauderdale Aqua Skiers practice their precision skiing in this picture. During the summer, this organization gives exhibitions out at Lauderdale and also on little Elkhorn Lake, which was formed when gravel was excavated for material to build Highway 12 as it bypassed the city.

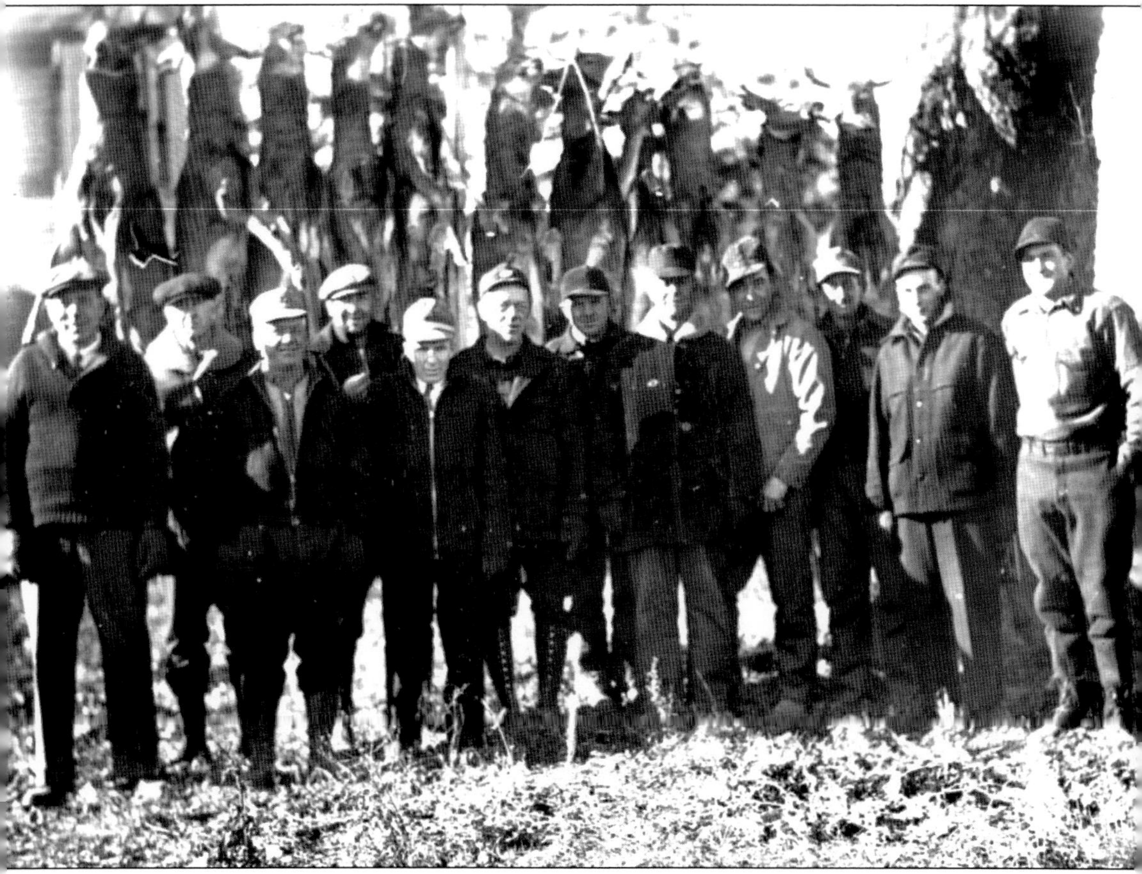

In the fall, a good percentage of the male population heads to northern Wisconsin for deer hunting. The state's deer herd has gradually worked its way south, however, and thrive on the corn and soy beans grown on the local farms. Each year now, many hunters get their venison within 20 miles of home.

Eight

The County Fair

The biggest thing that happens in Elkhorn is the County Fair. For one week, Elkhorn is a metropolis. Motels are filled. Streets are crowded. Motor homes and vans search for parking space. Music and announcements, magnified by the loud speaker, fill the air.

Most of the residents are involved with the fair. Some of them find employment taking tickets and parking cars. Others work in the buildings supervising the exhibits and judging entries. Some of them just buy a season's ticket and enjoy the six days. They look at farm machinery, eat junk food, watch harness racing, see great entertainers, and watch blue ribbons being handed out.

Maybe the best thing about the fair is that since its beginning in the 1850s, it has always been a "dry fair." No alcoholic beverages are sold on the grounds. Despite this, fairgoers still have fun.

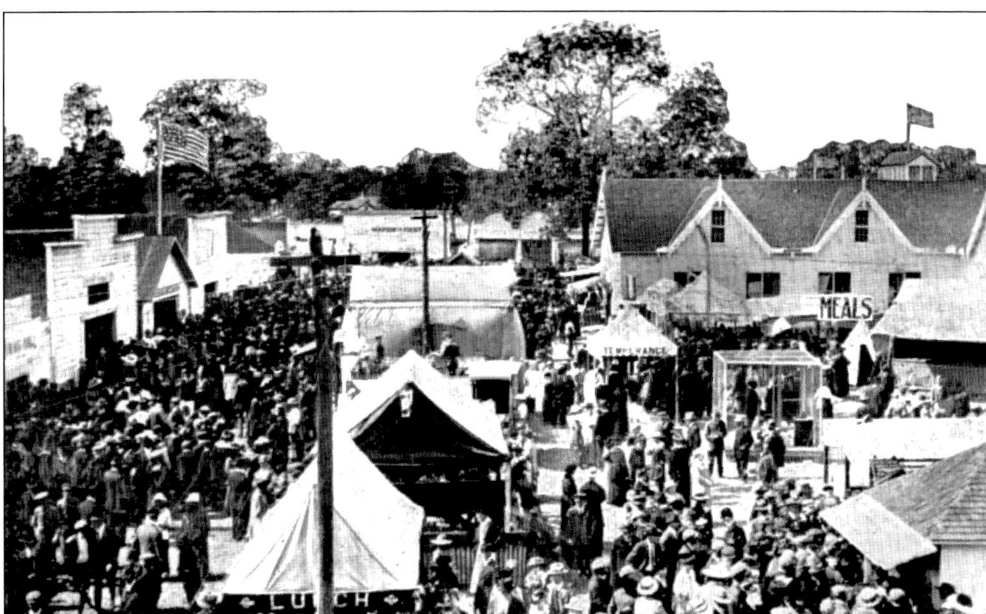

The Midway was crowded in 1919 as people sought a place to eat after the horse racing was over. Everyone was hungry. Sit-down dinners were offered in the permanent buildings. Plenty of other food was available from vendor lunch wagons and tents.

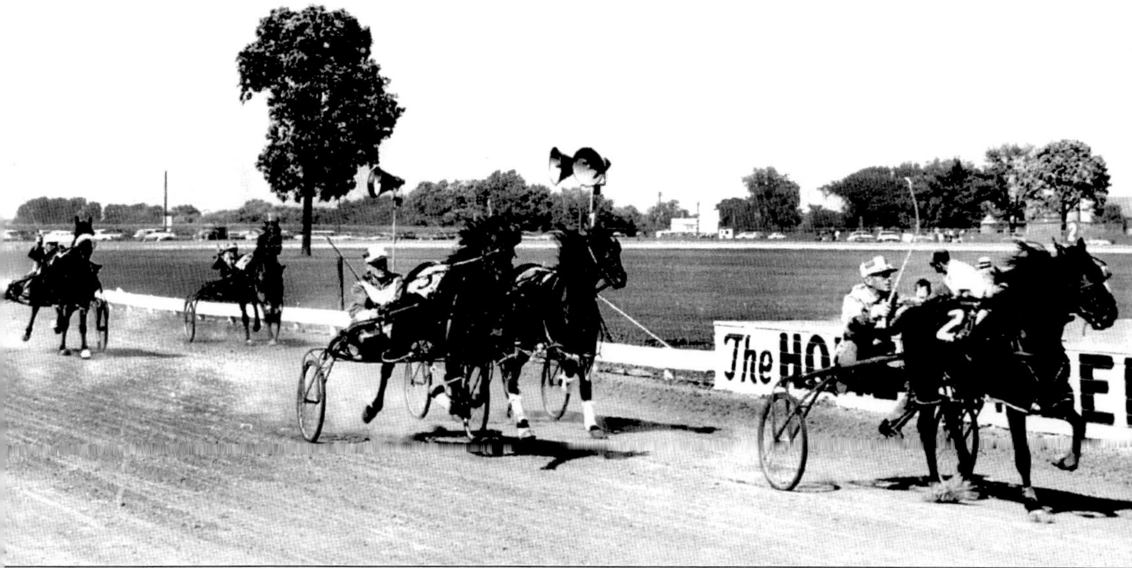

Harness racing is always an exciting part of the fair. The half mile oval is considered one of the best tracks on the circuit. Many local people own and train trotters and pacers. One of the drivers used to wear a helmet that said, "If you can read this, you are too close."

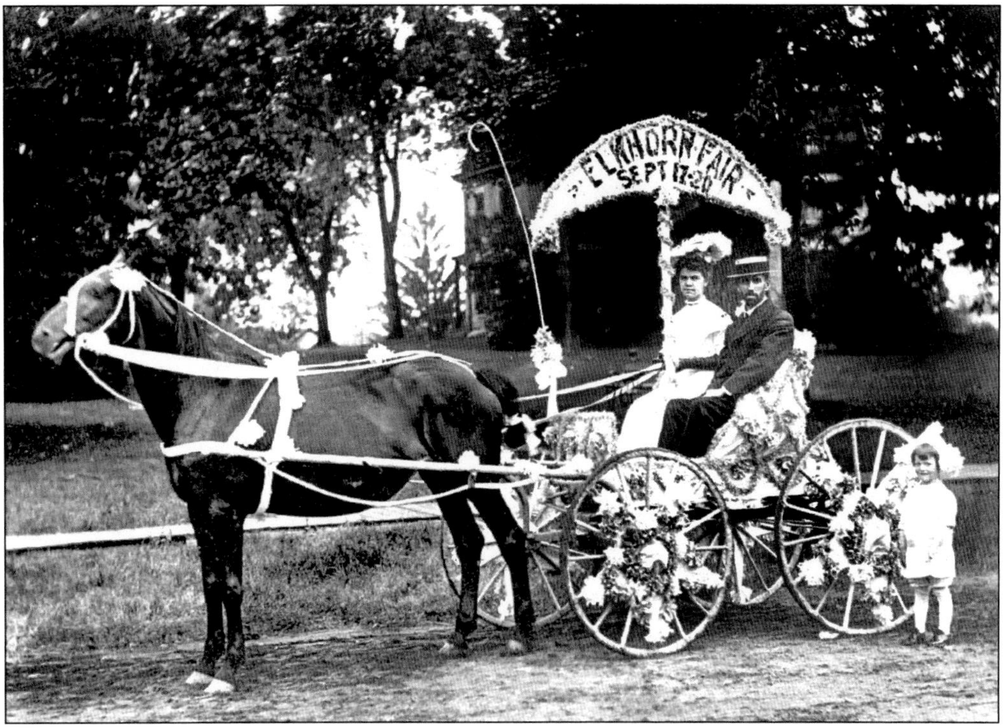

At one time, a parade signaled the opening of the fair. Local families decorated their buggies and vied for a blue ribbon.

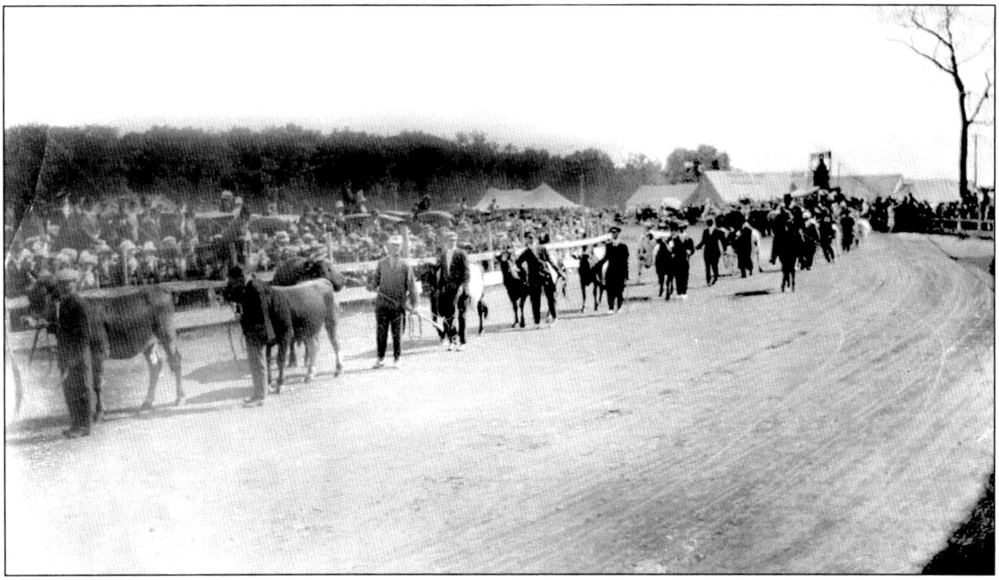

Another kind of parade in front of the grandstand was that of live stock. Farmers led their best cows down the track before judges awarded prizes.

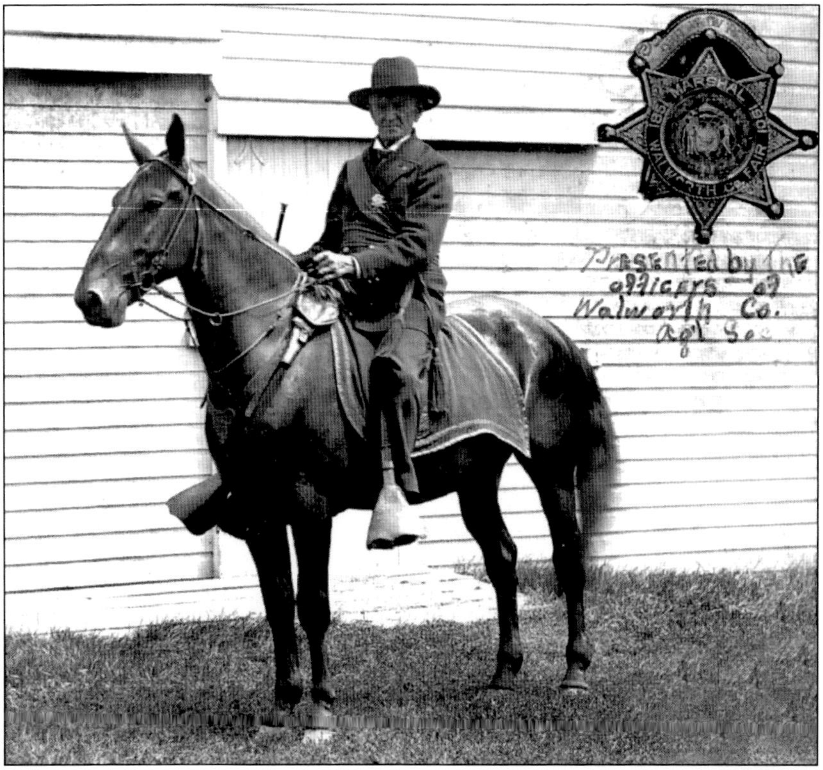

George Wylie was marshal of the fair for many years. He was a sterling example of those settlers who willingly served the city and county in many capacities. Wylie was on the board of supervisors and was sheriff for many years.

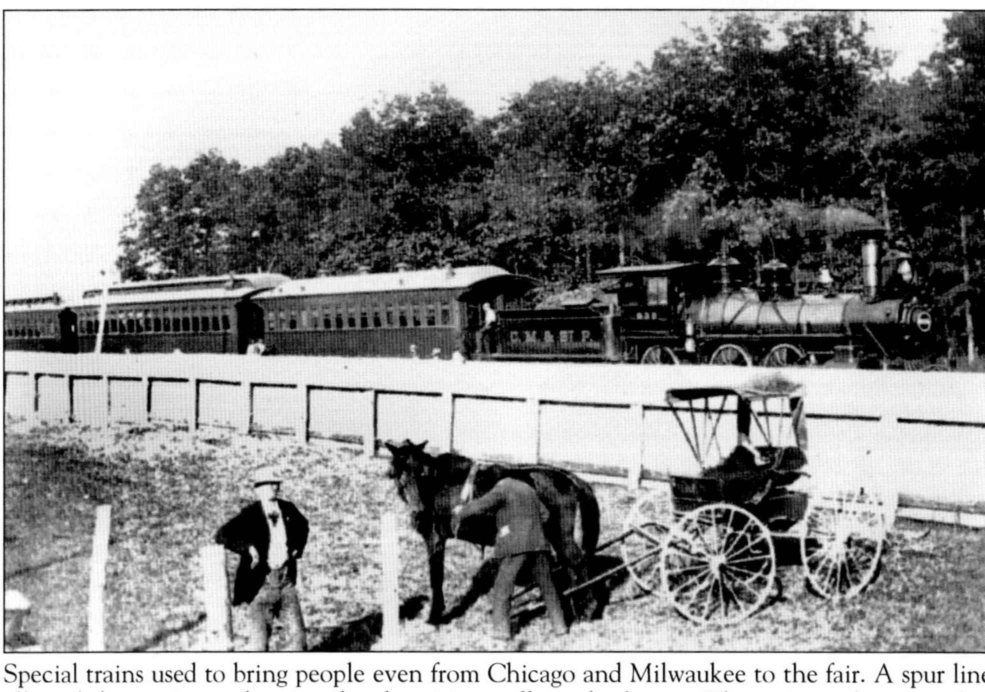

Special trains used to bring people even from Chicago and Milwaukee to the fair. A spur line allowed the engine and cars to let the visitors off at a back gate. The train no longer makes that trip, cars have taken over that job. On days or nights when there are super attractions, the parking lots are filled and the overflow has to park in the infield of the track.

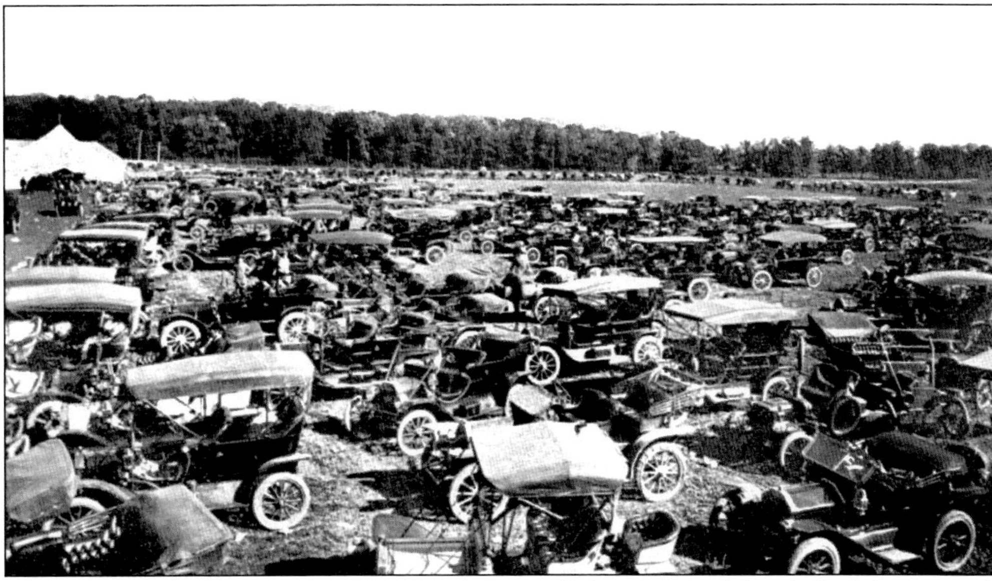

Even as early as 1913, many fairgoers came by car. All those automobiles choked the racetrack infield. Among them were roadsters and touring cars, with names like Hupmobile, Maxwell, and Mitchell.

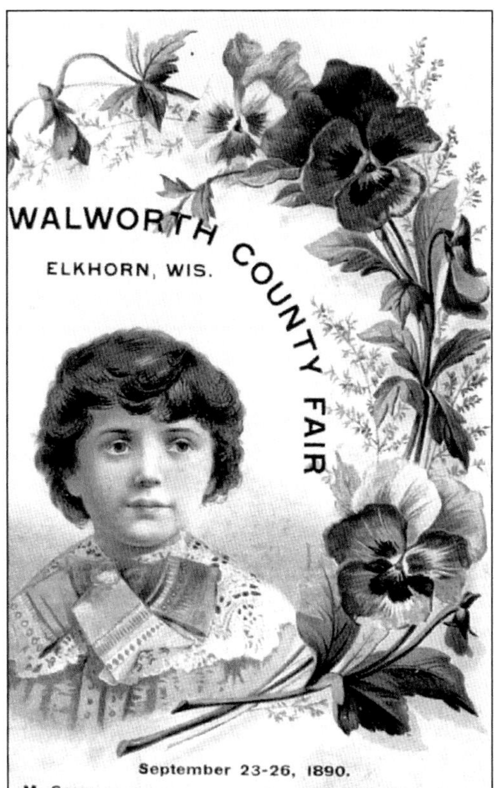

At the very early fairs, advertisers handed out souvenir cards that could be traded like baseball cards are today or, more likely, pasted into scrapbooks.

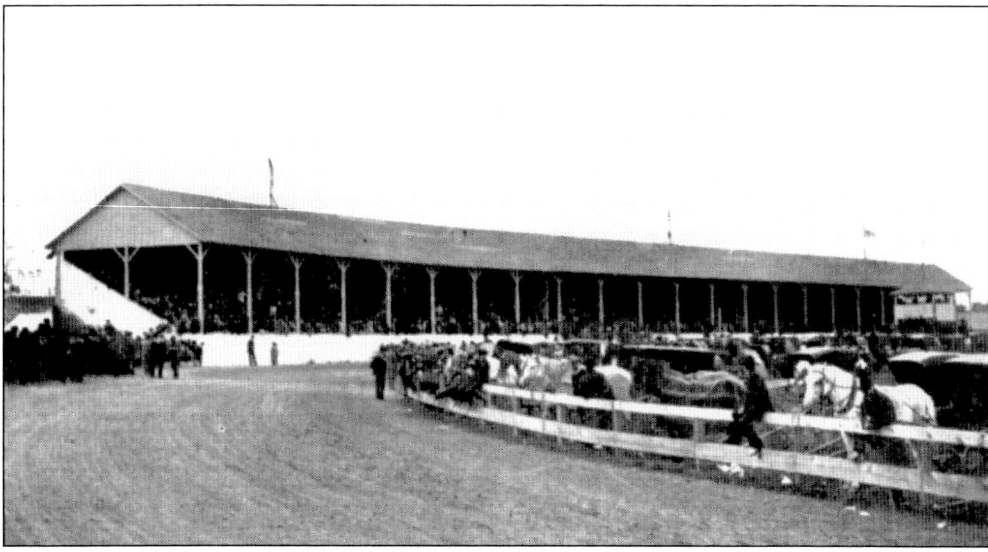

The old grandstand burned down some years ago only one month before opening day. The fair managed to open on time by borrowing temporary bleachers from neighboring football fields.

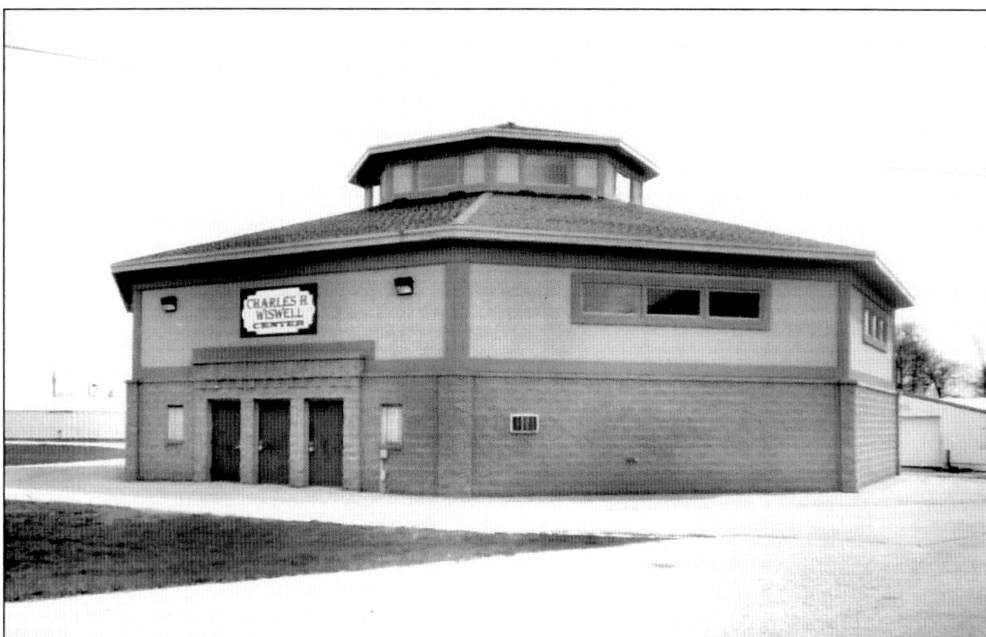

New buildings are added periodically. The Charles Wiswell Center replaced an earlier octagonal building which had become outmoded. It is there that livestock is judged. The Wiswell family in Elkhorn has been associated with telephone communication here since 1900 when the first telephone switchboard was set up.

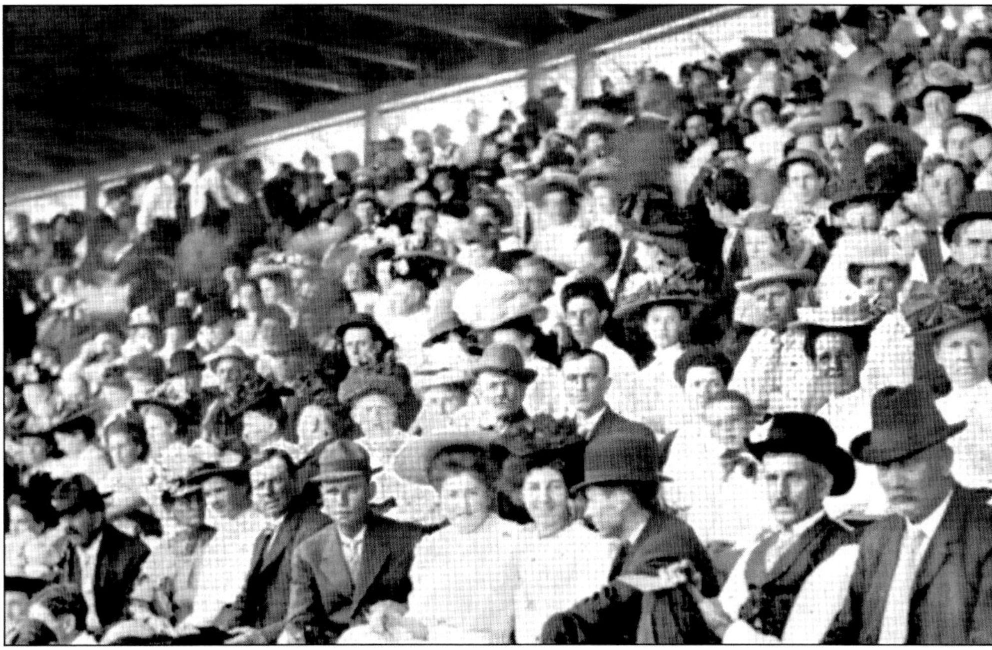

The grandstand was full in 1911 and it is filled every year the same way. The only difference is the way people dress. The people who watched the trotters go by used to dress conservatively. Men wore suit jackets, neckties, and hats. Women wore petticoats under their long skirts, blouses with long sleeves that buttoned right up to the neck, and a beribboned hat was important. How times have changed!

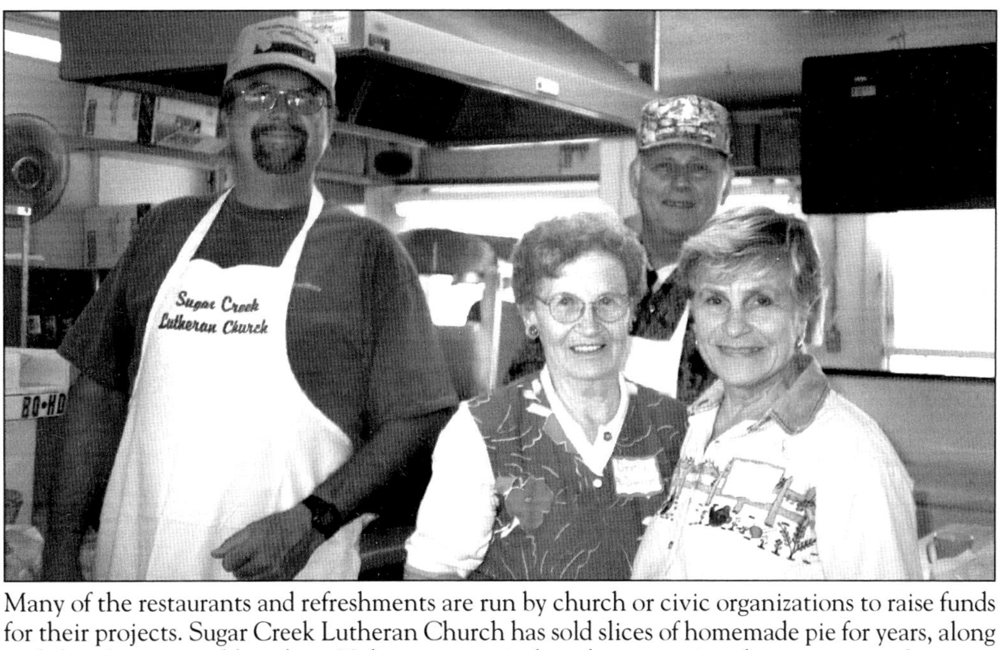

Many of the restaurants and refreshments are run by church or civic organizations to raise funds for their projects. Sugar Creek Lutheran Church has sold slices of homemade pie for years, along with hamburgers and hot dogs. Volunteers put in long hours serving the customers who come back year after year. Pictured from left to right are Harold Wodicka, Dorothy McDonough, Don Anderson, and Char Carlson.

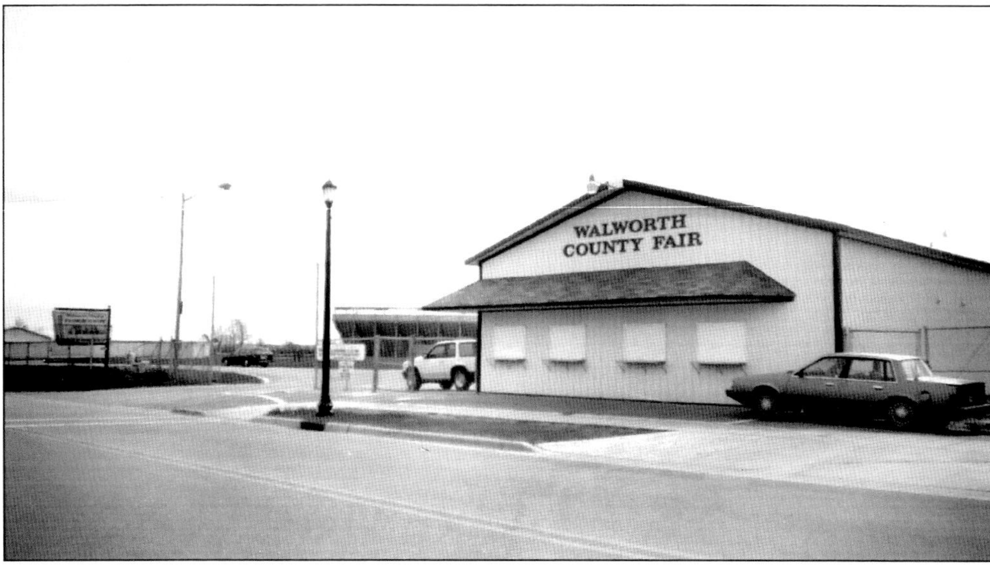

After Labor Day, everything seems pretty quiet at the fairgrounds. The vendors have left. The rides on the Midway have been dismantled. The livestock (horses, cows, sheep, goats, and rabbits) have returned to the farm.

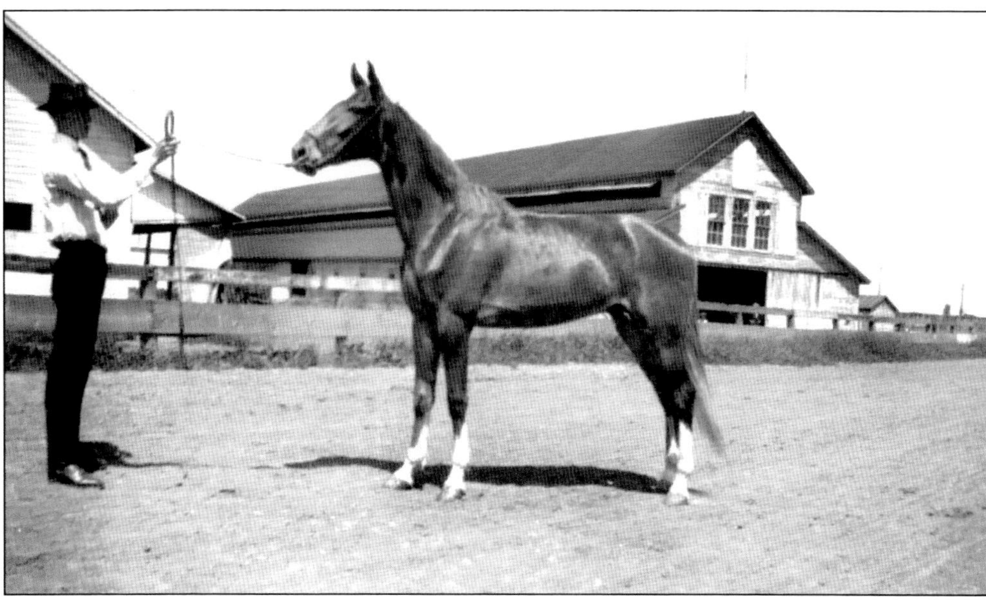

However, the grounds are not really deserted. Officials in the office are already planning the attractions for next year. The clop clop of the trotter's hoofs can be heard on the track because trainers work with their horses all year, getting then ready for future races. There are long horse barns at the far side of the fair grounds. The stalls are full most months.

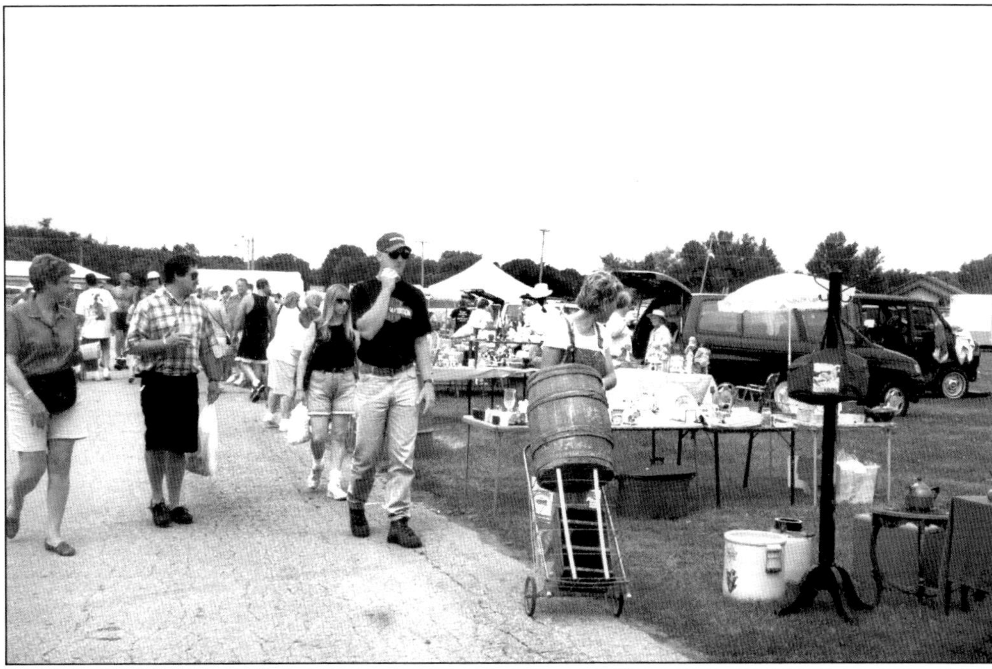

That lull following Labor Day is only a temporary one. There is something going on almost every weekend. The activities range from dog shows, family reunions, pork roasts, nostalgic classes in the one-room school house, to flea markets.

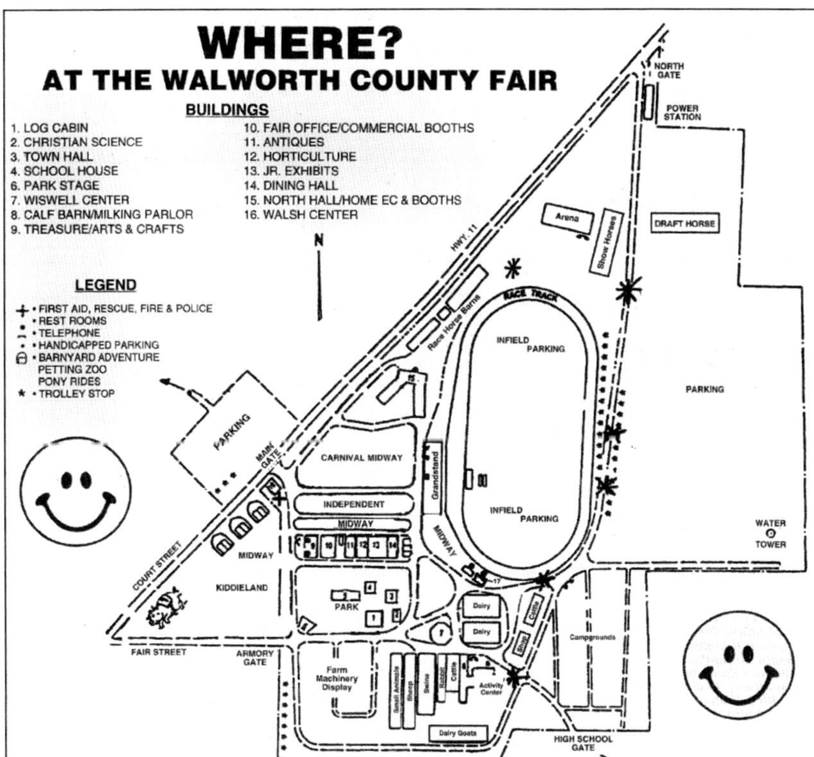

This map of the grounds reveals that there is room for many activities all year long at the fair grounds.

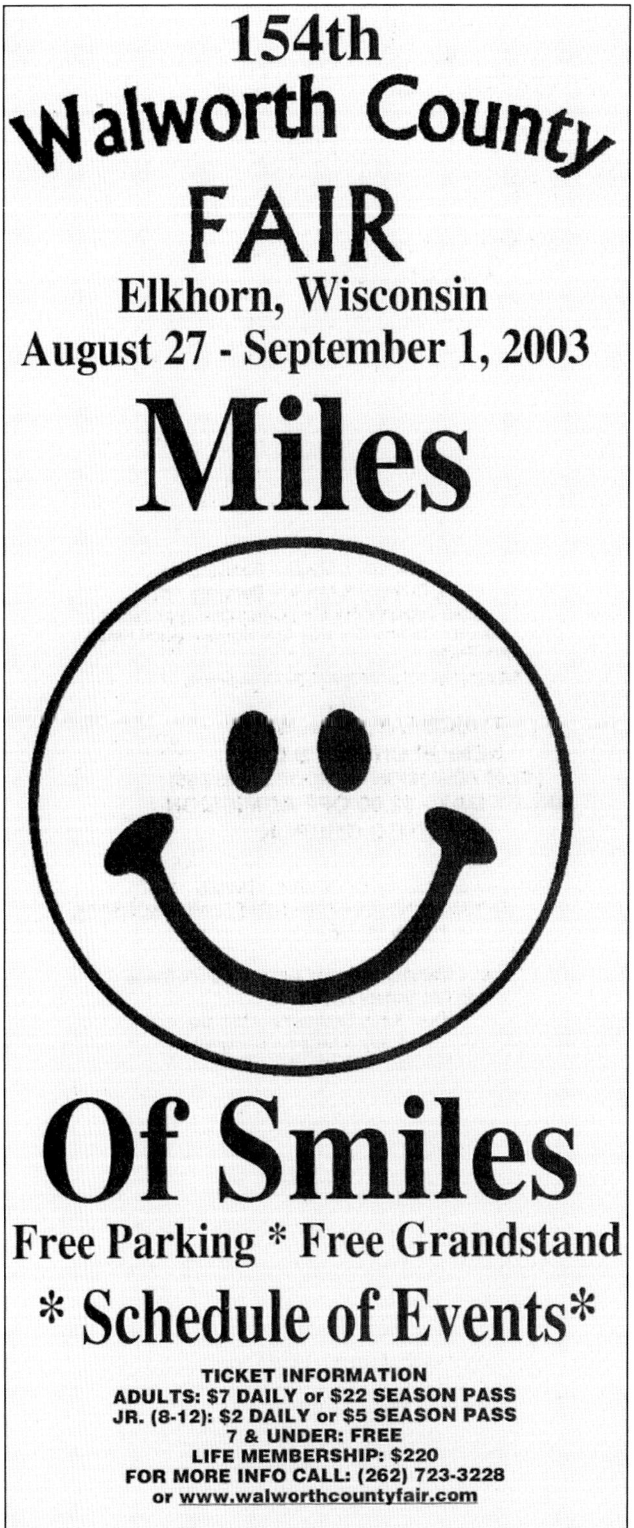

The importance to Elkhorn of the yearly fair cannot be overestimated. Like the county seat business which LeGrand Rockwell anticipated in his gamble back in 1836, it has caused the city to have a different character from the surrounding towns.

Nine

In the News

For a small city, Elkhorn has had its share of news headlines. Fortunately, most of the news has been good. There have been movie premieres and the capture of a most-wanted gangster. The city has starred in a national television show and has been featured on a series of Christmas cards.

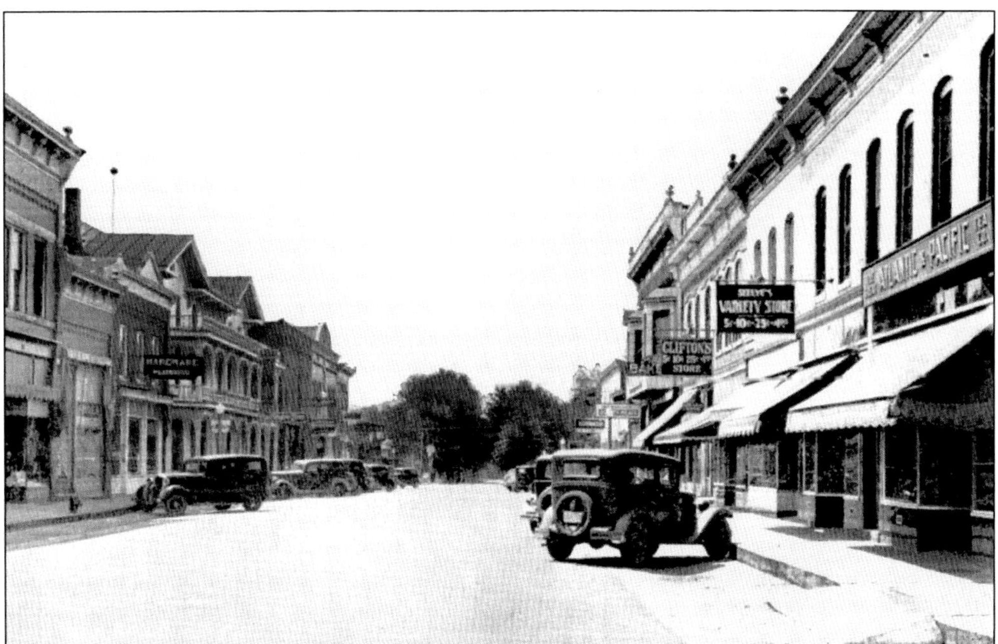

The street scene downtown shows a quiet city, peaceful and safe. Most of the time life is calm in Elkhorn. People like it that way.

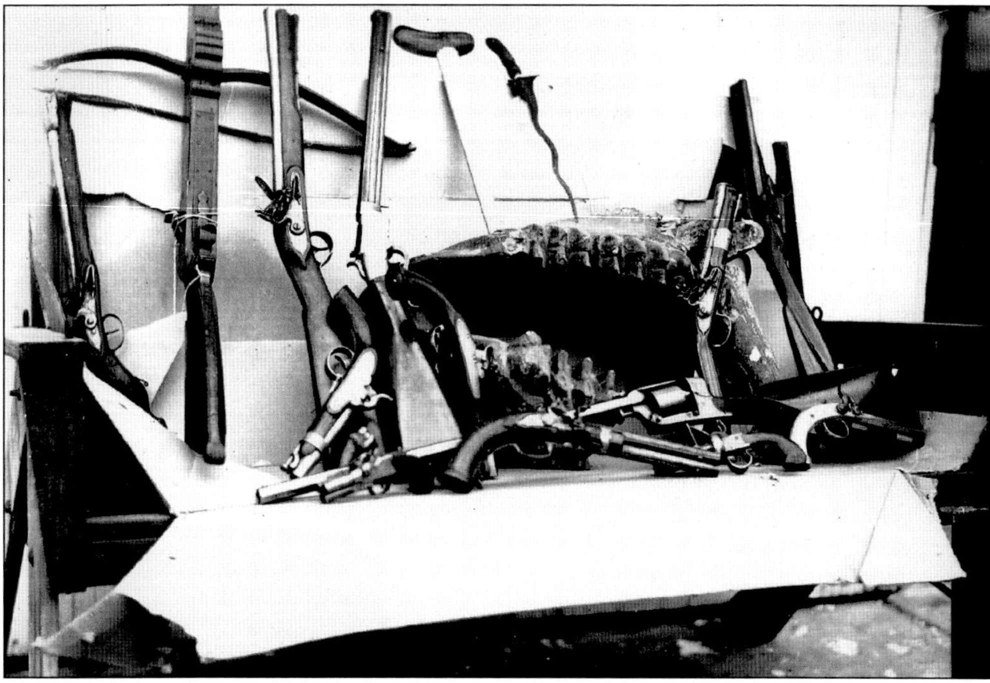

Probably the most exciting thing that ever happened was the unexpected capture in July 1933 of Roger Touhy, a Chicago racketeer. He and his men had hit a telephone pole outside of town and had left the scene. Their car was stopped when they entered Elkhorn and an arrest was made. Touhy gave a fictitious name and prepared to pay a fine. Officers, however, took a look at the powerful car and discovered guns.

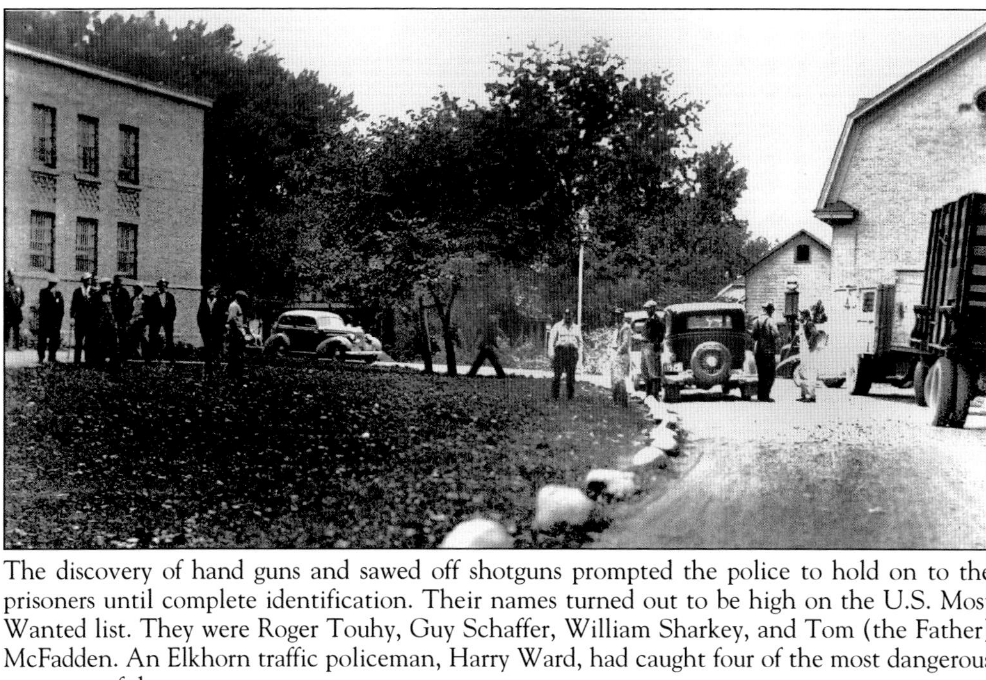

The discovery of hand guns and sawed off shotguns prompted the police to hold on to the prisoners until complete identification. Their names turned out to be high on the U.S. Most Wanted list. They were Roger Touhy, Guy Schaffer, William Sharkey, and Tom (the Father) McFadden. An Elkhorn traffic policeman, Harry Ward, had caught four of the most dangerous gangsters of that era.

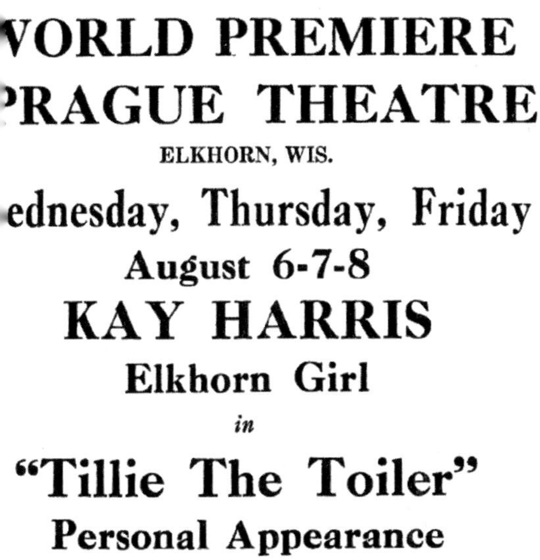

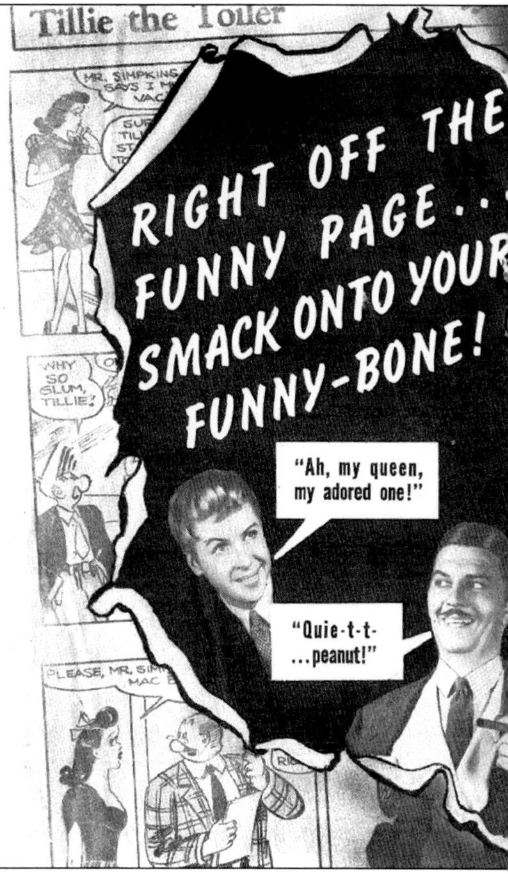

The Sprague Theater in downtown Elkhorn has been the locale for two movie premieres. One of them was in August 1941. The star of *Tillie the Toiler* was from this city, so the movie had its grand opening here. The street outside the theater was bright with spotlights and exploding flash bulbs when Kay Harris and her family appeared.

The theater had replaced the earlier Princess Theater and was considered an especially fine one. Owner Dan Kelliher explained that he had named it for the Sprague Opera House that had once stood on the corner.

A different kind of premiere occurred in 1952 when residents had the opportunity to see the half hour *March of Time* TV series entitled "Christmas Time in Elkhorn." A crew had spent a month in town filming aspects of small town living.

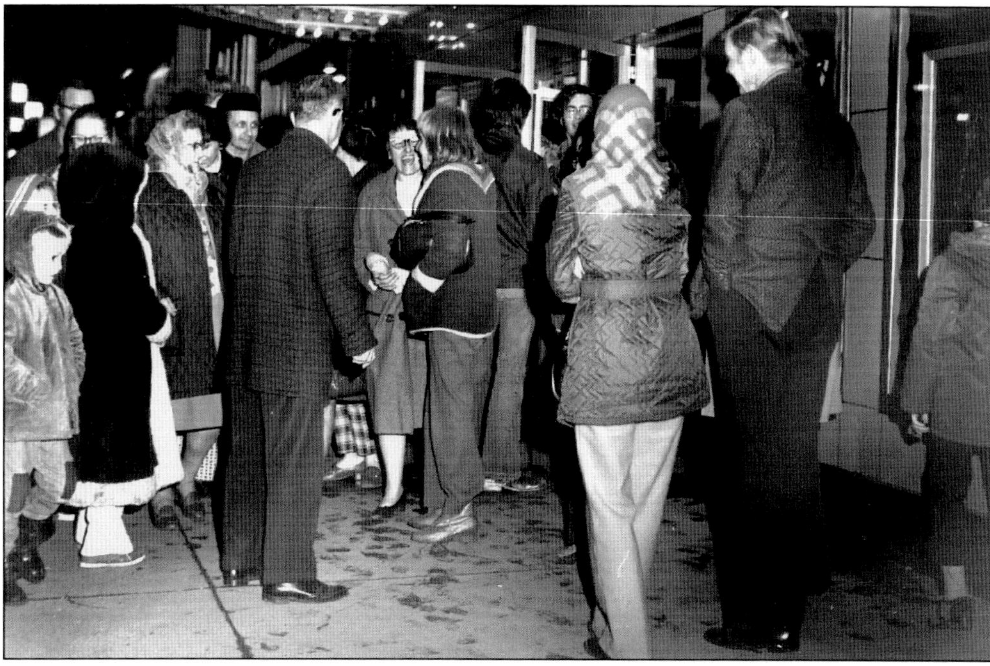

The world premiere of *The Book That Would Not Burn* took place in March 1974. Sugar Creek Lutheran Church had sponsored the film because missionary Laurel Johnson was a member and he had researched and written the script. The movie was about Christianity in Madagascar, so the Madagascar ambassador to the U.S. flew in from Washington to be present.

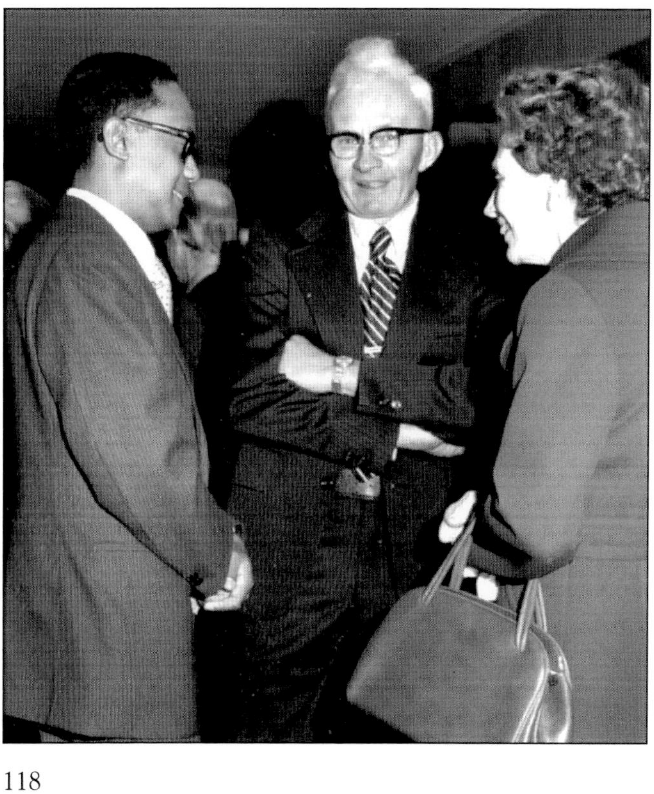

Distinctly different from Hollywood events, a reception was held afterwards at unglamorous Columbus Hall where cookies and hot chocolate were served. There the ambassador chatted with Allan and Alva Johnson. Allan was Laurel's brother and still farmed in the Norwegian settlement just west of Elkhorn.

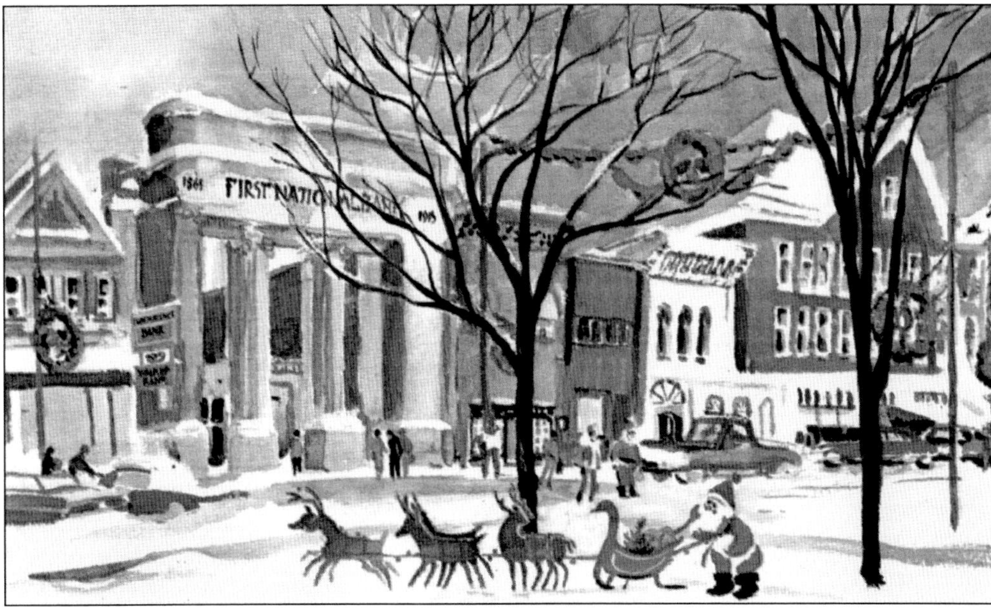

Each winter, the court house square is decorated with holiday scenes. Artist Cecile Johnson was so charmed by the park when she visited Elkhorn that she painted several water colors that were featured in a *Ford Times* magazine. Later, her pictures were selected by Hallmark for Christmas cards and Elkhorn became known as the Christmas Card City.

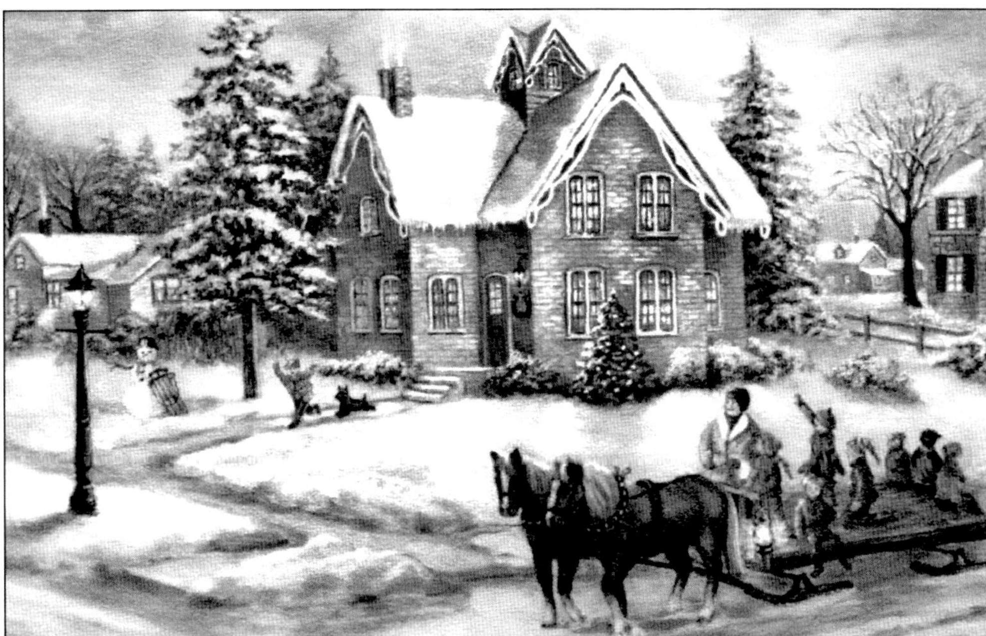

In recent years, Jan Castle-Reed, an Elkhorn artist, has continued the painting of Elkhorn scenes. She has been commissioned by the city to do a picture each year. One of her cards featured the 1857 home of Reverend Henry Webster, who penned the words for Joseph Webster's song "Lorena." The framed originals of all the cards hang in the main office of the Municipal Building. (Picture used with permission of Jan Castle-Reed.)

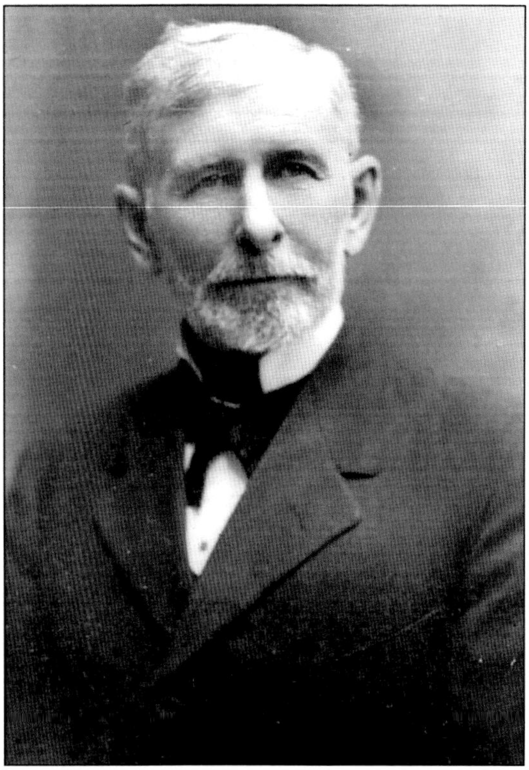

Elkhorn residents made the news also. The Tubbs family was in the headlines when Henry H. Tubbs ran for governor of Wisconsin (unsuccessfully) on the Prohibition ticket. Tubbs was city surveyor and publisher of *The Blade*, a short-lived newspaper. His wife, Helen, took over his duties at the paper whenever a surveying job took him out of town.

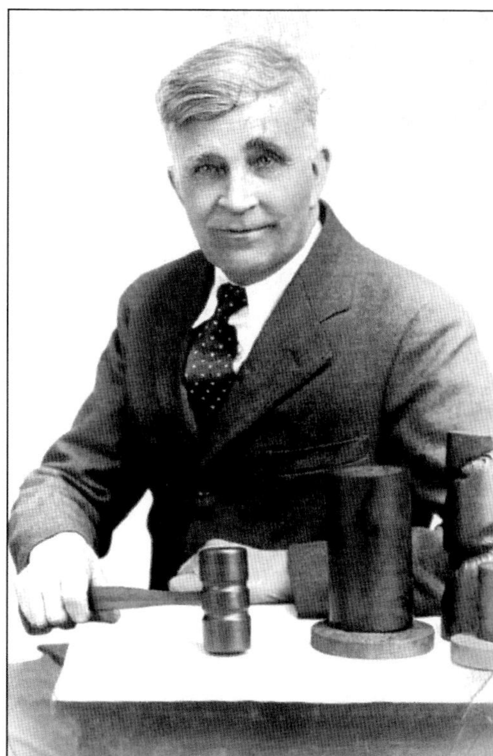

Alfred Olsen was on the front pages when he gave a special gavel to Vice President John Garner, who was noted for frequently breaking gavels when he presided over the Senate during Roosevelt's administration. Olsen had developed a special wood product called densewood, which was extremely light but very strong. One of its uses was in airplane construction. This densewood gavel was just what V.P. Garner needed.

Ten

CHANGE IS INEVITABLE

For many years, the population of Elkhorn hovered at around 3,500. At this writing in 2004, the figure has more than doubled. With that increase, there have necessarily been some changes.

Citizens no longer know everyone they see in the store or meet on the street. The freeways that link the town to larger cities 30 or 40 miles away let Elkhornites commute to those distant places for work. The same freeways, of course, bring people here to work and play. A surprising number of them decide it's a good place in which to settle and put down roots. A span of a hundred years separates these two views of the same Elkhorn downtown street.

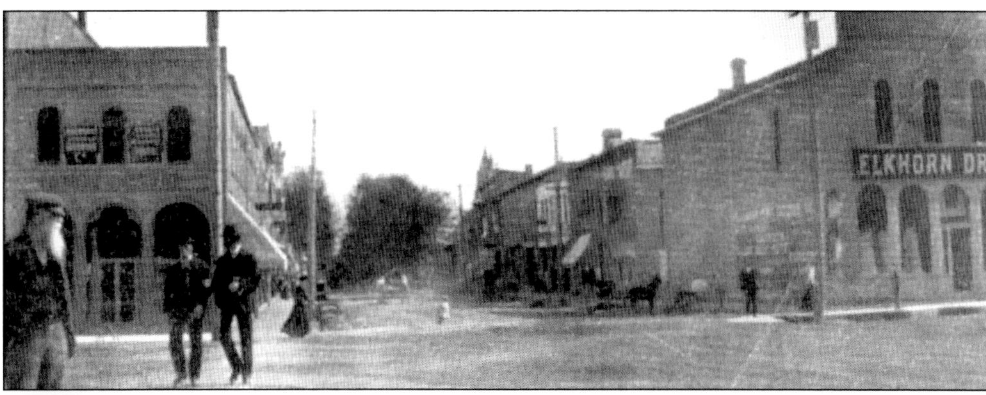

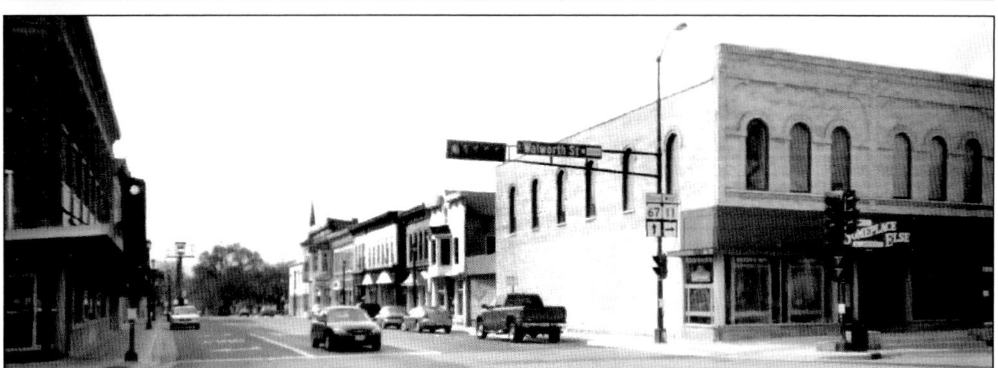

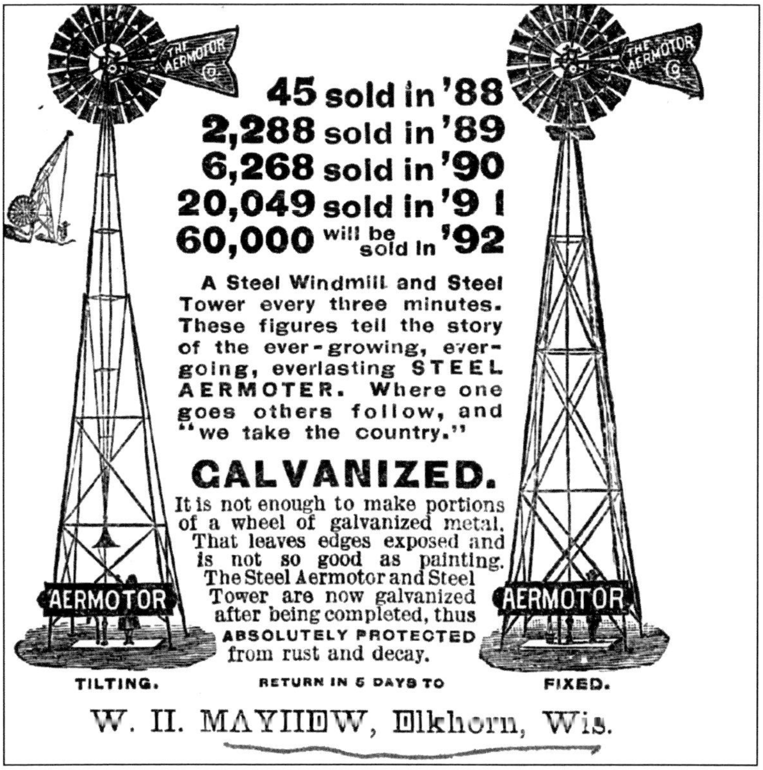

Businesses come and go. Once the sale of windmills to pump water was a profitable one. One of the most familiar sounds a hundred years ago was the squeak of the windmill blades when they were turned by the wind. Windmill farms to create electric power are being experimented with now, but the windmills look entirely different.

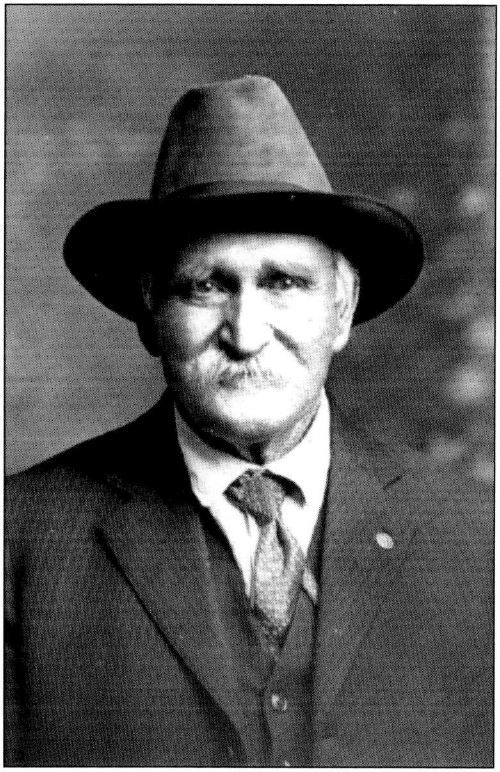

W.H. Mayhew sold windmills after the Civil War ended. He was Commander of Post No. 76 of the GAR (Grand Army of the Republic). It was organized here in 1883.

The need for water has increased constantly because modern appliances in the home require more of it and industrial growth uses great quantities too. Individual wells in the backyard of the city's homes were soon to be a thing of the past. Here, workers are pouring concrete that will hold the legs of one of Elkhorn's first water tanks. It was near St. Patrick's Church. Its construction took place in the fall of 1935.

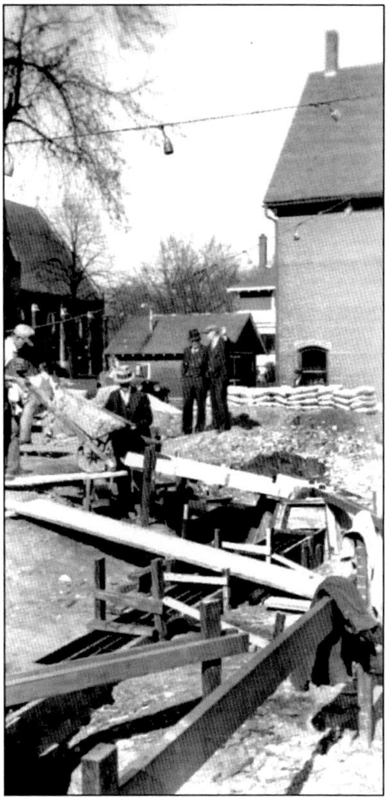

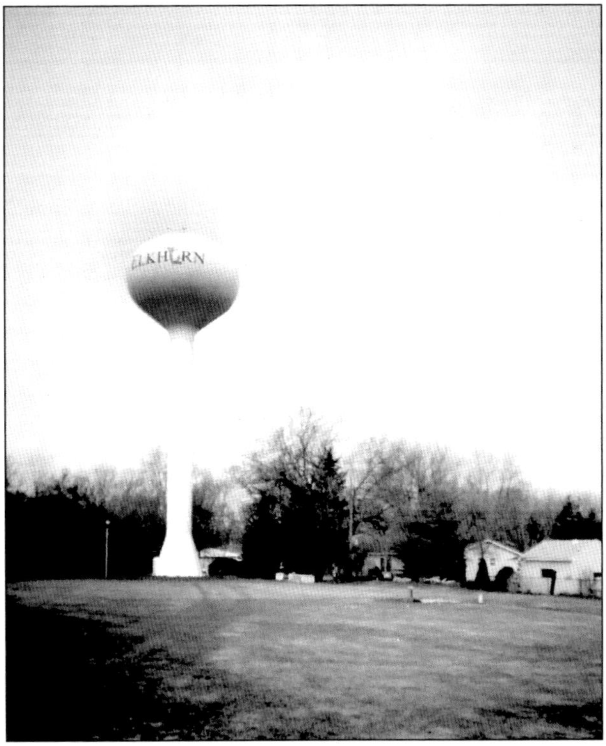

Modern water towers hold a much larger reserve of water. The city has more than one water tank today. They are no longer placed in the center of the city. Instead, they are located on the fringes and can be seen from miles away as one approaches Elkhorn.

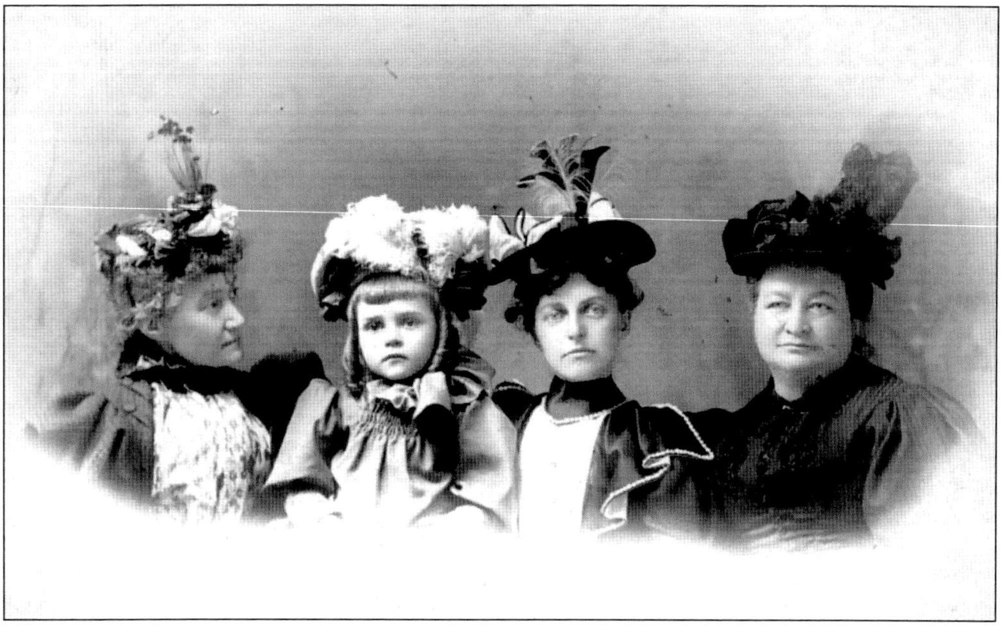

Supermarkets have replaced the individual shops that at one time made the downtown a big shopping district. Buildings that today are in use as offices were once grocery stores and meat markets. There used to be many stores where ladies could buy dresses and hats. Those places have left the downtown scene too.

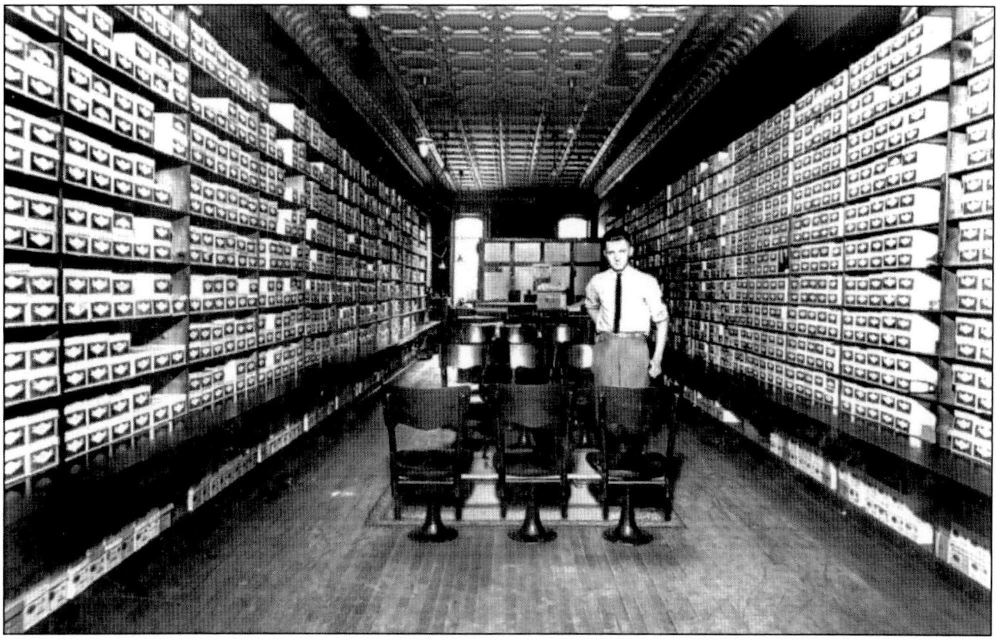

The local shoe store was a profitable business here at one time. Frank Strong waited for a customer in this photo. Self-service was unknown back then. The customers sat down on one of the seats in the aisle and the clerk brought shoes to be tried on. He also measured the foot first to be sure of correct fit.

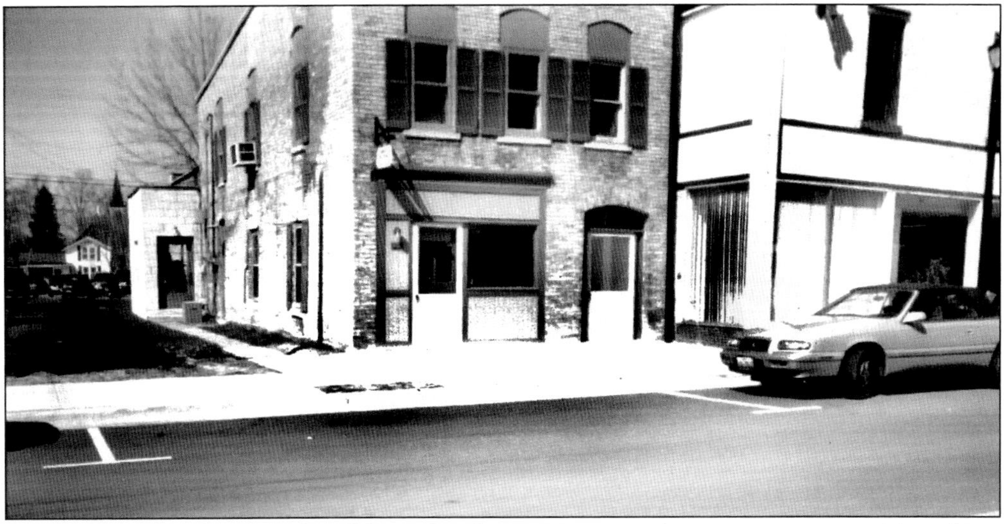

Unchanged is the fact that the Elkhorn fire department is a volunteer organization. Everything else about fire protection has undergone considerable improvement. The first fire station had one wide door to let the horse-pulled fire wagon emerge when the alarm was sounded. The old building still stands downtown, but has been made into a law office.

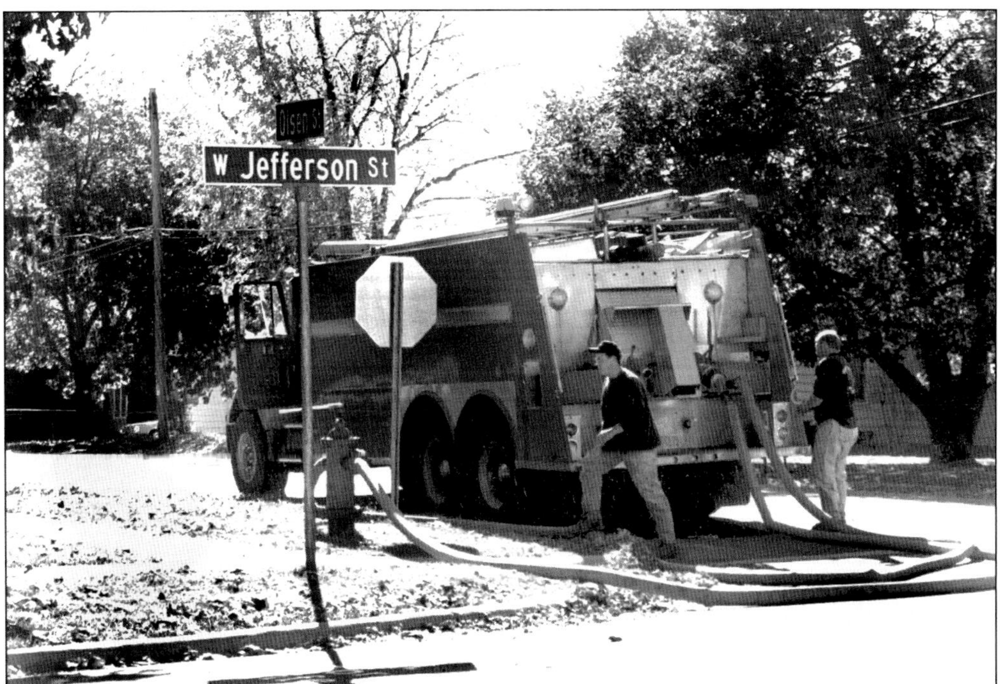

Modern fire trucks now reach burning buildings quickly and fire hydrants are placed at intervals along the streets providing a large volume of water. A fire whistle still blows when a fire has broken out. However, a beeper system that the volunteer firemen carry makes sure they hear the call.

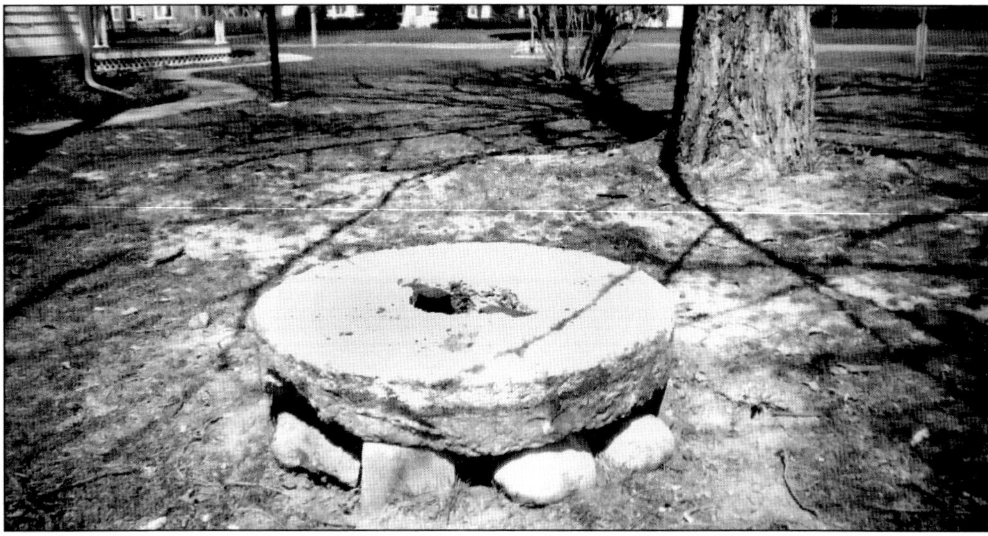

The round grindstone resting on the lawn of the Webster House Museum is a reminder of the time when farmers brought their corn, wheat, and oats to the mill on the north side of Elkhorn. Since the city did not have any water power, the Stearns mill was a Dutch style mill that relied on wind power. Patrons would wait for a windy day to go to town and do business at the mill. In 1893, a tornado blew it down and it was never rebuilt. All that remains is the heavy stone.

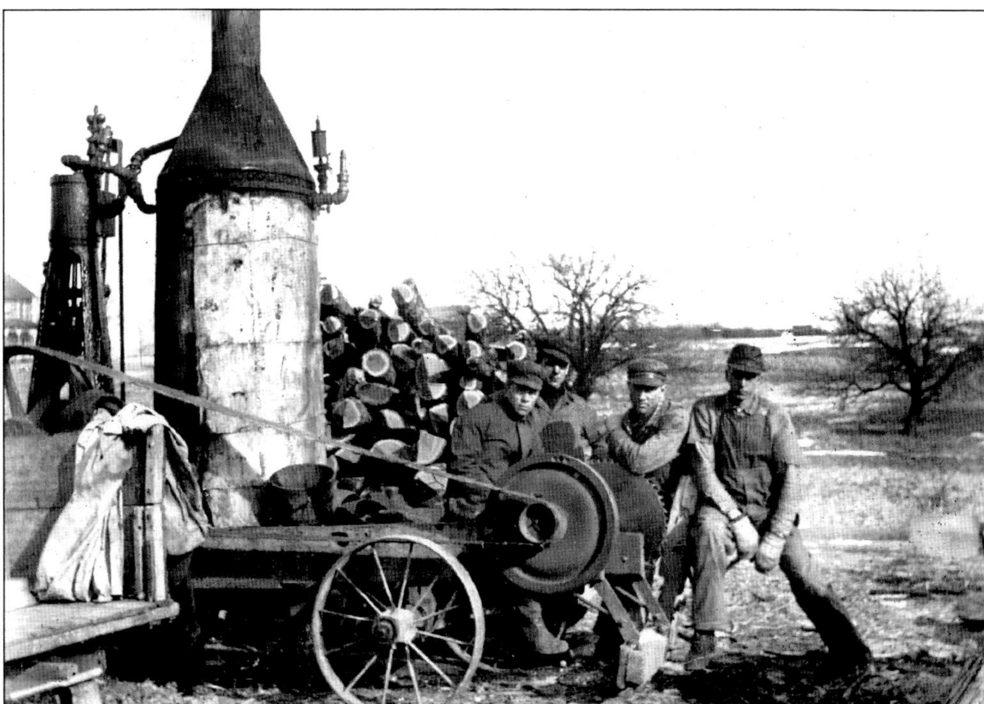

Electricity and natural gas make work easier today. A power saw has replaced this bulky steam engine in the task of cutting wood. In 1915, this crew went from farm to farm to cut the winter's supply of firewood for the family. Townspeople also wanted a big pile of wood before the snow came.

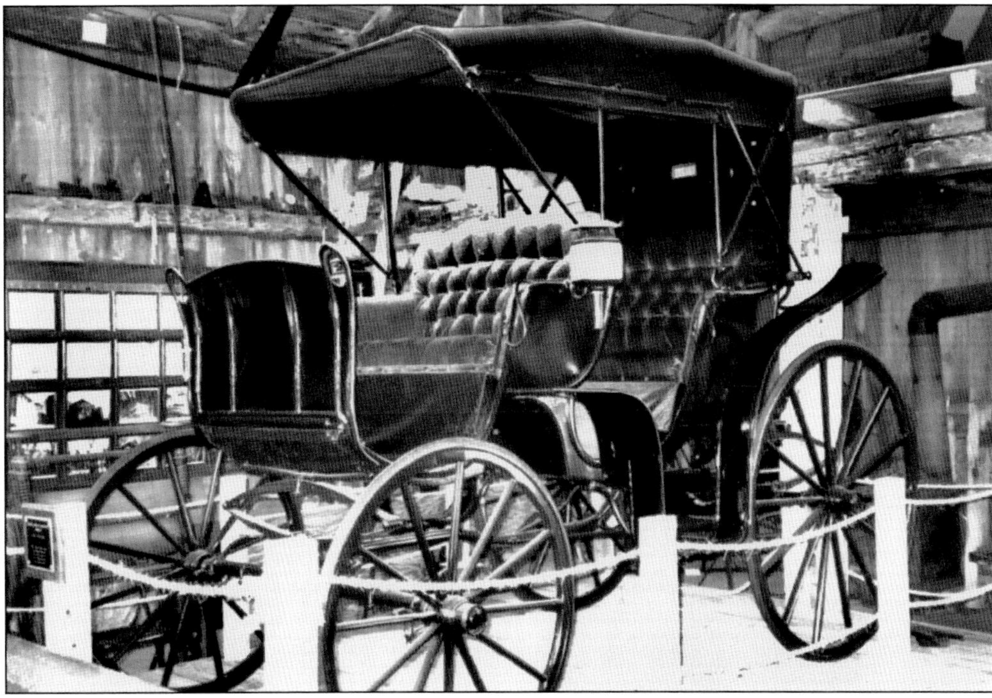

Transportation has probably changed more than anything else since the city was young. At one time, a handsome buggy with velvet cushioned seats was the dream of every man. The pictured buggy belonged to General Boyd, who was a delegate to the Wisconsin Constitutional Convention in the 1840s. In 2004, a buggy like this one is a museum piece instead of a realistic method of traveling.

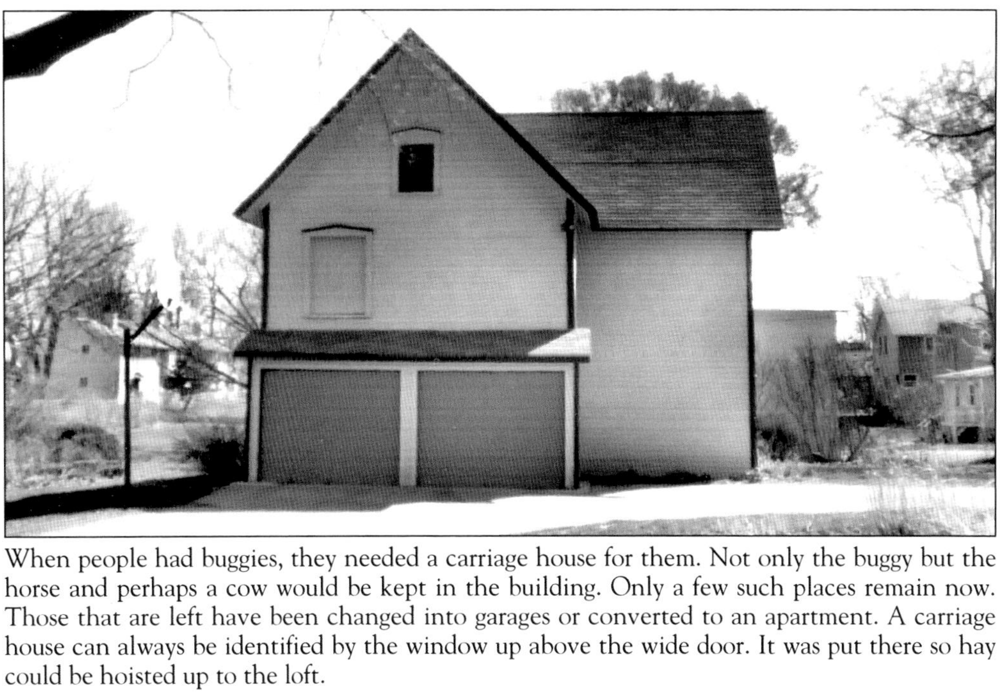

When people had buggies, they needed a carriage house for them. Not only the buggy but the horse and perhaps a cow would be kept in the building. Only a few such places remain now. Those that are left have been changed into garages or converted to an apartment. A carriage house can always be identified by the window up above the wide door. It was put there so hay could be hoisted up to the loft.

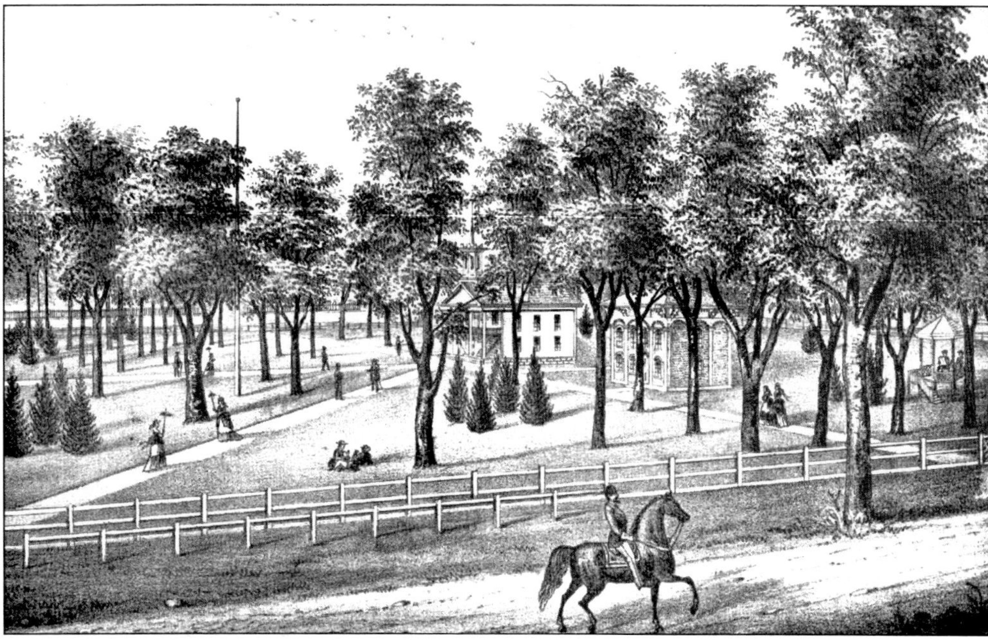

The Elkhorn book ends where it began, with its becoming the county seat. This is the sketch of the downtown park in the 1873 *Atlas of Walworth County*. The square has changed in appearance since 1873 and the buildings have been replaced with more modern ones. The court house square, though, remains the heart of Elkhorn.

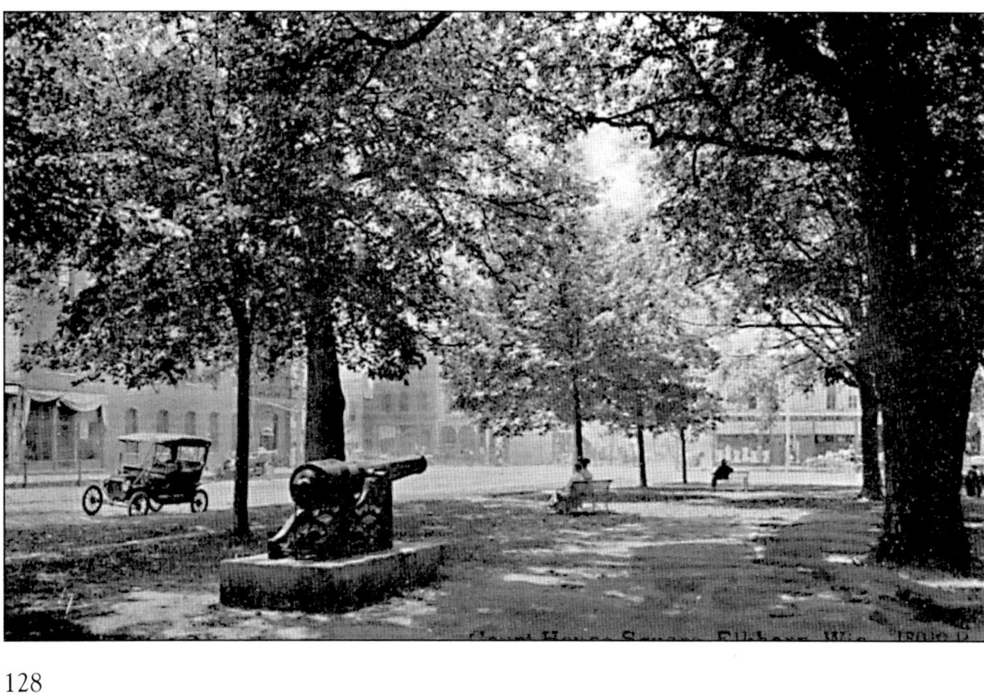